CRIME AND PUNI
IN ISLAMIC

Rudolph Peters' book is about crimes and their punishments as laid down in Islamic law. In recent years some Islamist regimes, such as those of Iran, Pakistan, Sudan and the northern states of Nigeria, have reintroduced Islamic law in place of Western criminal codes. This was after the abolition of Islamic criminal law in the nineteenth and twentieth centuries. Previously, during the pre-modern period, Islamic criminal law was applied across the Muslim world, and there are many examples of that application in the abundant archives and other sources of the period. Peters gives a detailed account of the classical doctrine and traces the enforcement of criminal law from the Ottoman period to the present day. The accounts of actual cases which range from theft to banditry, murder, fornication and apostasy shed light on the complexities of the law, and the sensitivity and perspicacity of the *qāḍīs* who implemented it. This is the first single-authored account of both the theory and practice of Islamic criminal law. It will be invaluable for students, and scholars in the field, as well as for professionals looking for comprehensive coverage of the topic.

RUDOLPH PETERS is Professor of Islamic law at Amsterdam University. He has published extensively on the subject. His books include *Jihad in Classical and Modern Islam* (1996) and *Sharia Criminal Law in Northern Nigeria* (2003).

THEMES IN ISLAMIC LAW 2

Series editor: Wael B. Hallaq

Themes in Islamic Law offers a series of state-of-the-art titles on the history of Islamic law, its application and its place in the modern world. The intention is to provide an analytic overview of the field with an emphasis on how law relates to the society in which it operates. Contributing authors, who all have distinguished reputations in their particular areas of scholarship, have been asked to interpret the complexities of the subject for those entering the field for the first time.

Titles in the series:
1. *The Origins and Evolution of Islamic Law*
WAEL B. HALLAQ

CRIME AND PUNISHMENT IN ISLAMIC LAW

Theory and Practice from the Sixteenth to the Twenty-first Century

RUDOLPH PETERS
Amsterdam University

CAMBRIDGE
UNIVERSITY PRESS

CAMBRIDGE UNIVERSITY PRESS
Cambridge, New York, Melbourne, Madrid, Cape Town, Singapore, São Paulo

Cambridge University Press
The Edinburgh Building, Cambridge CB2 8RU, UK

Published in the United States of America by Cambridge University Press, New York

www.cambridge.org
Information on this title: www.cambridge.org/9780521792264

First published 2005

A catalogue record for this publication is available from the British Library

ISBN 978-0-521-79226-4 hardback
ISBN 978-0-521-79670-5 paperback

Transferred to digital printing 2007

Contents

Acknowledgements

I owe a great debt of gratitude to the many persons and institutions that have contributed to the completion of this book. A fellowship awarded to me from September 2001 to March 2002 by the International Institute for the Study of Islam in the Modern World (ISIM) in Leiden enabled me to start writing it. I want to thank Muhammad Khalid Masud and Peter van der Veer, the two directors at that time, for giving me that opportunity. Parts of the book were written at the Department of Middle East Studies, New York University, which hosted me in February–March 2002, and at the Harvard Law School, where I worked as a guest researcher during April and May 2002. I am very grateful to Michael Gilsenan, director of the Department of Middle East Studies, NYU, and Frank Vogel and Peri Bearman of the Islamic Law Program of the Harvard Law School for inviting me. I am indebted to Marianne Nolte, then European Union Co-ordinator for Human Rights and Civil Society in Lagos, Nigeria, for being instrumental in securing EU funds that allowed me to visit Nigeria in September 2001 and study the reintroduction of Shariʿa criminal law in the north of the country. I want to thank Dr Sami Aldeeb of the Institut Suisse de Droit Comparé in Lausanne for his assistance in collecting the texts of the various Shariʿa penal codes enacted in the Muslim world. I am grateful to the Faculty of Humanities of the University of Amsterdam for awarding me travel grants to collect the necessary materials. During my stays in Cairo I was always able to use the facilities of the Nederlands-Vlaams Instituut in Cairo. I want to thank its successive directors Han den Heijer and Gert Borg and its librarian Anita Keizers for making me always feel at home. Khaled Fahmy offered me hospitality in New York and Cairo at various occasions. I thank him for his friendship and owe him a debt greater than he realises. Finally I want to express my thanks to the series editor Wael Hallaq for his comments and criticisms on the first draft of this book.

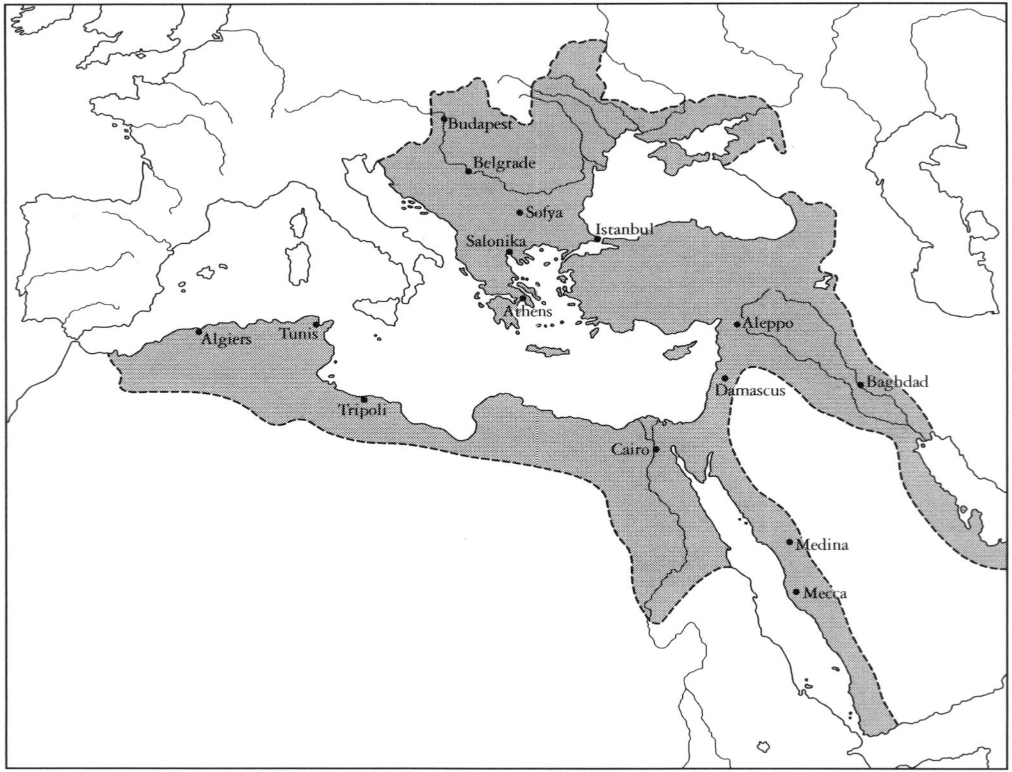

Map 1. The Ottoman Empire around 1600

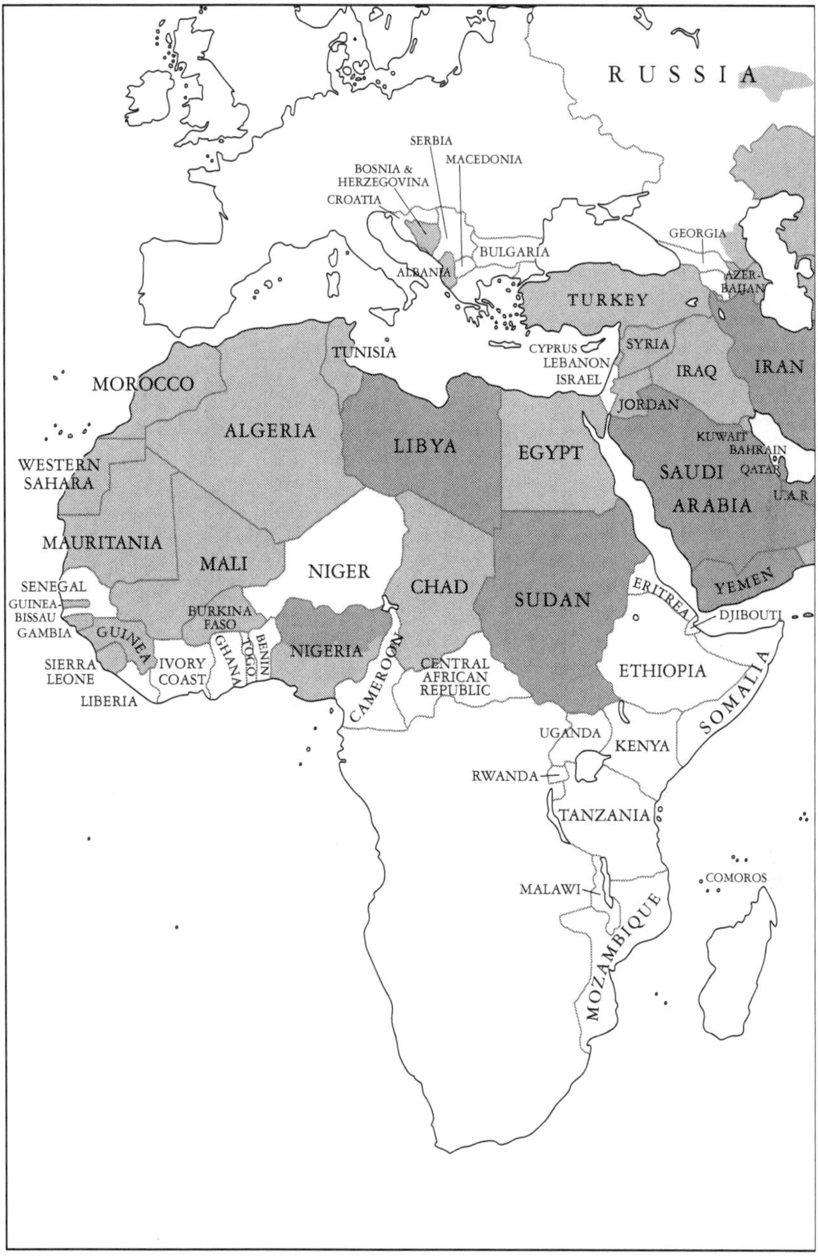

Map 2. Countries implementing Shariʿa criminal law (dark grey)

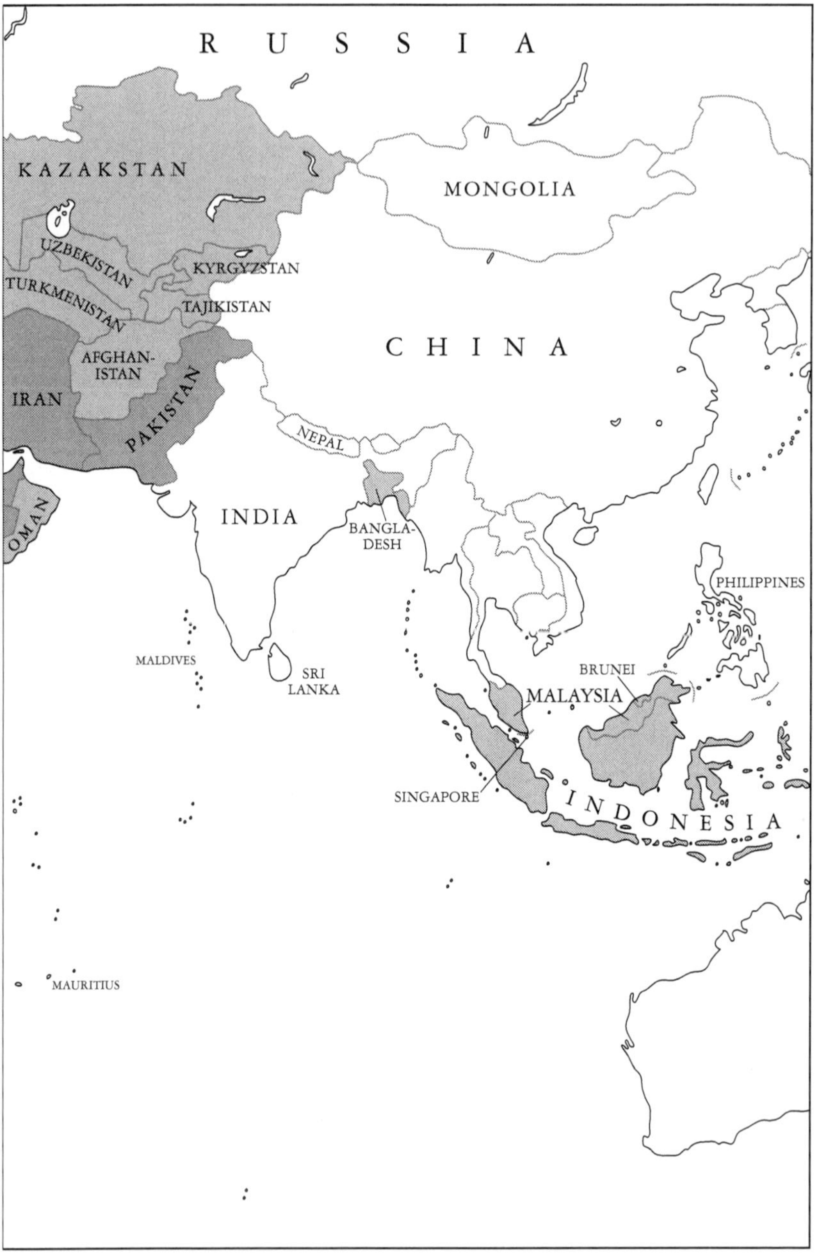
R U S S I A
KAZAKSTAN
MONGOLIA
UZBEKISTAN
KYRGYZSTAN
TURKMENISTAN
TAJIKISTAN
CHINA
AFGHAN-
ISTAN
IRAN
PAKISTAN
NEPAL
OMAN
INDIA
BANGLA-
DESH
PHILIPPINES
MALDIVES
SRI
LANKA
BRUNEI
MALAYSIA
SINGAPORE
INDONESIA
MAURITIUS

Map 2. (*cont.*)

Map 3. The spread of Shariʿa criminal law in Nigeria (dark grey)

CHAPTER I

Introduction

This book deals with criminal or penal law (I will use both terms indiscriminately), the body of law that regulates the power of the state to inflict punishment, i.e. suffering, on persons in order to enforce compliance with certain rules. Such rules typically protect public interests and values that society regards as crucial, even if the immediate interest that is protected is a private one. A case in point is theft. Many societies make the violation of private property rights a punishable offence, although the interests harmed by such violations are in the first place private ones. However, these societies regard the protection of property as essential for the social order and protect it by stronger remedies than those available under private law. The interests protected by penal sanctions vary from society to society. In some societies sexual acts between consenting adults are of no concern to the authorities, whereas in others the rules regulating sexual contact are regarded as so crucial for the maintenance of social order that violations are severely punished. The same is true, for instance, with regard to the consumption of alcohol and other psychotropic substances. Criminal laws, therefore, give an insight into what a society and its rulers regard as its core values.

Islamic law does not conform to the notion of law as found, for example, in common law or civil law systems. Rather than a uniform and unequivocal formulation of the law it is a scholarly discourse consisting of the opinions of religious scholars, who argue, on the basis of the text of the Koran, the Prophetic *ḥadīth* and the consensus of the first generations of Muslim scholars, what the law should be. Since these scholars interpreted the sources in different ways, we often find various opinions with regard to one legal issue. The jurists and the rulers developed ways to make these differences manageable for those who had to apply the law. The institution of the 'school of jurisprudence' (*madhhab*, plural *madhāhib*), uniting legal scholars around certain legal doctrines, brought greater coherence and consistency, because the adherents of such a school were bound to follow the opinions of the school's founding fathers. Moreover, rulers could instruct judges to adjudicate only according to opinions of one school. However, even within one law school, there are many controversies on essential legal issues. In order to organise and manage this doctrinal variety, the adherents of specific schools developed hierarchies of authority with regard to the different opinions.

In chapter 2 I will present this legal discourse on crime and punishment, paying attention to the various opinions. The aim of this study, however, goes beyond this: I intend also to show how the actual practice of Islamic criminal law was related to this discourse and how and to what extent this discourse was applied by the courts. This will be the subject of chapter 3. Chapter 4 deals with Islamic criminal law and modernisation. Since the first half of the nineteenth century, the application of Islamic criminal law has seen important changes. In most parts of the Islamic world, it was replaced by Western-type criminal codes. In some countries this happened at once, usually immediately after the establishment of colonial rule. Elsewhere it was a gradual process. It is this gradual process that I will analyse in chapter 4. Finally, chapter 5 is devoted to the importance of Islamic criminal law today, especially to the phenomenon of its return in some countries during the last decades of the twentieth century.

The presentation of the classical doctrine in chapter 2 forms the basis for the other chapters, in which I will examine its actual role in the criminal law systems in various periods and regions. The subject-matter is culled from the classical books of *fiqh* and I have tried to enliven and elucidate the doctrine by including specific and concrete cases from *fatwā* collections. I do not compare the Islamic criminal laws with modern criminal laws. However, in order to facilitate comparison, I have arranged the subject-matter according to what is customary in modern handbooks on criminal law: first I will discuss procedure and the law-enforcement officials; then the general concepts such as criminal liability, complicity and the penalties; and finally the specific offences. This arrangement enables those who are not familiar with Islamic law easily to identify the differences with their own criminal law systems. A completely comparative approach is, in my opinion, not meaningful and not feasible. It is not meaningful because it is not clear with what system of criminal law it must be compared. With a modern European or American system? Or with a pre-modern European system? Neither comparison will be very helpful in understanding the Islamic doctrine, whose early origins date back to the seventh century. Moreover, we are dealing with a fluid and often contradictory body of opinions and not with a uniform, unequivocal doctrine of criminal law. This makes comparison even more complicated.

This book differs from most studies on Islamic criminal law in that it is not limited to presenting the doctrine but also pays attention to how Islamic criminal law 'worked on the ground', i.e. how it was actually used in criminal law enforcement. We cannot assume that this was the same everywhere in the world of Islam during the entire pre-modern period. The levels of implementation of Islamic criminal law and the involvement of the different law-enforcing authorities (such as the *qāḍī*, the ruler and the executive officials) varied from region to region and from dynasty to dynasty. It depended on the form and organisation of the judicial institutions that states established. It is impossible to give a comprehensive picture covering the whole Muslim world from the eighth to the nineteenth centuries. This is a stage of scholarship that we have passed. We no longer try to find 'the Islamic essence' in the history of the institutions of the Muslim world, but rather confine ourselves to the study of specific regions and periods.

Thus, in order to study Islamic criminal law in practice, I have selected one specific state: the Ottoman Empire. There are two reasons for my choice. First, because this system is well documented, thanks to the preservation of the Ottoman Shariʿa court records. Of no other Islamic state in the past are we so well informed about its organisation and its legal practice. These records show that the Ottoman Empire, from the sixteenth to the eighteenth centuries, had a stable and fairly well-functioning system of criminal justice. The second reason for my choice is that legal and social historians have already done a great deal of research based on these records. I could use their studies as a starting point for my analysis of the Ottoman system of criminal law and of the role of the doctrine of Islamic criminal law in it. As I have done with my presentation of the classical doctrine, I will illustrate the way Ottoman criminal law worked with cases found in court records and in *fatwā* collections.

By selecting the Ottoman Empire I do not wish to suggest that the Ottoman system is somehow representative of 'the Islamic system of penal law'. The study of Ottoman criminal law is no more than a case study. Studies of other regions and periods that are now available (e.g. on Islamic Spain, see Further reading) show that there was a great diversity and that criminal justice was administered in very different ways. The division of labour and the delimitation of jurisdictions between the Shariʿa courts, the ruler and the executive officials varied considerably.

The emergence of Western hegemony in the nineteenth century greatly affected the legal systems in the Islamic world. In most Islamic countries that came under European colonial rule, Shariʿa criminal law was immediately substituted by Western-type penal codes. In some other countries, however, this was a gradual process: there the final abolition of Islamic criminal law took place after a period of reform, during which Islamic criminal law continued to be implemented. Chapter 4 will analyse this period of transition. The processes of reform during this period are of interest because they show us which precisely were the frictions between systems of penal law based on the Shariʿa and legal concepts based on Western law. I will use as examples two regions where reforms were introduced by Western colonial powers: India (between 1790 and 1807) and Northern Nigeria (between 1904 and 1960), and two regions where change was initiated by independent governments of centralising and modernising states: the Central Ottoman Empire (between 1839 and 1917) and Egypt (between 1830 and 1883), which at that time was an autonomous Ottoman province with its own legal system. In India and Nigeria, the colonial rulers directly interfered with the substance of Islamic criminal law and tried to mould it into something resembling Western criminal law, before replacing it entirely by a Western-type penal code. In Egypt and the Ottoman Empire the indigenous authorities reformed criminal law, building forth on the Ottoman system of dual jurisdiction in criminal law (i.e. the Shariʿa enforced by the *qāḍīs*' courts and *siyāsa* justice administered, at their discretion, by executive officials and the Sultan). Here the locus of reform was *siyāsa* justice: its administration was transferred from the ruler and individual officials to specialised courts and its arbitrariness was restricted by the enactment of penal laws codifying the domain of *siyāsa*. Shariʿa criminal law continued to be implemented without substantial changes by the *qāḍī* courts. For the greater part of the nineteenth century the entire legal system, both in Egypt and the Ottoman Empire, remained essentially Islamic. The new courts were not regarded as a challenge to Shariʿa justice but rather as a supplement to it. However, here too, Islamic criminal law was abolished in the end.

In the title of chapter 4 I deliberately chose the word 'eclipse' to convey the meaning that Islamic criminal law became invisible, without, however, ceasing to exist. The application of Islamic criminal law came to an end (except for some isolated instances, such as Saudi Arabia). Its doctrine, however, lived on. It is studied by Islamic scholars, discussed and taught to students. Islamist parties and groups, striving for the establishment of an Islamic state, regard its enforcement as their most prominent goal. Islamist regimes that came to power, and other regimes that were already in power but wanted to enhance their legitimacy, introduced Islamic criminal legislation, which became an icon for a regime's Islamicity. In chapter 5 this process is analysed. In this chapter I also pay attention to the question of whether these new Shari'a penal codes conform to internationally recognised human rights standards.

In conclusion a few technical remarks. Arabic and Ottoman terms and proper names are transliterated with diacritics according to the system used by *The International Journal for Middle Eastern Studies*. The main sources I have used are listed for each chapter or section in the first footnote. For quoting the Koran, I have in most cases used the translation by Mohammed Marmaduke Pickthall,[1] except that I have substituted the word 'Allah' with 'God'. For citing *ḥadīth*, I generally relied on al-'Asqalānī's compendium *Bulūgh al-marām min adillat al-aḥkām*.

[1] Mohammed Marmaduke Pickthall, *The meaning of the glorious Koran: an explanatory translation* (New York: Mentor Books, n.d.).

CHAPTER 2

The classical doctrine

2.1 INTRODUCTION

In this chapter I will discuss and analyse the classical doctrine of criminal law as found in the authoritative works of jurisprudence. I will pay attention to the various schools of jurisprudence (*madhhab*, plural *madhāhib*), including Shiite doctrine, and try to present the authoritative opinions of each school. This may seem somewhat confusing to the reader but it is necessary, first in order to convey how rich and variegated the legal discourse is, and second because I will refer to these opinions in the following chapters. To avoid further confusion, I will refrain from paying attention to the historical development of the doctrine, although I am well aware that the doctrine was not static and immutable. However, this is only recently recognised and there are still many gaps in our knowledge.

In order to make the variety of opinion manageable in practice and to impose some sort of order on it, two devices were used. The first and older one is the institution of the school of jurisprudence. Scholars tracing their doctrine to the same early authority regarded themselves as followers of the same school. Ultimately, there remained four of them in Sunni Islam: the Hanafites, Malikites, Shafiʿites and Hanbalites. These schools had, to some extent, a regional distribution: for instance, North Africa and Islamic Spain adhered to the Malikite school, Central Asia and the territory occupied by the Ottoman Empire was dominated by the Hanafites. In order to create greater legal certainty, rulers could direct the *qāḍīs* they appointed to follow one school. However, within one school there also existed various and contradictory opinions. In the course of time, jurists began to assess these different opinions and assign a hierarchy of authority. Some opinions were regarded as more correct than others. Although there was no complete unanimity about these hierarchies, they helped to make the legal discourse of one school manageable, especially for practitioners.[1]

[1] See Wael Hallaq, *Authority, continuity and change in Islamic law* (Cambridge: Cambridge University Press, 2001).

In the classical textbooks of *fiqh*, criminal law is not regarded as a single, unified branch of the law. It is discussed in three separate chapters:

(1) Provisions regarding offences against persons, i.e. homicide and wounding, subdivided into
 (a) those regarding retaliation (*qiṣāṣ*) and
 (b) those regarding financial compensation (*diya*).
(2) Provisions regarding offences mentioned in the Koran and constituting violations of the claims of God (*ḥuqūq Allāh*), with mandatory fixed punishments (*ḥadd*, plural *ḥudūd*); these offences are:
 (a) theft
 (b) banditry
 (c) unlawful sexual intercourse
 (d) the unfounded accusation of unlawful sexual intercourse (slander)
 (e) drinking alcohol
 (f) apostasy (according to some schools of jurisprudence).
(3) Provisions concerning discretionary punishment of sinful or forbidden behaviour or of acts endangering public order or state security (*taʿzīr* and *siyāsa*).

Categories (1 (a)) and (2) are expounded in the *fiqh* books with great precision and in painstaking detail. They may be regarded as constituting Islamic criminal law in its strict sense, with characteristic features that set it apart from other domains of the law, such as the absence of liability of minor and insane persons, the strict rules of evidence and the large part played by the concept of mistake (*shubha*) as a defence. Category (3) is a residual but comprehensive one under which the authorities are given wide-ranging powers. They may punish those who have committed offences mentioned under (1) and (2) but could not be convicted on procedural grounds (e.g. pardon by the heirs of a victim of manslaughter, or evidence that does not satisfy the strict requirements), and also those who have perpetrated acts that are similar to these offences but do not fall under their strict definitions. Moreover, under this heading the authorities can punish at their discretion all other forms of sinful or socially and politically undesirable behaviour. The punitive powers of the authorities are hardly restricted by law and, as a consequence, the doctrine offers little protection to the accused.

The provisions regarding bloodmoney (*diya*) (category (1 (b)) belong to the field of private law, since they deal not with punishment but with financial liability arising from a specific type of tort (i.e. homicide and wounding). Bloodmoney (*diya*) in cases of homicide or wounding is a financial compensation for damages suffered by the heirs of the victim (in cases of homicide) and for the victim himself (in cases of bodily harm). That this is no punishment is clear from the fact that in many situations it is not the perpetrator who is liable for the bloodprice, but his 'solidarity group' (*'āqila*), usually his agnatic male relatives. Nevertheless, I will discuss the rules on bloodmoney here, since the subject is intimately linked with the criminal law of homicide and bodily harm.

In setting forth the doctrine, I will arrange the material according to what is customary in modern handbooks on criminal law. I will first deal with the law-enforcing agencies and procedure in criminal cases. In section 2.3 some general rules will be discussed regarding criminal responsibility, unlawfulness of the punishable offence and complicity. The various penalties recognised in Islamic criminal law will be the subject-matter of section 2.4. Thereafter, I will expound the doctrine of substantive criminal law, according to the categories found in the classical texts, i.e. homicide and bodily harm (section 2.5), the *ḥadd* offences (section 2.6) and, finally, discretionary punishment (section 2.7).

2.2 ENFORCEMENT AND PROCEDURE

2.2.1 Law-enforcement agencies and procedure[2]

In classical Islamic theory of government the head of state has wide-ranging executive and judicial powers and may pass legislation within the limits set by the Shari'a. Specialised judicial organs, such as courts staffed by single judges (*qāḍī*s) operate on the basis of delegation by the head of state. The latter, however, retains judicial powers and may adjudicate certain cases himself or entrust other state agencies with hearing and deciding them. Moreover, he may issue instructions to the judicial organs with respect to their jurisdiction.

Classical doctrine recognises, apart from the head of state himself, three law enforcement agencies. The most prominent is the single judge, the *qāḍī*, adjudicating cases on the basis of the *fiqh* doctrine. However, officials in charge of public security, such as governors, military commanders and police officers, also have jurisdiction, especially in criminal cases. But unlike the *qāḍī*, they usually deal with crime according to political expediency rather than on the basis of the legal doctrine. This jurisdiction is called *siyāsa*. The delimitation of the jurisdictions of the *qāḍī* and the executive

[2] This part is mainly based on Christian Müller, *Gerichtspraxis im Stadtstaat Córdoba: Zum Recht der Gesellschaft in einer malikitisch-islamischen Rechtstradition des 5./11. Jahrhunderts* (Leiden: E. J. Brill, 1999) and Emile Tyan, *Histoire de l'organisation judiciaire en pays de l'islam*, 2nd rev. edn. (Leiden: E. J. Brill, 1960), pp. 567–650.

officials varies according to time and place. A final agency is the *muḥtasib* (also called *ṣāḥib al-sūq*, market inspector), an official supervising trade practices, public morals and the observance of religious duties.

The *qāḍī* may award punishment, but only on the strength of a sentence passed after a formal procedure. Trials before the *qāḍī* are adversarial, i.e. they aim at settling a dispute between a plaintiff and a defendant. The plaintiff, i.e. the victim or his heirs, must prove his claim against the suspected perpetrator, acting as the defendant. If the former succeeds, the *qāḍī*, after questioning the latter about whether he can produce evidence in his own defence (*iʿdhār*), will find for the plaintiff. The *qāḍī*'s role is passive, i.e. he does not investigate the facts of the case but only supervises the observance of the rules of procedure and evaluates the evidence produced by the parties. The plaintiff cannot force a defendant to appear in court, and statements must be made voluntarily: the doctrine is almost unanimous that a confession extracted under duress is invalid.

Criminal law enforcement by executive officials, such as police officers and military commanders, is mentioned only occasionally in the law books. These officials had wide, nearly unlimited powers in dealing with crime. The eleventh-century jurist al-Māwardī lists the differences between the way these officials handled suspects and the procedure followed by the *qāḍī*. The most important dissimilarities between the two types of criminal justice are related to evidence. The military commanders and police officials may decide whether or not the charge is probable on the basis of circumstantial evidence and the accused's prior convictions and reputation and inflict punishment if they find that, in their opinion, it is likely that he is guilty. They also may go by the testimonies of non-Muslims and other people who are otherwise not qualified to testify in court. By way of psychological pressure, the law enforcers may impose an exculpatory oath on the accused. Physical pressure is also allowed: during interrogation, the accused may be beaten, but only to urge upon him the need for truthfulness with regard to what he has been accused of, and not in order to force him to confess. If he confesses while being beaten, the beating must be stopped and his confession is effective only if repeated a second time. Other powers possessed by executive officials but not judges are that they may remand the accused into custody during the investigation and that they may send repeat offenders to prison for life if it is expected that the public will be harmed by their crimes.[3] Whereas al-Māwardī regarded the

[3] ʿAlī b. Muḥammad al-Māwardī, *al-Aḥkām al-sulṭaniyya* (Cairo: Muṣṭafā al-Bābī al-Ḥalabī, 1966), pp. 219–21.

enforcement of law and order by executive officials as falling outside the realm of the Shariʿa, this began to change during the thirteenth century. Since then many jurists have insisted that law enforcement by executive officials should also be governed by Shariʿa norms. However, in order to make it possible for this to be implemented in practice, they had to relax the strict rules of evidence and procedure.[4]

The most important of these executive officials were the chief of police (*ṣāḥib al-shurṭa* or *ṣāḥib al-madīna*) and the market inspector (*muḥtasib* or *ṣāḥib al-sūq*). The jurisdictions of these functionaries varied in place and time, but there were some common elements. The *shurṭa* were originally military elite troops who would protect the rulers and high officials of the state, enforce law and order and crush rebellions and disturbances. As a consequence of this last duty, they would also investigate crime, and try and punish criminals. In many documents dating from various periods we find that the police had the jurisdiction to try *ḥadd* crimes, homicide and offences against public security. They could impose punishment on the ground of public interest. Simple suspicion was sufficient for establishing guilt. An important task with which the police would usually be entrusted was the execution of the *qāḍīs*' decisions.

Another official dealing with crime was, as we have seen, the market inspector. He would check weights, measures and coins, the quality of the commodities sold in the markets and shops, and see to it that no dishonest trade practices were used. Further, he would supervise the public space, checking the state of public roads, traffic and buildings. He also had the power to supervise the functioning of judicial personnel, such as scribes, notaries, legal counsels and magistrates. As a true *censor morum* he would protect public morals, by enforcing dress codes and rules on the mixing of men and women in public, and supervising prostitutes and brothels. Finally, he would enforce the public observance of religious duties, such as fasting during Ramadan and attendance of Friday prayer. His powers were extensive: whenever he saw unlawful actions that fell under his jurisdiction, he could punish the culprit on the spot and impose discretionary punishments such as beating, exposure to public scorn and confiscation of property. However, as he did not have the authority to carry out inquiries or supervise formal litigation, he could only act if the facts of the case were undisputed, such as when the perpetrator had been caught *in flagrante delictu*.

[4] Baber Johansen, 'Signs as evidence: the doctrine of Ibn Taymiyya (1263–1328) and Ibn Qayyim al-Jawziyya (d. 1351) on proof', *Islamic Law and Society* 9, 2 (2002), 168–93.

Although the doctrine assumed that trial by the *qāḍī* was the rule, there is sufficient evidence that this was not always the case. Letters of appointments of *qāḍīs* quoted in an authoritative fourteenth-century manual for scribes, *Ṣubḥ al-aʿshā*, by the Egyptian author al-Qalqashandī, do usually not mention criminal justice as one of his tasks. When they do, it is restricted to the trial of *ḥadd* offences. In general, criminal law enforcement by the *qāḍī* was problematic. The rules of procedure followed in the *qāḍī*'s court were developed for litigation between two private parties, who would submit their dispute to the *qāḍī*. The *qāḍī* was not equipped to investigate the case himself nor did he have the staff to do so. He depended entirely on such facts as the parties were willing and able to establish. An official like a public prosecutor, who could investigate criminal offences and bring offenders to trial, did not exist in Islamic law. One can imagine that for a victim of crime it was much more effective to report the case to the police or to comparable authorities, who had the power to investigate the matter and arrest the suspects.

2.2.2 *Statute of limitation*

There is no unanimity on whether offences may be prosecuted indefinitely. Only Hanafite doctrine mentions a statute of limitation. Hanafite jurists hold that *ḥadd* crimes, with the exception of the unfounded allegation of unlawful intercourse (*qadhf*), may not be punished after the lapse of one month. With regard to drinking alcoholic beverages, the sentence must be pronounced before the smell of it has disappeared from the culprit's mouth. The term of one month only applies if the act is proven by witnesses without a legal excuse for not testifying immediately, and not if the evidence consists in a confession. The ground for this rule is that it is assumed that witnesses who choose to testify after having been silent for more than a month are suspected of being motivated by malice. That *qadhf* is excepted is due to the fact that this *ḥadd* offence violates both claims of God and claims of men and that the latter are not subject to extinction by the passage of time. This Hanafite statute of limitation is restricted to the sentencing to fixed punishments. If witnesses testify to an offence which might constitute a *ḥadd* crime more than a month after the event, the judge may impose discretionary punishment. In the Ottoman Empire, an imperial decree of 1550 forbade *qāḍīs* to hear cases if more than fifteen years had passed after the commission of the crime and the plaintiff had no legal excuse for not bringing the offence to the notice of the authorities.

2.2.3 Evidence

2.2.3.1 Evidence in criminal proceedings

The Islamic law of evidence is rational and very formalistic. The general rule is that the plaintiff must prove his claim and that he can do so by the testimony of witnesses or by the admission of the defendant. Oaths, or the refusal the swear an oath, can have probative force. Finally, the Hanafites, Shafiʿites and Shiites consider the *qāḍī*'s own knowledge, regardless of how he acquired it, as sufficient proof for a sentence. Evidence by witnesses is only admitted if two male, or one male and two female adult Muslim witnesses of good reputation (*ʿadl*) give concurring testimonies in the presence of the *qāḍī*. Testimonies conveying an admission made by the defendant out of court or what two other qualified witnesses have declared out of court (*shahāda ʿalā al-shahāda*) are accepted. Slight discrepancies in the testimonies make them invalid, even if they concur on the essentials. In the following homicide case, tried before the *qāḍī* of Tanta (Egypt) in 1860, the plaintiffs could not prove their claim, although there was no disagreement in the testimonies about the fact that the defendant had inflicted serious injuries on the victim. The court did not admit the evidence because of a minor inconsistency: one witness testified that the defendant had kicked the victim with his right foot whereas the other testified that he had done so with his left foot:

The plaintiffs, the heirs of the deceased, sued the *qāḍī* of Burullus, claiming 'that during a fight in his courtroom, he had struck the deceased with a thin palm branch twice, once on his head and once his face, that he had then chased the deceased from the courtroom and kicked him in the belly, that this had caused his belly and breast to bloat and that he had stayed in his bed until he died eight days later as a result of this assault'. The defendant replied that he had indeed struck the deceased for having been insolent during court proceedings, but only very lightly and on his turban. The plaintiffs produced three witnesses. The first one testified 'that he had seen that the deceased had attempted to prevent the *qāḍī* from sealing a deposition against him, that the *qāḍī* had struck him with his palm branch, that the deceased and the *qāḍī* had left the courtroom and that he had heard the deceased shouting [to the onlookers], "You must be my witnesses [to what is happening now]!"' The second witness stated 'that he was sitting outside the court and suddenly had seen the deceased coming out of the courtroom with the *qāḍī* pursuing him, that the *qāḍī* kicked him once in his belly with his left foot, which caused the deceased to fall, that the *qāḍī* then kicked him twice *with his right foot* in his belly and gave him two strokes with a medium-sized palm branch, once on his brow and once under his ear, that the deceased had lost consciousness, was carried to the district office and remained ill until he died as a result of the assault'. The third witness testified that he was also sitting outside the court, that he had suddenly seen the deceased coming bareheaded out of the courtroom, shouting, 'Be witness of this, folks,' that the *qāḍī* had come after him, that he had struck the deceased twice with a palm branch, once on his left ear and once on his right eye, that he had kicked him twice in his belly *with his left foot*, which had caused the deceased to fall down, that he was carried to the district officer and that he had remained in bed until he died as a result of the assault. After consultation of the Grand Mufti, the judge who heard this case decided that the testimony of the first witness was irrelevant as he had not seen the fatal blows and kicks and that the testimonies of the second and third witnesses were contradictory and could not serve as a basis for a sentence against the defendant.[5]

Oaths can under certain conditions corroborate incomplete evidence and render it full. Thus a plaintiff may prove his case with only one qualified witness, if he corroborates his claim with an oath. This is accepted by all schools but the Hanafites. The refusal to swear an oath, on the other hand, has also probative force. If the plaintiff cannot produce evidence, the defendant must swear that the plaintiff's claim is unfounded and then the *qāḍī* will find for the defendant. However, if the latter refuses to take this oath, the plaintiff's claim will be sustained.

The rules that I have summarised here are the general rules of evidence. For the trial of *ḥadd* crimes and, if the plaintiffs demand retaliation, of homicide and wounding, the standards of proof are stricter. The testimony of one witness corroborated by the plaintiff's oath, or the defendant's refusal to swear an oath, are not admitted as evidence. Moreover, only eyewitnesses may testify, and testimonies conveying the declarations of others are not admitted. In procedures regarding the adjudication of bloodmoney, the normal rules of evidence are followed, since the issue in these procedures is of a financial and not of a punitive nature.

For the trial of *ḥadd* offences, the rules of evidence are even more strict than those for retaliation. The *qāḍī*'s own knowledge is not recognised as sufficient proof for a verdict. Witnesses to *ḥadd* crimes are neither legally nor morally obliged to give testimony, and in cases of unlawful sexual intercourse it is even considered commendable not to notify the authorities or testify in court. Further, testimonies and confessions must be explicit in their wording and express the unlawfulness of the conduct that has been witnessed or is admitted. A testimony or confession to theft, therefore, must mention the word 'theft', and not just 'taking away', and a testimony to unlawful sexual intercourse (*zinā*) must use this technical term and not just any word meaning sexual intercourse. Only confessions made in court are

[5] Muḥammad al-ʿAbbāsī al-Mahdī, *al-Fatāwā al-Mahdiyya fī al-waqāʾiʿ al-Miṣriyya*, 7 vols. (Cairo: Maṭbaʿat al-Azhar, 1884 (1301 H)), vol. VI, p. 58.

valid: testimonies to the effect that the defendant, out of court, admitted that he committed the offence, which are valid in homicide trials, are not regarded as conclusive in cases of *ḥadd* offences. The rationale is that the judge, when a person confesses to having committed a *ḥadd* crime, must ascertain that he was of sound mind and acted voluntarily. Moreover, he must counsel the defendant that he is free to retract his statement. For the retraction of a confession will, until the moment of the execution of the punishment, invalidate the conviction (but not the civil liabilities arising from the judgment, such as the obligation to return stolen goods or to pay the proper brideprice (*mahr al-mithl*) in case of illegal sexual intercourse). Testimonies in *ḥadd* cases can also validly be retracted: each witness can nullify a sentence in a *ḥadd* case by withdrawing his testimony, which he may do until the moment of the execution of the sentence. This makes sentences in *ḥadd* cases somewhat precarious, unlike sentences of retaliation. As shown in the following case, tried in Egypt in 1880, law enforcers were well aware of the differences between a sentence in a *ḥadd* case and one in a homicide case. They would prefer a sentence of retaliation to one for robbery with manslaughter, because the latter could be affected by the withdrawal of confessions or testimonies. In the following case the Egyptian Khedive consulted the Grand Mufti about what could be done if the convicted robbers would retract their confessions:

Three men had attacked and robbed a person. During the assault, one of them had struck him with a sword, another had shot at him and the third had hit him with a stick. As a result the victim had died. His heirs demanded the death penalty as the fixed punishment for highway robbery with manslaughter. As the accused confessed to the crime, the *qāḍī* of Kordofan (Sudan) pronounced a death sentence for robbery. The verdict was later confirmed by the Court of Appeal in Cairo. As capital punishment could be carried out only on the strength of an order of the Khedive, the latter, before issuing the order, asked the Grand Mufti what would happen if the culprits retracted their confessions. The Mufti answered that in that case the heirs of the victim could sue the accused again for murder and demand capital punishment for them. They could prove their claim either by the eyewitnesses to the original crime or by witnesses testifying to the culprits' previous admissions.[6]

The requirements for proving unlawful sexual intercourse are even more strict than for the other *ḥadd* offences. On the strength of K 24:4[7] full evidence for this crime requires the concurring testimonies of four male eyewitnesses. They must have seen the act in its most intimate details, i.e.

[6] Ibid., vol. VI, pp. 505–7.

[7] 'And those who accuse honourable women but bring not four witnesses, scourge them [with] eighty stripes and never [afterwards] accept their testimony – They indeed are evil-doers.'

the penetration, or, in the terms of certain *ḥadīth*s, the witnesses must have observed the act just like 'a pencil going into a kohl container (*ka-l-mīl fī al-mikḥala*) or a bucket into a well (*ka-l-rashā' fī al-bi'r*)'. If their testimonies do not satisfy the requirements, the witnesses can be sentenced to eighty lashes, the fixed penalty for unfounded accusation of fornication (*qadhf*). The Shiites also admit the testimony of women regarding unlawful sexual intercourse, if there is at least one male witness. Thus, under Shiite law, it can be proven by the testimonies of two men and four women, or even one man and six women. By analogy to the requirement of the four witnesses, the Hanafites, Hanbalites and Shiites hold that a confession to unlawful intercourse must be repeated four times in court.

Circumstantial evidence is not admitted in the trial of *ḥadd* offences or of homicide and wounding if retaliation is demanded. The following sixteenth-century *fatwā* clarifies that a *ḥadd* offence (in this case drinking wine) can only be proven by witnesses to the act or a confession. Being in possession of an instrument with which the offence might have been committed is not sufficient for a conviction:

Question: [What happens] if a wine jar is found in Zeyd's possession?
Answer: It is related that Abū Ḥanīfa (may God have mercy on him) went on a Pilgrimage and that he, upon entering Medina, saw the people gathered around a man. They said: 'We found him with a wine-skin, and we wish to inflict the fixed punishment on him.' Abū Ḥanīfa replied: 'He's got the instrument of fornication with him, too. So stone him.' And they left the man and scattered.[8]

Malikite doctrine, however, admits circumstantial evidence in *ḥadd* cases in two instances: they accept as proof for drinking alcohol the testimony of two witnesses to the effect that the defendant reeks of alcohol (this opinion is also held by the Hanbalites) and they regard childbirth in the case of an unmarried woman, not being in the *'idda* period, as a proof of unlawful sexual intercourse. If in such a case she pleads that she was a victim of rape, she must, in order to corroborate her plea, produce circumstantial evidence (*amāra*), e.g. the fact that she came back to her village screaming for help. Other pleas, however, are accepted without corroboration, e.g. the defence that she was impregnated during her sleep unbeknownst to her, or that the conception was the result of heavy petting without penetration.[9]

8 Colin Imber, *Ebu's-Su'ud: the Islamic legal tradition* (Edinburgh: Edinburgh University Press, 1997), p. 211.

9 See e.g. Ṣāliḥ 'Abd al-Samī' al-Ābī, *Jawāhir al-Iklīl sharḥ Mukhtaṣar Khalīl*, 2 vols. (Cairo: 'Īsā al-Bābī al-Ḥalabī, n.d.), vol. II, p. 285; Ibn Farḥūn, *Tabṣirat al-ḥukkām fī uṣūl al-aqḍiya wa-manāhij al-aḥkām*, 2 vols. (Cairo: Maktabat al-Kulliyyāt al-Azhariyya, 1986), vol. II, p. 97 (ch. 64 on giving judgment on *zinā* on the strength of evidence of pregnancy).

If a person cannot be sentenced to a fixed punishment for a *ḥadd* offence because of lack of evidence, although it is otherwise plausible that he is guilty of it, he may be sentenced to a discretionary punishment (*taʿzīr).* For such sentences the strict rules of evidence do not apply. Circumstantial evidence is allowed, especially assumptions based on a person's reputation. Thus, a man who enters his house with a woman of bad reputation and remains there for some time cannot be punished with a fixed penalty, but he may be beaten and imprisoned at the *qāḍī*'s discretion. Similarly, a person may be convicted for theft on the strength of the presence of stolen goods in his home or because it is public knowledge that he keeps company with thieves, even if he denies the specific charge. In a case that occurred in Muslim Cordoba, persons were sentenced to a *taʿzīr* punishment of painful chastisement and long imprisonment for having entered a house with force, beaten up its residents and stolen property, on the basis of the confession of one of them and the testimony of several character witnesses who testified that they knew all the defendants as wicked villains and wine bibbers.[10] Such assumptions based on reputation also play an important role in the assessment of evidence and the acceptance of statements at their face value without further proof. In the following *fatwā* given by a sixteenth-century Ottoman mufti, establishing the bad reputation of a person who allegedly tried to rape a beardless youth (*amrad*, the prototypical object of male homosexual desires), suffices for accepting the victim's statement without further corroboration:

Question: When Zeyd wished to sodomise the beardless ʿAmr, the latter killed Zeyd with a knife, having no other way of escaping. He explains the case in the presence of the judge, and the people of the village bring testimony, saying: "Amr is truthful.' Is the [testimony] heard?
Answer: There is no need for testimony. So long as Zeyd is a wicked person, ʿAmr cannot be touched. Their testimony [merely] reinforces [his claim].[11]

2.2.3.2 *The* qasāma *procedure*

As we saw, oaths do not count as evidence in the law of homicide, except in litigation about financial compensation for the next of kin. There is, however, one exception, the *qasāma* procedure, which is an anomalous way of substantiating suspicions. The procedure aims to determine the liability for a killing by the swearing of fifty oaths in cases where a body is found

[10] Aḥmad b. Yahyā al-Wansharīsī, *al-Miʿyār al-muʿrab wa-l-jāmiʿ al-mughrib ʿan fatāwā ʿulamāʾ Ifrīqiyya wa-l-Maghrib*, 13 vols. (Beirut: Dār al-Gharb al-Islāmī, 1981), vol. II, p. 412.
[11] Imber, *Ebu's-Suʿud*, p. 250.

showing marks of violence. The schools differ on its conditions and on its legal effects. According to most schools the oaths are sworn on the side of the plaintiffs. According to the Hanafites, however, it is the defendants who must swear the oaths, which is more in accordance with the general rules of evidence.

For all schools but the Hanafites, the *qasāma* procedure is a means to complement insufficient evidence, whenever there is a strong suspicion (*lawth*) as to the identity of the murderer. In such cases the plaintiffs, i.e. the victim's heirs, or, in Malikite law, if intentional homicide is the issue, his prosecutors (cf. § 2.5.4.1), after duly having proven the circumstances giving rise to this suspicion, may swear fifty oaths (twenty-five under Shiite law in cases of unintentional killing) in order to substantiate the suspicion. This then establishes the liability for the bloodprice. According to the Malikites and Hanbalites, the procedure may even result in a death sentence for the defendant, if the prosecutors swear that the killing was intentional. The strong suspicion required for initiating the *qasāma* procedure is usually circumstantial, e.g. the fact that a body is found in a hostile village or among an enemy tribe, the fact that a dead person was found lying on the ground just after a group of people had dispersed from that spot, or if the victim is found covered with blood in an isolated place, and in his vicinity another person with blood on his clothes or carrying a blood-stained knife. However, this suspicion may also consist in incomplete evidence, e.g. an accusation by the dying victim, the testimony of one single witness to the killing or the testimony of one or two witnesses to the effect that a person was seen attacking or beating the victim but not actually killing him.

The following case, from twelfth-century Muslim Spain, is a good example of the possibilities of the use of the *qasāma* procedure under Malikite law:

In February 1123, a certain Muḥammad ibn Bāṭir, a wealthy notable living in one of the towns of Muslim Spain, was found strangled in his apartment. He was involved in money lending and people knew that he was rich and usually had large amounts of cash in his house. His apartment, consisting of two rooms, was located in a building owned by him. This was further inhabited by trustworthy men and women. People visiting him had to pass through a gate, which would be locked at night after evening prayer. However, the backside of his apartment faced a hill and between this hill and the building rubble from a demolished wall had amassed. Therefore it was possible to enter this apartment through its window. Every morning the man would wake up the other residents for dawn prayer. One morning, however, he did not do so. Assuming that he had overslept, the neighbours knocked on his door, but there was no answer. Alarmed they notified one of his relatives who also knocked, but again to no avail. Then they unhinged the door and found him dead, lying naked in his bed, tied up and strangled. His moneybox had been prised open and its contents were missing. Suspicion fastened on a young man, hailing from the victim's native village, whom he had befriended. The boy used to assist the man in collecting debts and running errands, and the latter had given him some capital to set him up in business. The youth visited him nearly every night and sometimes spent the whole night in his apartment. When he came late at night or left late, the residents of the building would open the outer gate for him. The night before the victim was found, the residents had opened the door for him to let him in, but had not seen him leaving the building. Since in the morning he had disappeared, he must have escaped through the window in the back of the room. Their suspicion was fed further by the fact that they had seen him before in the company of wicked people, looking as if they were conspiring. When they went in search of him, they found that he had fled, together with his brother-in-law, one of those disreputable companions. Their houses were also empty. Later, one of the victim's neighbours, a woman, told that the youth's sister, the wife of his companion who had also absconded, had come to her before the body had been found and promised her a sum of money if they would not tell anybody that the youth had visited the man the night before. In the end the suspects were found and put in prison, where they were regularly beaten to make them confess. At this point the mufti, Ibn Rushd (the Grandfather, d. 1126), was consulted about what could be done against them if they persisted in their denial. His answer was that this was a case of strong suspicion (*lawth*) and that the victim's agnatic relatives could swear fifty oaths to make the evidence against the youth and his brother-in-law complete and demand their death.[12]

According to Hanafite doctrine the defendants and not the plaintiffs must swear the oaths. If a body showing traces of violence is found in a house, on a person's land, in a city quarter or in a village or its vicinity (within shouting distance), and there is no evidence as to the identity of the killer, the victim's heirs can introduce a claim against the owner of the house or the land or against any one of the inhabitants of the quarter or village. If the defendant denies the claim, the heirs can start the *qasāma* procedure and demand fifty oaths of denial to be sworn by the owner of the house or of the land or by fifty inhabitants, to be selected by the plaintiffs, of the quarter or village. This then establishes liability for the payment of the bloodprice. Within Hanafite doctrine there is some controversy about who is liable if the victim's body was found in a private house or on private ground: the actual users or the owner, or their solidarity groups (*ʿāqila*, see § 2.5.5.1). The victim's heirs forfeit their rights if they first sue someone else. The following case, tried in Egypt in 1861, shows that this procedure could have satisfying results (at least if we assume the plaintiff's claim to be well founded):

[12] Wansharīsī, *Miʿyār*, vol. II, pp. 302–10.

The mother of Faṭṭūma, the deceased, representing the heirs, sued Faṭṭūma's husband alleging that he had taken hold of her in the presence of his other wife and his adult daughter, thrown her on the floor, stripped her and hit her about five hundred times with the soft branch of a quince tree, that thereafter she stayed in bed for three days and died. The husband, one of the village sheikhs, denied the accusation and claimed that his wife had died from an illness she had caught about six days before her death. The plaintiff produced two witnesses (apparently the women who had washed the body and prepared it for burial) who testified that they had seen the naked body of the deceased after her death and that there were traces of beating and wounds on it, but that they did not know who had hit her. The judge did not admit this as legal evidence against the defendant but allowed the plaintiffs to start the *qasāma* procedure. Since the defendant was the owner of the house where the deceased had been found, the *qāḍī* made him swear fifty oaths to the effect that he had not killed her and did not know who had. Having established that the defendant had no *ʿāqila*, the *qāḍī* sentenced him to pay his wife's bloodprice to her heirs.[13]

2.3 GENERAL PRINCIPLES OF SUBSTANTIVE CRIMINAL LAW

There are very few general principles in Islamic criminal law. The classical books of *fiqh* do not contain chapters dealing with general notions or rules. Those that exist are either mentioned in each separate chapter devoted to a specific crime or they must be found by deduction. General principles of criminal responsibility for homicide, bodily harm, and *ḥadd* crimes can be deduced from the defences or pleas that the law recognises. However, one must be aware that although they may preclude the application of fixed punishments or retaliation, the offender can in many cases still be punished with a discretionary punishment. In the following the term 'criminal responsibility' refers to criminal responsibility for *ḥadd* crimes, homicide and bodily harm, not for *taʿzīr*, nor for civil liability for killing or bodily harm. With regard to *taʿzīr* and *siyāsa* the judicial authorities have a great latitude in imposing punishment. And as for *diya*, the liability is based on tort. For tortious liability it is only required that someone has caused the damage (i.e. the victim's death or wounds), not that he was at fault, for example by acting intentionally or negligently. As a consequence, children and insane persons can be held financially liable for any harm caused by them.

In the following I will discuss the rules determining the criminal responsibility of the offender (the requirement of the *mens rea*, the 'guilty mind'),

[13] Mahdī, *Fatāwā*, vol. VI, p. 78.

the general characteristics of a punishable offence (*actus reus*), the effect of repentance after having committed a crime and, finally, the rules with regard to complicity. There is no theory of attempted crime in Islamic law.

2.3.1 *Criminal responsibility*

Islamic criminal law is based on the principle of individual responsibility. Persons are punished for their own acts. Collective punishment is not allowed, although there are exceptional cases of collective liability, such as in the Hanafite *qasāma* doctrine, where the inhabitants of a house or village can be held liable for the financial consequences of a homicide with an unknown perpetrator, committed in the house or village (see § 2.2.3.2). Under certain circumstances a person who has committed an offence is not responsible for the consequences. Some of these circumstances are connected with the absence of *mens rea*, the 'guilty mind' or the blameworthiness of the defendant, for instance because the offence was committed by a minor or an insane person. In such cases the offence cannot be imputed to the offender. Other circumstances cause the offence to lose its unlawful character (*actus reus*): an act which contains all the elements of a crime and can be imputed to the person who has committed it must sometimes be regarded as lawful because of a justifying circumstance, such as for instance self-defence.

2.3.2 Mens rea

Muslim jurists explain that there are three requirements for the application of legal punishment: the offender must have had the power to commit or not to commit the act (*qudra*); he must have known (*ʿilm*) that the act was an offence; and he must have acted with intent (*qaṣd*).[14] This can be regarded as a framework for a theory of *mens rea* in regard to offences punishable with retaliation and *ḥadd* offences. It implies that minors and the insane are not held responsible for their offences, because they are presumed not to be aware of the unlawfulness of their acts and, moreover, lack criminal intent. Further, this framework is a starting point for considering coercion as a defence in criminal proceedings. Finally, it provides the theoretical basis for the concept of uncertainty (*shubha*) as a legal defence: actual or presumed ignorance of the unlawfulness of an act is a legal defence in cases of homicide and *ḥadd* offences.

14 Aḥmad b. Idrīs Qarāfī, *Anwār al-burūq fī anwāʿ al-furūq*, 4 vols. (Beirut: ʿĀlam al-Kutub, n.d.), vol. I, p. 162.

Table 2.1: *Age before which puberty cannot be established*

	Hanafites	Malikites	Shafi'ites	Hanbalites	Shiites
Boys	12	9	9	10	–
Girls	9	9	9	9	–

Table 2.2: *Age after which absence of puberty cannot be established*

	Hanafites	Malikites	Shafi'ites	Hanbalites	Shiites
Men	15	18	15	15	15
Women	15	18	15	15	9

2.3.2.1 Minority, insanity and unconsciousness

There is no *mens rea* if the perpetrator of an offence, according to the law, lacks the intellectual capacity to realise fully the implications of his conduct. This is the case with minors and the insane. Minority ends with (physical) puberty. There is, however, an irrebuttable presumption that children cannot have reached puberty before a certain age (defined differently by the various schools) and must have reached it after a certain age. Only the Shiites do not fix a minimum age. The positions of the schools are shown in tables 2.1 and 2.2.

Between the age limits, puberty can be proven by establishing that a person has the physical signs of sexual maturity. Minority and insanity make the imputation of crimes to the offender impossible and prevent his conviction. However, they do not preclude financial liability, since liability arising from torts only requires causation and not that the damage has been caused by fault. Unconsciousness also removes criminal responsibility, unless it was the result of drunkenness, since this is in itself an offence. With regard to offences punishable at the *qāḍī*'s discretion, the only requirement in respect of the perpetrator is that he is possessed of reason (*'aql*), i.e. the understanding that he acted wrongly. If he is a minor, he may be punished in order to discipline him (*ta'dīb*).

2.3.2.2 Uncertainty (shubha)

An important category of defences falls under the heading of *shubha*, i.e. uncertainty regarding the unlawfulness of the offender's act. This defence is based on a saying of the Prophet Mohammed: 'Ward off the fixed punishments from the Muslims on the strength of *shubha* as much as you can.'[15] The doctrine of uncertainty is only relevant in connection with homicide and *ḥadd* crimes. The classification and terminology of the different types of uncertainty and the examples given vary among the schools. Here I will try to present the gist of it, avoiding the rather fluid terminology. *Shubha* can be of two kinds: uncertainty as to the facts and uncertainty as to the law. Uncertainty as to the facts exists if a person believes that his conduct is lawful because he excusably erred in the identity of persons or objects. Uncertainty as to the law exists if a person's belief in the permissibility of his acts derives from an erroneous understanding of the law.

There exists uncertainty regarding the facts if, for example, a person strikes what he believes to be a dead body, but actually kills a sleeping person or if a blind man finds a woman in his bed and has intercourse with her, erroneously assuming that she is his slave. Or if a man marries a woman and sleeps with her, after which he discovers that she is his foster sister. Their marriage is null and void, but they cannot be convicted for unlawful sexual intercourse, on the grounds of excusable ignorance.

Uncertainty regarding the law can be the consequence of ignorance of either the essentials or the details of the law. Ignorance of the essentials of the law, such as ignorance of the prohibition of stealing, of drinking wine, or of fornication, i.e. ignorance of rules that are based on clear texts from Koran or *ḥadīth* or on consensus (*ijmā* ʿ), is only excusable if the offender is a recent convert to Islam, coming from outside the territory of Islam, or if he recently came from the wilds far from civilisation. Uncertainty on the details of the law is almost always regarded as excusable. Standard examples are the killing of a person at his own request, stealing from one's children in the belief that one is entitled to their property, sleeping with a slave woman belonging to one's wife assuming that such intercourse is lawful, or drinking wine for medicinal purposes. In such cases the defendant will not be sentenced to a fixed penalty for committing a *ḥadd* offence.

With regard to some pleas, uncertainty is assumed to exist: only the facts on which the uncertainty is based must be proven, and the defendant is not required to plead a mistaken belief. This is the case if the mistaken belief is founded on a text from Koran or *ḥadīth* which has been abrogated by another text or is interpreted differently by the majority of the jurisprudents, or if the belief is based on a minority opinion. Standard examples of this

[15] Ibn Ḥajr al-ʿAsqalānī, *Bulūgh al-marām min adillat al-aḥkām* (Cairo: Dār al-Kitāb al-ʿArabī, n.d.), no. 1044.

kind of uncertainty are the father who kills his son, steals his property or sleeps with his female slave, believing that he is allowed to do so on the strength of the *ḥadīth* 'You and your property belong to your father.'[16] The Hanafites add another type of uncertainty regarding the law, called *shubhat al-'aqd* (uncertainty regarding a contract), which is presumed to exist if there is a formal semblance of right, for instance if there is a void marriage contract, even if its nullity derives from a Koranic text or from the consensus of the jurisprudents and even if the defendant knew that the marriage was invalid.

2.3.2.3 *Duress (ikrāh)*

Duress can be a defence with regard to *ḥadd* crimes. A person will not be punished if someone forces him to commit a crime by threatening to kill him or to inflict severe injuries, resulting in the loss of bodily organs, if he refuses. Similar threats against one's child and, according to some schools, against one's parents are also regarded as duress. It is not sufficient that such a threat was uttered; the person who acted under duress must have actually believed that the person uttering the threats was ready to carry them out and was capable of doing so. The person who acted under duress is regarded as a mere instrument in the hands of the one who coerced him and the chain of causality (*ḥukm al-sabab*) between the latter and the offence remains intact. Unlawful orders by the head of state or state officials are also regarded as duress, even if no specific threats were uttered. There is some controversy about when precisely a power relationship is assumed to imply coercion and when not. In the following case, which was decided in Egypt in the 1860s, there was a difference of opinion about this very issue between a *qāḍī* and the Egyptian Hanafite Grand Mufti:

> Ibrāhīm Agha, the commander of an Egyptian cavalry regiment stationed in the Sudanese town of al-Ubayyiḍ, had ordered a soldier to give fifty strokes of the cane to Bābā 'Abd Allāh, a soldier who, pleading illness, had refused to carry out a command. As a result of this chastisement the soldier died the same day. In the trial before the *qāḍī*, the provincial governor acting as the representative of the state (the victim did not have any relatives) demanded from Ibrāhīm Agha, the defendant, his due according to the law. After the governor had proven his accusations, the *qāḍī* sentenced the defendant to pay the deceased soldier's bloodprice to the state. The defendant's plea that not he but the soldier who had administered the beating had actually caused the victim's death was not accepted. His orders, just like those of the sultan, must be regarded as constituting duress. The actual perpetrator was,

[16] Ibn Māja, *Sunan* (Cairo: Dār al-Ḥadīth, 1998), p. 64; Ibn Ḥanbal, *Musnad*, 6 vols. (Cairo: Maṭba' al-Maymūniyya, 1985), vol. II, 179, 204, 214.

according to the *qāḍī*, no more than an instrument in the hands of his commanding officer and the latter was held responsible. The Grand Mufti, however, opined that in this case a plea of duress could only succeed if the defendant could prove that he had reason to fear for life and limb if he disobeyed the order.[17]

Opinions differ on the question of whether duress is also a defence in homicide cases. The problematic aspect here is that, objectively, the evils between which one must choose are equal. The discussion of this problem hinges on whether the person who acted under duress can be regarded as having acted out of his own free will, or must be seen as an instrument in the hands of the person who uttered the threats. If he can be assumed to have exercised a choice in killing the victim, even if he did not want to do so, he must be held responsible. This is the position of the majority of the jurists, who argue that the chain of causality between the person who exercised the coercion and the victim's death was interrupted by the actual killer since the latter had the choice to act or not to act. An additional argument is that there appears to exist a general rule stating that one may not sacrifice the life of another person in order to save one's own life, for it is generally accepted that during a famine it is not permitted to kill a person in order to survive by eating his flesh. For these reasons, the actual killer is held responsible for the homicide and may be sentenced to retaliation. The jurists differ on whether the person who uttered the threats may also be sentenced to retaliation. The Malikites, Hanbalites and some Shafiʿites hold that this is the case, arguing that he has used a method that is usually effective. Otherwise, he is liable to discretionary punishment. The Hanafites, however (with the exception of Abū Yūsuf, d. 798 CE) differ from the other schools and permit duress as a defence in homicide cases. They hold that the person who was forced to kill did not want the victim's death and was no more than an instrument in the hands of the one who forced him to act. They compare him with a man who is thrown from the roof of a house and lands on a passer-by, as a result of which the latter dies.

2.3.3 Actus reus

For behaviour to constitute a punishable offence (*actus reus*), it must be unlawful, i.e. it must infringe upon the claims of men or of God. For some offences the unlawfulness of the act is connected with a person's religion: drinking alcoholic beverages or changing one's religion is only unlawful for Muslims. For others, such as homicide and bodily harm, it is connected

[17] Mahdī, *Fatāwā*, vol. VI, p. 68.

with the question of whether the victim's life and body were legally protected (*ʿiṣma*).

Self-defence or halting a crime in progress may also make lawful an act that would normally be a crime. Thus killing or wounding an attacker in defence of life, honour or property of oneself or of one's relatives is lawful if the act of self-defence is proportional to the acts of the attacker, i.e. if such an act does not exceed the level of violence necessary to ward off the aggressor. Self-defence is closely related to, and partly overlaps with, the plea of halting a crime in progress. This plea can be made by a person who used proportional violence against another person to prevent him from continuing with a crime he was in the process of committing.

According to all schools, except the Hanbalites, it is obligatory to defend one's life against attacks, even at the expense of the life of the assailant. They infer this from K 2:195 ('. . . and be not cast by your own hands to ruin . . .') reading this text as a prohibition for Muslims to be the cause of their own deaths, if they can prevent it. Defence of one's life is also a valid defence if a person, while being on the point of starvation, kills the owner of food necessary to save his life, after the latter's refusal to give it to him. For in that case the victim acted unlawfully against the killer. This is to be distinguished from the case of a person killing another during a famine in order to save his life by eating the victim's flesh, which is never allowed. Killing or wounding in self-defence entail neither criminal nor financial liability. The acts of violence necessary for this defence have become lawful due to the fact that in such cases the attacker is deemed to have lost his legal protection (*ʿiṣma*). In fact, the aggressor's death or injuries are regarded as a form of lawful retaliation for his aggression.

Defence of one's honour occurs when a woman is sexually assaulted and fights back. This is obligatory for her if she is capable of it. If she fails to defend herself, in spite of being capable of it, she is regarded as having consented to intercourse. She is allowed to use all means to ward off the attack, including killing the attacker if this is the only way to defend herself. Such a fight is even qualified as 'an act of Holy War (*ghazā*)', implying that if she is killed during the fight, she is a martyr (*shahīd*) and goes straight to Paradise.[18] In the following *fatwā*, Ebūʿs-Suʿūd, a sixteenth-century Hanafite mufti, expounds the legal position of a woman who knows that she has been divorced by her husband, whereas the latter denies the repudiation and demands his marital rights.

[18] Ebussuud Efendi and Mehmet Ertuğrul Düzdağ, *Şeyhülislam Ebussuud Efendi Fetvaları ışığında 16. asır Türk hayatı*, 2nd edn. (Istanbul: Enderun Kitabevi, 1983), no. 781.

Question: If Zeyd, after saying, 'If I perform such an act, my wife will be triply divorced,' does perform that act, and if his wife knows this but is unable to prove it, is she sinning if Zeyd makes [sexual] advances to her [and she accepts them]? *Answer*: This is unlawful sexual intercourse, which she must never commit voluntarily. It is necessary that she offers [him] everything that she possesses in order to obtain *khul*ʿ [consensual divorce against a consideration given by the wife]. If he intends to have intercourse with her and she cannot escape by other means, it is lawful for her to add poison to his food. [In that case] she does not commit a sin and is not liable for his bloodprice.[19]

As to men, their honour is impugned by illicit sexual behaviour of their wives or female relatives. Therefore, if a man catches his wife or one of his female relatives in a compromising situation with a man, he is permitted to kill his wife or relative and her lover, provided that killing is the only way to stop the continuation of the crime. Here two grounds for impunity coincide: defence of one's honour and the necessity of halting a crime in progress. Opinions differ regarding the evidence that the defendant must produce in order for this defence to be accepted. The Hanafites and Shafiʿites require that the act of unlawful sexual intercourse be proven by four male eyewitnesses, whereas the other schools accept the testimony of two witnesses, arguing that the proof for fornication in this case is not required for convicting the culprits, but only as a defence against a charge of homicide.

Finally, defence of one's property is a valid plea against charges of homicide or wounding. In the following *fatwā*, authored by a nineteenth-century Malikite mufti in Egypt, it is made clear that a high level of violence is allowed if the lawful owners of stolen property are resisted in taking it back. In fact, the liability for homicide in this case depended on the issue of the ownership of the calf that was the immediate cause of the scuffle:

Two brothers went in search of one of their calves that had gone astray. Near a neighbouring village they found a calf which they thought was theirs. However, when they wanted to take it, they were stopped by a man called Yūsuf, who was accompanied by some of his nephews, and a fight broke out. One of the brothers died in the fight and the other brother accused Yūsuf of having killed him. Yūsuf however denied this, saying that the victim had struck him on the face with his stick, after which he had lost consciousness. When he regained his consciousness he saw his nephews standing around the victim. Therefore, he accused his nephews of having killed the victim. They claimed, however, that their uncle had been the killer. The case was submitted to the mufti who explained that everything depended on the ownership of the calf. If the calf was the property of the two brothers, then

[19] Ebussuud and Düzdağ, *Fetvaları*, no. 780.

Yūsuf and his relatives had acted unlawfully against them. Since in that case they were all accomplices in the homicide, they all deserved capital punishment, if the victim's heirs could prove that nobody else could have killed him [The Malikites recognise collective responsibility in homicide cases, see § 2.3.5]. However, if the calf belonged to Yūsuf or his relatives, the two brothers were acting unlawfully and, if it could be established that Yūsuf and his nephews could only have warded them off and protected their property by killing them, they were not liable for the murder.[20]

2.3.4 *Repentance* (tawba)

A very special form of exemption from punishment can in some cases be brought about by repentance. It is an interesting defence that does not fit in Western theories of criminal law, because it is connected neither with the *mens rea* nor with the unlawfulness of the act. The explanation is that, if a criminal offence does not violate the claims of men, one of the objectives of the punishment is the rehabilitation of the offender. By showing his repentance, the offender actually proves that he has already been reformed and does not need to be punished anymore. According to all Sunnite schools, repentance prevents the punishment for apostasy (except for apostasy on the ground of insulting the Prophet Mohammed) and, on the strength of K 5:33–4,[21] the penalty for banditry. The apostate is given a term during which he can repent and return to Islam and thus obtain impunity. Repentance in the case of banditry is only accepted if it occurs before the bandit is caught. It consists in the expression of one's intention to abandon crime and to lead a straight life. Some schools specify a term during which the defendant must give evidence of the seriousness of his intentions. The Malikites require in addition that the bandit give himself up to the authorities. Repentance resulting in the lapse of the *ḥadd* penalties for banditry does not affect the liability for homicide, bodily harm or theft, since these are claims of men. According to Shiite law, and some minority opinions among the Shafiʿites and Hanbalites, repentance expressed before the crime has been proven in court prevents the enforcement of all fixed punishments barring the punishment for unfounded accusation of

[20] Muḥammad ʿIllaysh, *Fatḥ al-ʿalī al-mālik fī al-fatwā ʿalā madhhab al-Imām Mālik*, 2 vols. (Cairo: Maṭbaʿa al-Taqaddum al-ʿIlmiyya, 1902–3), vol. II, p. 286.

[21] 'The only reward of those who make war upon God and His messenger and strive after corruption in the land will be that they will be killed or crucified, or have their hands and feet on alternate sides cut off, or will be expelled out of the land. Such will be their degradation in the world, and in the Hereafter theirs will be an awful doom' (5:33); 'Save those who repent before ye overpower them. For know that God is Forgiving, Merciful' (5:34).

unlawful intercourse (*qadhf*), since this is connected with a claim of men. The criminal responsibility on the strength of *ta'zīr*, however, remains.

2.3.5 *Complicity and plurality of perpetrators*

The rules with regard to duress excepted, there is no general doctrine of complicity nor is there a legal distinction between primary and secondary participation. The jurists, however, do discuss rules for establishing criminal liability if more than one perpetrator is involved in an offence. For most schools, participants in a punishable offence are liable only if they have individually carried out all elements of the offence. If one of two thieves breaks into and enters a house at night, takes a precious necklace and throws it through the window to his partner, whereupon the latter runs away with it, neither one can be punished with the fixed punishment for theft, because they have not individually carried out all the acts essential to the definition of theft (see § 2.6.2). The Hanafites go even further and require in addition that the value of what each person has stolen amounts to the minimum value necessary for the application of the fixed punishment (*niṣāb*).

The only form of collective criminal liability in the law of *ḥadd* is to be found in the doctrine of banditry, where the aggravating circumstances causing an increase in the punishment are not individualised. This means that if one of the persons participating in an incident of banditry seizes property of one of the victims, all participants will be sentenced to amputation of the right hand and left foot, the punishment for banditry with misappropriation (see § 2.6.3). But this principle of collectivity also works the other way: if one of the participants cannot be convicted because he is a minor or because of some other circumstance (except repentance, which affects only the person who has repented), none of the others can.

With regard to homicide, all schools (except the Malikites who, as I will explain, follow a doctrine of collective liability) hold that if a person is assailed by more than one perpetrator, the plaintiff, in introducing his claim against the perpetrators, must specify whose actions actually caused the victim's death. If the plaintiff cannot attribute the fatal blow to one of the attackers, his claim is not admitted. This is made clear in the following Hanafite *fatwā* given in connection with a case tried in Egypt in 1858. Incidentally, the fact that the *qāḍī* dismissed the claim does not mean that the culprits were not punished. As I will explain in § 4.3.2 on nineteenth-century Egypt, crimes were tried both by the *qāḍī* and by state courts.

A man was attacked by two persons, one of whom hit him on the head with a rock. When he was found, just before he died from his wounds, he told that he had been attacked by two men, whom he identified, and that one of them had hit him on the head with the rock, but that he did not know which of them it had been. The mufti, upon the *qāḍī*'s request, explained that the *qāḍī* should dismiss such a claim, since it did not identify the person who actually had caused the victim's death.[22]

For establishing liability in cases of more than one attacker, it is also necessary that the plaintiff specifies whether the acts of each of them, provided they would have been lethal if carried out separately, were committed simultaneously or in succession. If the perpetrators acted simultaneously and if criminal intent (*ʿamd*) is proven, they can all be sentenced to death. If they acted in succession, the one who first attacked the victim is liable if the victim dies within a day after the attack. Otherwise the victim's death is ascribed to the last attacker. In both situations, the other assailants are to be punished by a discretionary punishment. How complicated these rules are is illustrated by the following case that was brought to an Egyptian court in 1879:

Two men had entered the cattle pen of Muḥammad Bey ʿAbd Allāh at night [probably to steal cattle, although this is not mentioned in the record] and killed a certain Ramaḍān Mūsā, who was sleeping there. The first defendant had hit him on the head with a big stone and the second one, when the victim still showed signs of life, had stabbed him in the belly with his knife. Ramaḍān died two days after the attack. During the trial the first defendant confessed that he, together with the second defendant, had murdered Ramaḍān. Further it was established that both acts would have been lethal if they had been carried out separately. Against the second defendant, who did not confess, nothing was proven. Asked for his opinion, the Grand Mufti argued that the first defendant could not be sentenced to retaliation. Since the hitting with a stone and the stabbing with the knife had been consecutive acts and the victim had lived for more than one day after the attack, the cause of his death was to be ascribed to the second defendant, against whom nothing was proven legally. The first defendant, the Mufti explained, was to be punished by the state authorities on the strength of *taʿzīr*.[23]

As mentioned before, the Malikites take a different stand. They hold liable not only the person who by his acts has directly caused the victim's death, but all other persons who were involved in the crime, e.g. through abetting or offering assistance. Therefore, under Malikite law, both the person who prepared poison, knowing that it would be used to kill someone, and the person who actually administered it can be sentenced to death by way of retaliation. The same is true if, for instance, three men drag a person to an isolated place and only one of them actually shoots him.

[22] Mahdī, *Fatāwā*, vol. VI, p. 25. [23] Ibid., vol. VI, p. 480.

Sometimes one of the perpetrators in a homicide case is not liable for retaliation because of some personal circumstance excluding such liability, such as minority or certain forms of kinship between victim and perpetrator (as we shall see in § 2.5.4.4, a father cannot be sentenced to death for killing his child). In such a situation, the Hanafites, contrary to the other schools, hold that none of the perpetrators can be sentenced to retaliation.

2.4 THE PENALTIES

2.4.1 Aims of punishment and rules of execution

As in most Western penal systems, punishment is justified in Islamic law by deterrence, retribution, rehabilitation and, finally, the idea of protecting society by incapacitating the offender. In addition, the rules regarding punishment are, as we shall see, closely intertwined with those of redress by means of damages, not only in the law of homicide, but also with regard to theft and unlawful sexual intercourse. Since the Shariʿa is religious law, some of the laws of punishment also have a 'vertical' dimension, in that they relate to reward and punishment in the Hereafter. This is the case with the law of *ḥadd* and the institution of *kaffāra* (see § 2.5.1).

Deterrence (*zajr*) is the underlying principle of all fields of Islamic criminal law. Since, according to the jurists, the threat of punishment in the Hereafter does not sufficiently deter people from committing forbidden acts, punishment in this world is a necessity. For the fixed punishments, deterrence is referred to by the words 'an exemplary punishment' in K 5:38 and its importance is clear from the rule that *ḥadd* penalties must be carried out in public. Although the law of homicide is based on retribution, the notion of deterrence also plays a role: K 2:179 proclaims: 'And there is life for you in retaliation, O men of understanding, that ye may ward off [evil].' This is usually understood as meaning that retaliation will deter people from killing.

The importance of retribution is most evident in the punishment of retaliation for homicide and bodily harm (*qiṣāṣ* or *qawad*), which is based on the idea of 'a life for a life, an eye for an eye and a tooth for a tooth'. The retributive character is emphasised by the majority view that the way of executing the death penalty for homicide must be similar to the way the victim was killed, and that, under supervision of the authorities, the heirs may carry out the death penalty themselves (see § 2.4.11.1). Retribution also plays a role in the *ḥadd* penalties: witness Koranic verses such as K 5:33[24]

[24] See n. 21.

and 5:38[25] that characterise the punishments for theft and banditry as the recompense of those who have committed these crimes.

Rehabilitation of the offender, i.e. trying to deter a culprit from repeating his crimes and bringing him back to the straight path, is the main justification of discretionary punishment, which, as we shall see, must be meted out in accordance with the special circumstances of the accused in order to achieve an optimal effect.

Finally, punishment can be a means of protecting society by incapacitating the offender, by execution, banishment or lifelong imprisonment. It is the main rationale of *siyāsa* punishment, i.e. punitive measures imposed by the executive authorities for political expediency or the maintenance of public security (see § 2.7.2). Not all forms of capital punishment serve this objective. The execution of a murderer on the strength of retaliation serves retribution, rather than the protection of society, witness the fact that the imposition of the death penalty depends on the will of private individuals, i.e. the victim's heirs. Protection of society is also the principal aim in taking action against recidivists: 'With regard to repeated offenders who are not deterred by the prescribed punishments, the executive officials are allowed, if the people suffer harm from their crimes, to keep them permanently imprisoned until they die, so as to protect the people from their harm. Their food and clothing must be provided from the treasury (*bayt al-māl*).'[26]

According to all schools except the Hanafites, fixed punishments have a special religious rationale: the notion that by being subjected to the fixed punishment, the culprit atones for his sins and will not be punished for it in the Hereafter. As the Prophet has allegedly said: 'The hand of the repentant thief precedes him to heaven.'[27] The Hanafites argue, however, that this atonement is brought about by sincere repentance (*tawba*) and not by the application of the fixed penalty.

The execution of criminal sentences is the exclusive competence of the state. There are, however, two exceptions. According to the Malikite and Shafiʿite schools, the prosecutors (the victim's next of kin), with the *qāḍī*'s permission, are entitled to carry out the death penalty for homicide personally. And all schools except the Hanafites hold that the execution of criminal sentences against slaves is the authority of their masters. The Malikites, however, here make an exception for the punishment of amputation, which should be carried out by an official executioner.

25 'As for the thief, both male and female, cut off their hands. It is the reward (*jazāʾ*) of their own deeds, an exemplary punishment from God. God is Mighty, Wise.'

26 Māwardī, *al-Aḥkām al-sulṭaniyya*, p. 220.

27 Frank E. Vogel, *Islamic law and legal system: studies of Saudi Arabia* (Leiden: Brill, 2000), p. 241. The *ḥadīth* is not found in any of the authoritative collections.

In principle, criminal sentences are carried out immediately after the passing of the sentence. However, if there are circumstances of a temporary nature endangering the life of the person who is to undergo corporal punishment, such as illness or extreme climatic conditions, the execution of the sentence may be postponed until circumstances allow the punishment to be inflicted without the risk that the convict dies. In order to protect the life of the unborn child, a pregnant woman is not subjected to corporal punishment; the sentence will be carried out after delivery. In case of a death sentence, the execution is stayed until after the weaning of the child.

If a person, having committed several crimes, is sentenced to a number of different penalties, each of them must be carried out. If this is physically impossible, the authorities must first execute those sentences that are founded on the claims of men and then those resulting from the claims of God. The death penalty has priority over, and cancels, the other penalties within the same class. If, for instance, someone has been convicted for theft, slander and drinking alcohol, all penalties must be inflicted, i.e. amputation of the right hand, eighty lashes and again eighty lashes, respectively. If a person has been sentenced to the removal of his eye by way of retaliation, to eighty lashes for slander, to a hundred lashes for unlawful intercourse and to amputation of the right hand, the head of state or his agent must first carry out the gouging out of the eye because that is a claim of man, then imprison him until the wound has healed, then carry out the punishment for calumny, which is also a claim of man. Thereafter he may choose which penalty he carries out first. If, in this example, the punishment for illicit intercourse would have been lapidation, this must be executed after the removal of the eye and the infliction of eighty lashes for calumny, both being claims of men. As the death penalty has priority over the other penalties, lapidation must be carried out first, cancelling the other *ḥadd* penalties, since these are claims of God.

The following is a list of the various punishments mentioned in the books on *fiqh*. The list is not exhaustive, since *qāḍī*s and executive officials may, at their discretion, impose any penalty that they hold suitable. They may also subject the culprit to practical measures in order to prevent him from repeating his crimes. Thus we find for instance that a young male homosexual prostitute was sentenced to house arrest at his parents' home and that a procuress was forced by a *qāḍī* to live among pious people and that the house from where she plied her trade was bricked up.[28]

[28] Wansharīsī, *Mi'yār*, vol. II, pp. 409, 415.

2.4.2 *Reprimand*

The lightest form of discretionary punishment is a verbal reprimand or 'a frown from the *qāḍī*', i.e. signs and gestures showing his displeasure. These light forms of rebuke are recommended especially for members of the elite, since these are very likely to mend their ways after an admonition, especially if made in public.

2.4.3 *Fines*

Pecuniary punishments must be distinguished from liability for blood-money, since the latter is a form of compensation or damages due to the victim or his heirs, whereas the distinctive feature of the former is that they are to be paid to the state. Moreover, in many cases blood-money is not paid by the perpetrator, but by his solidarity group (*ʿāqila*). Only the Malikite scholars unanimously allow fining as a *taʿzīr* punishment. Within the other schools opinions differ. The controversy stems from uncertainty as to the legal grounds justifying the seizing of a person's property by the state. Within the Hanafite school only Abū Yūsuf regarded it as lawful – not, however, as a form of confiscation of property, but as a deposit guaranteeing the offender's future proper behaviour. However, in spite of the legal hesitations, fining was a common form of punishment. In the following *fatwā*, issued by the sixteenth-century Hanafite mufti Ebu's-Suʿud, Abū Yūsuf's minority position is presented as the authoritative one, thus justifying the Ottoman practice of fining offenders.

Question: If the judge or governor sees fit to impose a money fine (*taʿzīr bi'l-mal*), is this permissible in law?
Answer: I have heard from a reliable person that a money fine is permissible if the judge or governor sees fit. A case in point is when a man does not attend Friday prayer. It is permissible to punish him with a fine. *Khulasa*.
In which case, in what manner is the fine imposed?
Answer: A fine is permissible if [the judge or governor] sees benefit (*maṣlaḥa*) in it. Our Lord the Seal of *Mujtahids* Rukn al-Din al-Vanjani al-Khurazmi said: 'This means that we take his property and place it in deposit. If he repents, it is returned to him, as is the custom with horses and weapons belonging to rebels.' The Imam Zuhr al-Din al-Timirtashi al-Khurazmi upholds him in this. It is said that a case in point is that, when a man does not attend Friday prayer, it is permissible to fine him.[29]

[29] Imber, *Ebu's-Su'ud*, pp. 224–5.

2.4.4 *Public exposure to scorn* (tashhīr)

A common form of discretionary punishment was the exposure of the offender to public scorn, which was often imposed in combination with other penalties. Examples are the shaving of a culprit's head, the blackening of his face with soot – a punishment especially reserved for false witnesses – and parading him through the streets, on foot or seated back-to-front on a donkey accompanied by a town-crier announcing the culprit's offences.

2.4.5 *Banishment* (nafy, taghrīb)

Banishment is mentioned as a penalty in connection with two *ḥadd* offences. It occurs in K 5:33,[30] apropos of banditry, and in a Prophetic *ḥadīth* in connection with unlawful intercourse.[31] However, banishment as a punishment for banditry is interpreted by most schools as imprisonment until the culprits show repentance. Only the Malikites regard it as real deportation, but apply it only to male bandits. As to illicit sex committed by a person who is not a *muḥṣan* (see § 2.6.4), banishment for a year is a complementary punishment according to all Sunnite schools except the Hanafites. The Malikites and Shiites apply it, however, only to men, since the banishment of women means that they are forced to live far from their male relatives and may, therefore, lead to debauchery. The other schools, for the same reason, require that a woman who is sentenced to banishment must be accompanied, at her own expense, by a close male relative to stay with her and watch over her. In Shiite law, banishment is also an additional penalty for pimping (*qiyāda*).

2.4.6 *Imprisonment* (ḥabs)

The most common function of imprisonment lies outside the domain of penal law. It is the ultimate means of coercion in private law to force debtors to fulfil their obligations. They can be imprisoned by the *qāḍī* until they pay their debts or carry out their obligations or prove that they are indigent or incapable of fulfilling their obligations. The law also allows imprisonment as a form of pre-trial custody, pending the investigation of the crime. As a punitive measure it occurs under two headings. As we have seen in the preceding paragraph, the common interpretation of banishment as a fixed punishment for bandits is imprisonment. Further, imprisonment can be

30 See n. 21. 31 See the *ḥadīth* of Unays, quoted in § 2.6.4.

imposed as *ta'zīr* punishment. The length of imprisonment is left to the discretion of the authority imposing it. It can be a matter of some days or months, or until the culprit repents, or even until his death. The Hanafite school adds a third instance of imprisonment, namely as a punishment for theft after two previous sentences of amputation. In principle prisoners must support themselves. However, if they do not have sufficient means, the state must feed and clothe them.

2.4.7 *Flogging* (jald)

Flogging, to be administered by a leather whip, is a very common penalty. A generally accepted rule is that the executioner, in administering the lashes, may not raise his hand above his head to the extent that the armpit is visible. The force with which the lashes are administered varies with the crime: flogging for unlawful intercourse must be more painful than flogging for calumny, and the latter more painful than flogging for drinking alcohol. Flogging for drinking alcohol may, therefore, also be inflicted by palm leaves, twined cloth or shoes. The Shafi'ites and Hanbalites in fact regard this way of inflicting the penalty as compulsory. There is a difference of opinion regarding flogging as *ta'zīr* punishment. According to some, it must be more severe than whipping for unlawful sex, whereas others hold that it must be milder than flogging for drinking alcohol.

Men are as a rule flogged while standing, whereas women are whipped while seated. Men are stripped to the waist (except while being flogged for calumny), unlike women, who may leave their clothes on. However, furs and leather clothing are to be removed as they would protect the offender against the pain. On the strength of K 24:2[32] it is commendable to carry out the punishment in public. The blows must be equally distributed over the body, with the exception of dangerous spots such as the head and the genital area. The Malikites hold that the blows may only be aimed at the back. These provisions are meant as precautions so that the lashing will not be fatal. If the culprit is weakened by a serious and incurable illness, the fixed punishment of lashing, which may not be waived after judgment has been given, is administered in a lightened form, for instance with a twined piece of cloth, a shoe, or, in extreme situations, with a bundle of fifty or a hundred twigs. In the latter case, provided that care is taken that all twigs

[32] 'The adulterer and the adulteress, scourge ye each one of them [with] a hundred stripes. And let not pity for the twain withhold you from obedience to God, if ye believe in God and the Last Day. And let a party of believers witness their punishment.'

touch the body of the condemned, only one or two blows are needed for administering the required hundred lashes.

2.4.8 *Amputation* (qaṭʿ) *of the right hand*

Amputation of the hand means severing the hand from the wrist, or, according the Shiites, the cutting off of the four fingers. The wound is then cauterised in boiling oil at the expense of the condemned. If the thief's right hand is paralysed, or has already been amputated as a consequence of a previous conviction, the left foot is to be cut off. In case of further offences, the Hanafites prescribe prison sentences, whereas the other schools hold that the offender's remaining extremities may be removed.

2.4.9 *Cross-amputation* (al-qaṭʿ min khilāf)

Cross-amputation means that a person's right hand and left foot are amputated. Under Shiite law, only the four fingers of the hand and the forefoot are cut off. In case of a second offence the left hand and right foot are severed. It is one of the penalties for banditry and was sometimes inflicted also on rebels.

2.4.10 *Retaliation for injuries* (qiṣāṣ mā dūn al-nafs)

The amputation of members, the infliction of wounds and blinding may be imposed by way of retaliation upon someone who has wilfully inflicted such injuries on another person. The Malikites and Hanafites hold that the punishment must not be carried out until the victim's wounds have healed so that it is clear that no liability for his death arises, which would replace the liability for bodily harm. The other schools allow immediate execution. According to the Malikites the operation must be carried out by a physician, to be paid by the plaintiff.

2.4.11 *The death penalty*

The normal way of executing the death penalty is beheading by the sword, but, as we shall see below, in certain cases different forms of execution are prescribed. Sometimes the *qāḍī* is free to choose from a number of modes of execution: in Shiite law, homosexual intercourse entails the fixed punishment of death, whereby the *qāḍī* has the choice between beheading, lapidation, burning or dropping the convict from a high wall. A woman will not be put to death during pregnancy. The execution is postponed until she has delivered and weaned the child.

2.4.11.1 The death penalty as retaliation

The death penalty for intentional homicide must, according to most schools, be carried out by an executioner. The Malikites and Shafiʿites, however, hold, on the basis of K 17:33,[33] that the death penalty may be executed, with the permission and under the supervision of the authorities, by one of the heirs of the victim. If one of them kills the perpetrator without official permission, he is not liable for retaliation but only for disciplinary punishment. The Hanafites and Shiites allow only execution by the sword, whereas the other schools, on the basis of K 16:126[34] and 2:194,[35] hold that death shall be inflicted in exactly the same way as the victim was killed. Only if this would result in protracted torture is the death penalty to be carried out by the sword. Government officials must inspect the weapon and examine whether the heir who is going to execute the offender is able to handle the weapon with skill. If this is not the case he must find another person to do it for him. If such a person is only willing to perform this task against a remuneration, this is to be paid from the offender's estate.

2.4.11.2 The death penalty by stoning (rajm)

Lapidation or stoning to death is administered by a crowd, throwing stones at the condemned with the aim of ultimately killing him or her. The stones may not be too small nor too large: if they are too small it would take too long to kill the condemned and if they are too large, he would die too soon. The right size is that of a stone that fills a hand. According to some schools women may be dug into the earth up to their waists. The Hanafites hold that the witnesses, if the conviction is based on testimony, must throw the first stones to show that they have not withdrawn their testimonies, and that the head of the state or his representative (the *qāḍī*) must do so if the conviction is based on a confession.

2.4.11.3 The death penalty through or in combination with crucifixion (ṣalb)

Crucifixion is mentioned in the Koran (K 5:33) as one of the punishments for banditry. Most schools explain crucifixion as exposure of the body of

[33] 'And slay not the life which God hath forbidden save with right. Whoso is slain wrongfully, We have given power unto his heir, but let him not commit excess in slaying. Lo! he will be helped.'

[34] 'If ye punish, then punish with the like of that wherewith ye were afflicted.'

[35] 'The forbidden month for the forbidden month, and forbidden things in retaliation. And one who attacketh you, attack him in like manner as he attacked you. Observe your duty to God, and know that God is with those who ward off [evil].'

the bandit after his execution. The majority of the Malikites, however, hold that the bandit must be crucified first, and then brought to death by stabbing him in the breast. For the Shiites, finally, the punishment consists of crucifying the bandit for a period of three days. If after this period the culprit is still alive, his life will be spared.

2.4.12 Complementary penalties

There are a few complementary penalties that cannot be imposed independently. For instance, a person who has been convicted of calumny (*qadhf*) loses his capacity to testify, according to the Hanafites forever and according to the other schools until his repentance.

2.5 HOMICIDE AND BODILY HARM

2.5.1 Introduction

Killing or wounding a person will only entail punishment or financial liability if it is committed unjustly or unlawfully (*ʿudwān^an^, taʿaddiy^an^* or *ẓulm^an^*). This means that the acts of killing or of inflicting injuries must have been committed without a legal justification. Such a justification can be the fact that the killing was a lawful execution, or that it was justified by the interest of the Muslim community as a whole, such as in the case of the killing of Muslims used as shields by the enemy during a siege or a battle. Killing a person is also allowed if he lacks legal protection (*ʿiṣma*) as in the case of apostates (*murtadd*) or of unbelievers residing outside the territory of Islam (*ḥarbī*). Killing an apostate, therefore, is not homicide and will not entail retaliation or a liability for bloodmoney, but only a discretionary punishment for obstructing the proper procedure to be followed. This is explained in the following *fatwā*, issued by the Egyptian Grand Mufti in 1861:

> A Muslim, on trial for having intentionally killed a Christian merchant, pleaded that he had acted with just cause because the Christian had once converted to Islam and then returned to his old faith. Therefore he was an apostate, whose life is not protected by law. The Mufti ruled that if the defendant could prove his plea, he could not be sentenced to retaliation or to the payment of bloodmoney, but would only be liable for disciplinary punishment (*taʾdīb*) for not having given the apostate an opportunity to reconvert to Islam.[36]

[36] Mahdī, *Fatāwā*, vol. VI, p. 91.

The Islamic law of homicide and bodily harm is governed by three principles:

(a) the principle of private prosecution;

(b) the principle that redress consists in retaliation or financial compensation;

(c) the principle of equivalence, which means that retaliation is only allowed if the monetary value of the victim is the same as or higher than that of the perpetrator.

The most salient aspect of the Islamic law of homicide and bodily harm is the principle of private prosecution. The claims of the victim or of his next of kin are regarded as claims of men and not as claims of God. This means that the plaintiff is the *dominus litis* and that the prosecution, the continuation of the trial and the execution of the sentence are conditional upon his will. Prior to the execution of the sentence, the prosecutors may pardon the defendant or accept a financial settlement. The judge cannot interfere and acts merely as an arbiter who supervises the procedure, assesses the admissibility of evidence, and finally pronounces judgment on the basis of the plaintiff's claim and the evidence produced by him. The state only plays a subsidiary role in cases of homicide and hurt. If there are no terms for retaliation, state authorities or the court may inflict punishment by way of *taʿzīr*. In Malikite law the *taʿzīr* penalty is fixed: a person who commits wilful homicide but cannot be sentenced to retaliation for procedural reasons (because e.g. the victim's next of kin pardon him) must be sentenced to one year's imprisonment and a hundred lashes.

In cases of homicide and bodily harm the plaintiffs may demand either retaliation or financial compensation. Retaliation, i.e. a death sentence or the infliction on the perpetrator of wounds similar to the ones the victim has undergone, is only permitted if the killing or wounding was intentional. In that case, the standards of proof are higher (see § 2.2.3.1). If there are no terms for retaliation, although during the trial it is established that the defendant has caused the death or the injuries, the plaintiff may demand bloodmoney. This is not a form of fining: it accrues to the plaintiff(s) and not to the state, its amount is negotiable between the plaintiff and the defendant, and, finally, in many cases it is not the perpetrator who must pay the compensation, but his clan.

Since this domain of the law regulates the private claims of individuals, it is governed by the notion of equivalence (*mumāthala*) between the inflicted damage (death or bodily harm) and the retaliation or financial compensation. The yardstick for determining equivalence is a person's status, to which a monetary value is attached. This status, as we shall see

(see § 2.5.4.2) is determined by sex, religion and by whether a person is a slave or a free person. The principle of equivalence prescribes that a person may not be sentenced to death for killing a person of a lower monetary value. Shiite doctrine, however, allows such death sentences but upholds the principle of equivalence by the stipulation that such a sentence may only be carried out if the plaintiffs (i.e. the victim's heirs) pay the difference in monetary value to the heirs of the murderer. With regard to retaliation for bodily harm, not only must there be equivalence between victim and perpetrator, but also equivalence between the injuries of the victim and those to which the attacker will be subjected. If an injury similar to the one suffered by the victim cannot be inflicted without a serious risk for the life of the condemned, retaliation lapses and is replaced by financial compensation.

The origins of this part of the law go back to the pre-Islamic custom of feuding, which allowed revenge for killing and bodily harm on all members of the tribe of the perpetrator. This often resulted in feuds that could last for generations. These feuds would cease if the victim's tribe would accept compensation, to be paid collectively by all members of the tribe. With the advent of Islam, this institution of revenge was drastically modified. The Koran introduces these reforms in K 2:178–9,[37] 4:92[38] and 5:45.[39] The most important reforms were that revenge in kind could only be taken on the person of the offender and only after due trial. Yet this part of the law retains many archaic traits, such as the collective liability for the bloodprice in many cases and the provisions concerning *qasāma*, a collective oath imposed in order to establish liability in cases of homicide (see § 2.2.3.2).

Homicide creates a bar to succession: the killer cannot inherit from his victim. There is some difference of opinion among the schools about what

[37] 'O ye who believe! Retaliation is prescribed for you in the matter of the murdered; the freeman for the freeman, and the slave for the slave, and the female for the female. And for him who is forgiven somewhat by his [injured] brother, prosecution according to usage and payment unto him in kindness. This is an alleviation and a mercy from your Lord. He who transgresseth after this will have a painful doom. And there is life for you in retaliation, O men of understanding, that ye may ward off [evil].'

[38] 'It is not for a believer to kill a believer unless [it be] by mistake. He who hath killed a believer by mistake must set free a believing slave, and pay the blood-money to the family of the slain, unless they remit it as a charity. If he [the victim] be of a people hostile unto you, and he is a believer, then [the penance is] to set free a believing slave. And if he cometh of a folk between whom and you there is a covenant, then the blood-money must be paid unto his folk and [also] a believing slave must be set free. And whoso hath not the wherewithal must fast two consecutive months. A penance from God. God is Knower, Wise.'

[39] 'And We prescribed for them therein: The life for the life, and the eye for the eye, and the nose for the nose, and the ear for the ear, and the tooth for the tooth, and for wounds retaliation. But whoso forgoeth it [in the way of charity] it shall be expiation for him. Whoso judgeth not by that which God hath revealed: such are wrong-doers.'

Table 2.3: *Types of homicide creating a bar to succession*

	unlawfulness	direct causation	intent	legal capacity
Shafi'ites	–	–	–	–
Hanbalites	+	–	–	–
Hanafites	+	+	–	+
Malikites	+	–	+	–
Shiites	+	–	+	+

types of homicide produce this bar. The Shafi'ite doctrine is most comprehensive in this respect: all forms of killing, intentional or unintentional, direct or indirect (i.e. without a direct physical act between the victim and his attacker), and even lawful killing, such as killing in self-defence or by way of a lawful execution, create such an impediment. The Hanbalites take the same position, except that, in their view, lawful killing does not create such a bar. Hanafite opinion is that only direct, unlawful killing creates an impediment to inheritance, regardless of whether the killing was intended or accidental. Finally, under Malikite and Shiite law a person who has killed accidentally is not excluded from inheriting from his victim, but he is not entitled to a share in the bloodprice. Although minors and insane people are liable for bloodmoney if they kill, this does not create a bar to inheritance according to Hanafite and Shiite opinion. Table 2.3 marks with + the various conditions that, according to the different schools, are required for killing to create a bar to inheritance.

K 4:92 requires that Muslims, under certain conditions, must also atone for the shedding of blood in a purely religious way, by performing an expiation (*kaffāra*) consisting in the freeing of a slave, or, if one does not possess slaves, fasting for two months. This comes in addition to the obligations imposed by the court as a result of the trial. On the basis of K 4:92 it is obligatory in cases of unintentional and semi-intentional homicide (*qatl khaṭa'* and *qatl shibh 'amd*). The Shafi'ites and Shiites, however, hold that intentional homicide also entails the obligation to atone. *Kaffāra*, being a purely religious institution just like the ritual duties, falls outside the sphere of the law (in the Western sense) and is of no concern to the *qāḍī*.

2.5.2 *Causation*

For a sentence of retaliation it is required that the killing was the result of a direct act by the killer, and that he used an instrument or a method that normally causes death. With regard to financial liability, the chain of causation between the act and the result may be longer. Thus witnesses who give false testimonies on the strength of which the defendant is sentenced to retaliation are, according to most schools, each liable for half the bloodprice if they retract their statements after the execution. The general rule for establishing financial liability for homicide is that death must have been caused by an act of the killer. Whether the killer could foresee the result in such a situation is of no consequence: if a person takes another man's minor son, without the father's permission, to a region or city afflicted by plague and the minor dies as a result of it, he is liable for the boy's bloodprice, regardless of whether or not he knew about the epidemic. Moreover, it is required that no voluntary human act intervened in the chain of causation between the act of the killer and the victim's death. This point is made clear in the following *fatwā* given by a Hanafite mufti:

Question: Zeyd's wife Hind co-operates with ʿAmr in killing the said Zeyd, by getting him to drink poison. If they confess voluntarily, for what are they liable? *Answer*: If they made him drink with their own hands, they are liable for bloodmoney. If Zeyd drank it himself, they are liable for a severe chastisement and a long imprisonment.[40]

There is difference of opinion regarding the liability for retaliation if death was caused by criminal omission. The Hanafites do not recognise this as wilful homicide, since they require for retaliation that the perpetrator have committed a positive act that has directly caused the victim's death. Shafiʿite and Hanbalite scholars admit such a liability but only if the omission is linked to a positive act. Examples mentioned by them are the imprisoning of a person and withholding food and drink from him, or the negligence of a midwife who fails to tie off the umbilical cord after cutting it. The Malikite view, finally, is that if a person fails to act when acting is obligatory, and if this omission inevitably results in the death of another person, the former can be sentenced to retaliation for homicide. A nineteenth-century Malikite mufti was asked whether a group of Bedouin was liable for the death of one of them, after he had strayed from the caravan and they had continued their journey after an unsuccessful search for him. The mufti opined that they were not liable for his death since their actions had not inevitably resulted in the victim's death.[41]

40 Ebussuud and Düzdağ, *Fetvaları*, no. 755.

41 ʿIllaysh, *Fatḥ al-ʿalī*, vol. II, p. 296.

2.5.3 *Degrees of criminal intent*

The legal effects of killing and inflicting bodily harm depend very much upon the perpetrator's intent. Retaliation can only be awarded if the killing was wilful or intentional; otherwise the victim or his heirs are entitled to financial compensation. The basic distinction is between intentional (*ʿamd*) and accidental (*khaṭaʾ*) homicide or wounding. In addition, all schools but the Malikites recognise an intermediate category of semi-intentional homicide (*shibh ʿamd*), which creates a liability for the enhanced bloodprice (*diya mughallaẓa*; see § 2.5.5.2).

Various definitions are given to demarcate these categories from each other. The clearest one, in my view, is the definition adopted by the Shafiʿites and Hanbalites: homicide or bodily harm are intentional if both the act against the victim and its results (death or injury) were intended. The offence is accidental if neither the act nor the result was intended, such as when a person aims his gun at an animal, wanting to shoot it, but hits a person. Semi-intentional (*shibh ʿamd*) is when only the act, not the result was intended; for instance, if a person beats another with a cane or throws a pebble at him by way of jest and the other person dies or loses an eye as a result.

Since the jurists felt that it is impossible to establish a person's state of mind, such as the intent to kill, they adopted an external, objective criterion for determining whether or not a killing or wounding was intended: the weapon or means that were employed. If the act was intended, the intention to kill or wound is assumed to exist if the weapon or means were such that they normally would produce death or the injury that was inflicted upon the victim. The Hanafites Abū Yūsuf (d. 798) and al-Shaybānī (d. 805) also follow these principles. Abū Ḥanīfa (d. 767), however, adopted a slightly different definition. In his view, homicide is regarded as intentional if the killer used fire or a sharp weapon or instrument that can cut through the body (such as a sword, a sharp piece of wood or a sharp stone), whereas killing by all other weapons and instruments (hitting with a blunt instrument such as a stick or a large stone, drowning or poisoning) is classified as semi-intentional. According to the doctrine of Abū Ḥanīfa, many forms of wilful manslaughter could not be punished with death. The Malikites and Shiites do not only look at the weapon to establish intent. If the victim's death is caused by an instrument or an act that normally would not be fatal, they try to establish whether or not the intention to kill or wound existed by looking at other circumstances, such as anger or hatred on the part of the offender. Therefore, they have no need for the category of semi-intentional killing. On the other hand, the Malikites have introduced an additional legal category, *qatl ghīla* (heinous murder), not known by the others. It is defined as 'killing a person for his money after having him treacherously brought to an isolated place'.[42] In such cases of murder, the killer can be sentenced to capital punishment, regardless of the pardon of the next of kin or the lack of equivalence between victim and killer.

Accidental homicide or wounding exists if a person has caused another person's wounds or death without the intention to wound or kill the victim. Examples of accidental homicide are that of a man cutting down a tree which fatally hits another person; of a man trying to kill a person but, missing him, killing another; and a man who during a hunt aims at an animal but inadvertently hits a human being. If the act itself was not intended either, as in the case of a mother turning over in her sleep and thereby smothering her baby, the jurists speak of semi-accidental (*shibh khaṭa'*). This distinction, however, does not affect the liability for bloodmoney. Negligence is not required. Homicide or the infliction of injuries by minors or insane people, even if they were intended, can create only a financial liability.

Finally there exists the category of indirect killing or indirectly causing bodily harm (*qatl bi-sabab, jarḥ bi-sabab*), when a person creates the necessary conditions for a fatal accident, but does not directly cause it. The classic example is that of a man who died or was injured because he fell into a well dug by someone else. In these circumstances the man who dug the well is liable only if he dug the well unlawfully, for example because he did so on another person's (or public) property.

2.5.4 Retaliation (qiṣāṣ)

2.5.4.1 The prosecutors (awliyā' al-dam)

Retaliation for homicide can only take place if it is demanded by the victim's next of kin, the prosecutors (*walī al-dam*, plural *awliyā' al-dam*). If there are no next of kin, the head of state, or his representative, acts as a prosecutor. In Sunnite law a sentence of retaliation can be passed only if all prosecutors demand it: if one of them chooses to pardon the killer, retaliation cannot take place. Shiite law follows the reverse principle: retaliation can take place if at least one of the prosecutors demands it. But then he (or they) must compensate the other prosecutors for not receiving bloodmoney.

There is some difference of opinion regarding the question of who the legal prosecutors are. All schools except the Malikites hold that the

[42] Ibn Qudāma, *al-Mughnī*, 11 vols. (Beirut: Dār Iḥyā'al-Turāth al-ʿArabī, n.d.), vol. VII, pp. 648–9.

prosecutors are the victim's heirs regardless of their sex, with the exception, at least for the Shafi'ites and the Shiites, of the spouse relict. Malikite law, however, is different in this respect. Here the pre-Islamic tribal agnatic group asserts itself and retaliation must be demanded by the victim's closest adult male agnatic relatives. The rules governing the inheritance of the agnatic relatives determine which relatives have the right to pardon the killer. The agnatic relatives are divided into five classes:

(a) the descendants
(b) the ascendants
(c) the descendants of the first ascendant (i.e. brothers, nephews etc.)
(d) the descendants of the second ascendant (paternal uncles, cousins, etc.)
(e) the descendants of the third ascendant (paternal great-uncles and their offspring)

Relatives of a higher class exclude those of a lower class. A son or grandson excludes a father or grandfather, a father or grandfather excludes a brother, etc. Within each class, closer relatives exclude more remote ones. Thus, a son excludes a grandson, a father excludes a grandfather and a paternal uncle a cousin. A final rule is that the strength of the blood-tie is relevant. A germane brother and his offspring exclude a consanguine brother. Retaliation cannot take place if the closest male agnate (or, if there are more in the same degree, one of them), pardons the defendant. Female relatives have no say in it, except in the case that there are close female relatives (e.g. daughters), whereas the male agnates are related to the victim in a more remote degree (e.g. brothers). In such a case there must be at least one in each group who is in favour of pardon. If there are only female relatives and no male agnates, the head of state must endorse a pardon by the female relative(s).

A complicating circumstance is the presence of minors among the prosecutors. In Malikite law this creates no problem since only adult relatives have a say in this matter. But for the other Sunnite schools there is a problem since for retaliation the assent of all heirs is required, and a minor cannot validly express his will. In such a situation, a *qāḍī* cannot award retaliation until the youngest minor heir has reached majority. As a remedy the jurists have introduced the rule that the minor's father or, in Hanafite law, his other close relatives, may speak for him if they are also heirs of the victim. This, however, does not resolve the problem in all situations, for a murderer who has killed a father of minor children may thus have to spend long years in prison before the last child has become of age and is legally capable to express his will.

There is a fundamental difference of opinion regarding the nature of the right of the prosecutors. According to the Hanafites and Malikites they only have the right to demand retaliation or to forfeit this right, thereby pardoning the killer. They cannot claim bloodmoney or any other financial consideration without the agreement of the killer. The other schools are of the opinion that the prosecutors are entitled to a triple choice: they may demand retaliation, pardon the culprit without a consideration or pardon him in exchange for the payment of the bloodprice. The implications of the difference become clear if the murderer dies before his execution. In Shafiʿite, Hanbalite and Shiite law the victim's next of kin can still demand the bloodprice from the murderer's heirs, whereas, according to the other schools, the victim's next of kin have lost their rights as a result of the killer's death. The other controversy about the nature of the right of the prosecutors is whether they have an independent right or merely act as the victim's agents. If the latter is the case they are bound by any declaration made by the victim before his death: if he has pardoned the perpetrator, they cannot demand retaliation, whereas on the strength of the first opinion, all the available options are still open for them.

In the following *fatwā* some of these points are brought up:

Question: Zeyd is shooting a gun in some place and hits ʿAmr, who dies on the third day. If he hit him accidentally, must the said Zeyd pay bloodmoney?
Answer: Yes. *In which case,* ʿAmr dies within three days but, while he is still able to move every limb, he says: 'I have forgiven [Zeyd]. Do not seek [compensation for] my blood.' Can Zeyd, simply because ʿAmr said this, not pay bloodmoney to his heirs?
Answer: If the killing was deliberate, he can refuse unconditionally. If it was accidental, his absolution is valid from the third [part of the estate, which he can bequeath by testament.] If the third of his property suffices [to cover the full] amount of his bloodmoney, yes, [Zeyd can refuse to pay.] Otherwise he must pay the shortfall.[43]

The mufti here follows the Hanafite doctrine that in cases of intentional homicide the prosecutors are not entitled to financial compensation, as opposed to cases of accidental homicide. A further Hanafite rule applied here is that the heirs are bound by declarations the victim made before he died. In addition the mufti shows that if the killing was accidental, and the heirs would have been entitled to demand the bloodprice, the remittance of the bloodprice by the victim must be regarded as a gift made during a terminal illness (*maraḍ al-mawt*), subject to the same restrictions as testaments are, namely that its value may not exceed the value of one-third of the estate. This means that if the victim's bloodprice is

[43] Imber, *Ebu's-Suʿud*, pp. 248–9.

less than the value of one-third of his estate, the killer is not obliged to pay. However, if his bloodprice is higher, then Zeyd must pay the difference between the value of the bloodmoney and that of one-third of the estate.

2.5.4.2 *Equivalence between the offender and the victim*

According to most schools, retaliation for homicide or bodily harm is only allowed if the victim's bloodprice is the same as or higher than the offender's. As a consequence, a person cannot be sentenced to retaliation if he has killed a person with a lower bloodprice: a free man cannot be executed for having killed a slave, nor a Muslim for having killed a *dhimmī* (protected non-Muslim resident). The only exception is that a man may be executed for having killed a woman, although her bloodprice is only half that of a man. The Hanafites, however, follow a different criterion with regard to retaliation for homicide. For them the permanent protection of life (*ʿisma*) is the basis of the required equivalence and not the value of the bloodprice. Thus in Hanafite law a Muslim may be executed for killing a *dhimmī* (but not for killing a *mustaʾmin* because his protection is only temporary), and a free man for killing a slave.

The Shiites have a somewhat different and more businesslike approach: they do allow retaliation also if the value of the offender is higher than that of the victim, but in that case the victim or his heirs have to pay the difference to the offender or his heirs. Thus, if a woman is killed by a man, the latter may be sentenced to death if the woman's heirs demand it, but they must pay one half of the bloodprice of a free man to the heirs of the perpetrator by way of compensation, since the bloodprice of a woman is half that of a man. The same rule is applied if several people participate in the killing of one person. They all can be sentenced to death, but the heirs of the victim must pay compensation to the heirs of the perpetrators if the sum of their bloodprices amounts to more than the bloodprice of the victim. If, on the other hand, the bloodprice of the victim or victims (i.e. the sum of their bloodprices) have a higher value than the bloodprice of the killer, such as when a slave kills a free person, or one free person kills two, then the next of kin do not have a choice: retaliation is in these cases obligatory. These rules also apply to bodily harm.

With regard to injuries, there is also another form of equivalence that must be considered: if the member or organ of the offender that is to be removed is paralysed, partly amputated or otherwise defective, this cannot be taken in exchange for a sound one. In this case financial compensation must be paid.

2.5.4.3 *The practical limits of retaliation*

Retaliation for homicide is not subject to special restrictions, except that the execution of a pregnant woman must await delivery and the weaning of the child, because otherwise two lives would be taken. Retaliation for bodily harm is allowed only if it is medically possible to inflict exactly the same injury without endangering the life of the person who is to undergo this penalty. This means that retaliation can be awarded for loss of hands, feet, arms, legs, testicles, noses, ears, eyes and teeth. As to loss of the senses, only the loss of eyesight can entail retaliation. Retaliation will not be awarded in the case of a deep head wound, a fractured spine or sternum or if a member has been cut off through the bone and not through the joint. In the latter case, however, the Shafiʿites follow a different rule: they allow retaliation from the closest joint between the victim's wound and the end of the arm or leg and award a financial compensation for the part that could not be amputated. The jurists discuss in detail the various types of wounds in order to determine whether or not retaliation is possible. For the wound called *mūḍiḥa*, a wound that lays bare the bone, or less serious injuries, retaliation can be exacted, but not for severe wounds, such as the *maʾmūma* (a head wound reaching the cerebral membrane, *umm al-raʾs*). With regard to fractures there is considerable difference of opinion between the schools about which ones allow retaliation and which not. If retaliation is not possible, it is replaced by financial compensation.

2.5.4.4 *Further conditions*

Sometimes the relationship between the murderer and his victim, or between the next of kin and the offender, prevent retaliation. All schools agree that a father, and according to some, any ascendant, cannot be put to death for killing his child (or descendant). Neither, according to the Hanafite, Shafiʿite and Hanbalite schools, does retaliation take place if a child of the offender is among the heirs of the victim, a situation which may arise for example after a family quarrel that got out of hand. The following legal riddle is constructed around this rule: what can a man who has murdered his mother-in-law do to escape capital punishment? The answer is that he must (unless the marriage is childless) kill his wife, for in that case his wife's right to demand retaliation against him for the murder of her mother is inherited by their children. Since then the perpetrator's children are among the prosecutors, retaliation cannot be demanded. For the same reason he cannot be sentenced to capital punishment for the killing of his wife.

Under Shafiʿite and Hanbalite law, no retaliation takes place if the offender himself inherits the right to demand the death penalty against himself. Since a killer cannot inherit from his victim, he can only acquire this right by inheriting it from someone else. Such a situation occurs if, for instance, a man has killed his wife's childless brother. His wife is then one of the prosecutors. If she dies before the sentence, the perpetrator himself inherits this right.

Although, as noted earlier, the Hanafites stipulate capital punishment in the case of a freeman murdering a slave, this penalty is waived if the murderer is himself the slave's master, since he is the prosecutor. The waiver also applies to wounding his slave. In neither case is he entitled to bloodmoney, since the slave is his property. He is, however liable to *taʿzīr* punishment. In the following sixteenth-century *fatwā* it is emphasised that such behaviour constitutes a grave sin:

Question: If Zeyd pulls out the eyes of his slave ʿAmr, what is incumbent upon him?
Answer: A great torture in the next world. In this world a severe chastisement is necessary.[44]

2.5.5 *Financial compensation* (diya)

In cases where someone has accidentally (*khaṭaʾ*) or semi-intentionally (*shibh ʿamd*) caused a person's death or bodily harm, or if someone has done so intentionally but a sentence of retaliation could not be pronounced, e.g. because the victim's bloodprice is lower than the killer's, or because there is a child of the killer among the prosecutors, a liability for the bloodprice or financial compensation (*diya*, *ʿaql*, *arsh*, *ḥukūmat ʿadl*) is created. The bloodprice for homicide accrues to the victim's estate except that under Shafiʿite and Malikite law, the spouse relict has no share in it.

2.5.5.1 *Liability for bloodprice, the solidarity group* (ʿāqila)

One of the indications that bloodmoney (*diya*) is not a form of punishment is the fact that as a rule it is not to be paid by the perpetrator but by his solidarity group (*ʿāqila*). This is the survival of a pre-Islamic institution. The solidarity group is liable if the killing or wounding is accidental, or semi-intentional. However, if, during the legal proceedings, the offender was instrumental in establishing the liability, e.g. by confessing to the act in the presence of witnesses, or by concluding a settlement with the victim's

44 Ebussuud and Düzdağ, *Fetvaları*, no. 538.

heirs, the liability of the solidarity group lapses and the offender himself must pay. The solidarity group is not liable for offences against slaves, because such offences are regarded as the infliction of damage to property. But the owner's solidarity group is liable for acts of homicide and wounding committed by slaves, to a maximum of the slave's value.

Originally the *ʿāqila* consisted of the adult able-bodied tribesmen, who had the duty to protect all members of their tribe. This is still the basis of the legal definition adopted by the Malikites, the Hanbalites and the Shiites, for whom the *ʿāqila* consists of all male agnatic relatives of the killer, including minors. The Shafiʿites define the *ʿāqila* as the adult male agnatic relatives who are also heirs. They exclude, however, the ascendants and descendants. The Hanafite definition, finally, reflects the urban and military milieu in Iraq, where tribalism was losing its strength. The Hanafites hold that other groups can also function as *ʿāqila*. For them the test is whether there exists a solidarity (*tanāṣur*) within such a group to the extent that if a person's house were to burn down, the others would offer him assistance. This applies under Hanafite law for instance to soldiers belonging to the same payroll (*dīwān*) and to traders in the same market. For a freedman his patron (*mawlā*), i.e. his former owner and the latter's male agnatic relatives, form the solidarity group, at least if the freedman himself does not have agnatic relatives or if these are indigent. If a person has no *ʿāqila* the treasury is liable, but only if the offender was a Muslim.

If the full bloodprice is due, the solidarity group can pay it in three annual instalments. If the compensation for injuries is less than one-third of the full bloodprice, the amount must be paid after one year; if it is between one- and two-thirds, the amount is due in two annual instalments. There are some limits to the *ʿāqila*'s liability. The compensation for injuries is to be paid by the perpetrator if the amount is smaller than one-twentieth (Hanafites and Shiites) or one-third (Malikites, Hanbalites) of the full bloodprice. In Shafiʿite law there is no threshold value for the liability of the solidarity group. The Hanafites, Shafiʿites and Hanbalites have put a maximum to what each individual member of the *ʿāqila* has to contribute. For the Hanafites this is 3 dirhams per year, which would mean that some 1,100 men are needed to cover the full bloodprice of 10,000 dirhams or 1,000 dinars. The Shafiʿites and Hanbalites introduced a much higher limit: half a dinar for the rich and one quarter of a dinar for the middle groups per year. The poor are exempt from this obligation.

2.5.5.2 The amount of the bloodprice (diya) *for homicide*

The bloodprice for a free Muslim man is the standard against which the values of all other categories of persons are measured, both for life and for injuries. There are two kinds: the normal bloodprice, due in cases of unintentional homicide, and the enhanced bloodprice (*diya mughallaẓa*), for intentional and semi-intentional homicide. The normal bloodprice is 100 camels of various specifications as to age and sex. The enhanced bloodprice is also 100 camels, but of more expensive specifications. In early Islam the standard bloodprice was given a monetary value of 1,000 dinars or 12,000 (according to the Hanafites 10,000) dirhams. This equals 29.7 or 35.64 kg of silver or 4.25 kg of gold.[45] In monetary value there is no difference between the normal and the enhanced bloodprice. In Hanbalite and Shiite law, there is another form of enhanced bloodprice which is due if homicide takes place in the holy months or in the holy precinct in Mecca (*al-ḥaram*), or if the victim is a female close relative of the offender (*maḥram raḥam*). In these cases the bloodprice is increased by one-third.

The value of the bloodprice varies with the victim's sex, religion and legal status, i.e. freedom or slavery. This reflects the differences in legal capacity. The bloodprice of a woman is half that of a man. The value of the bloodprice of a *dhimmī* is fixed differently by the schools: the Hanafites and Hanbalites hold that it is the same as that of a Muslim. According to the Malikites it is one-half of the bloodprice of a Muslim and according to the Shafiʿites one-third. The Shiites assign to it the extremely low value of 800 dirhams. The bloodprice of a slave is his market value, with a maximum, according to some, of the bloodprice of a free person. The compensation for an embryo (*ghurra*) after a miscarriage as a result of violence against the mother is one-tenth of the bloodprice of the mother, ergo one-twentieth of the bloodprice of a free Muslim man. The embryo must show human characteristics such as nails or hair, or, according to others, life (*rūḥ*) must have entered it. In Shiite law the full bloodprice is due as soon as life has entered the embryo, and then sex is taken into account; but Shiite law is exceptional in that it extends the protection of the body to the period before a person is alive. Shiite jurists distinguish five stages of development of the embryo before life enters it, and assign values to each of them, ranging from 10 to 100 dinars. The first stage is that of sperm. The ultimate logical consequence is a curious rule in Shiite law that if a person disturbs a man during sexual intercourse with *coitus interruptus* as a result, he must pay 10 dinars, the bloodprice of a foetus in its very first stage (*nuṭfa*). The money is to be shared equally between the husband and wife. The same amount is due to the wife if her husband practises *coitus interruptus*

45 Based on the weights of the coins that were current after the monetary reforms introduced by Caliph ʿAbd al-Malik in 715–16 CE, i.e. 2.97 of silver for the dirham and 4.25 g of gold for the dinar.

without her consent.[46] The Shiites also extend the protection of the human body after death. Mutilation of a dead body creates a liability for financial compensation. The bloodprice to be paid for cutting off the head of a body – or any part without which a man cannot survive – is 100 dinars, both for men and women, and the bloodprice for other parts is calculated in the same way as in the case of a living person as fractions of 100 dinars. This compensation does not belong to the heirs, but to the deceased himself and must be spent on his behalf, e.g. on charity or in order to perform the *ḥajj* for him.

2.5.5.3 Financial compensation for bodily harm (arsh, ḥukūmat ʿadl)

Financial compensation for injuries is fixed in two different ways. There is a tariff list for the loss of members, faculties and certain wounds. Compensation based on this tariff list is called *arsh* or *diya*. For other injuries the damages are assessed by having recourse to experts on the market price of slaves. The amount due as compensation is that part of the full bloodprice that is proportional to the loss in value of a slave with a similar defect. This assessed compensation is called *ḥukūmat ʿadl.*

The tariff list is based on a number of principles. One of these is that the full bloodprice is due for loss of members, faculties or organs of which the human body has only one, and half of the bloodprice for members that come in pairs. Thus the compensation for the loss of the nose, the tongue, the male member or the faculties of sight or hearing is the full bloodprice, whereas for the loss of a hand, an eye or a lip, half of the full bloodprice is due. According to the same logic, a finger or a toe is compensated with one-tenth, and one tooth with one-twentieth of the *diya*. For the wounds called *maʾmūma* (a head wound laying bare the cerebral membrane) and *jāʾifa* (a wound in the body that reaches one of the inner cavities) the compensation is one-third, for the *munaqqila* (a wound whereby a bone is displaced) three-twentieths, and for the *mūḍiḥa* (a wound that lays bare the bone) one-twentieth of the full bloodprice must be paid. These compensations are cumulative: if several injuries have been inflicted, the offender must pay the sum of their individual compensations, even if this amounts to more than the full bloodprice. The members and organs for which compensation is sought must have been sound. If this was not the case the assessed compensation (*ḥukūma*) is due.

46 ʿAwaḍ Aḥmad Idrīs, *al-Diya bayn al-ʿuqūba wa-l-taʿwīḍ fī al-fiqh al-Islāmī al-muqāran* (Beirut: Dār wa-Maktabat al-Hilāl, 1986), pp. 244–7.

The above-mentioned fractions are portions of the bloodprice of the person who has suffered the injuries. Thus a woman's eye is half the value of that of a man. The Malikites, however, make an exception for injuries with a value of less than one-third of the full bloodprice. For such injuries the compensation for a woman is equal to that for a man. This leads to the curious consequence that for the loss of three fingers a woman gets 300 dinars, but for the loss of four fingers, only 200. With regard to injured slaves, most schools determine the compensation to be paid by relating the above-mentioned fractions to his market price. But here again the Malikites take a different position: they regard him in this context entirely as property and hold that the offender must pay for the real damages, i.e. the reduction of his market value as a result of his injuries.

2.6 *ḤADD* OFFENCES

2.6.1 Introduction

Ḥadd crimes are defined as offences with fixed, mandatory punishments (*ʿuqūbāt muqaddara*) that are based on the Koran or the Sunna. This definition encompasses not only the specific offences mentioned in the Koran, but also intentional homicide and wounding. Hanafite and Shiite authors, however, add another element to the definition, i.e. that a *ḥadd* crime must be entirely or predominantly a violation of a claim of God, i.e. violation of a public interest, which excludes homicide and wounding, since retaliation is a claim of men. The distinguishing feature is that claims of God, unlike claims of men, cannot be waived by men. For practical reasons I follow the Hanafite and Shiite classification. The crimes with fixed punishments are:

- theft (*sariqa*)
- banditry (*qaṭʿ al-ṭarīq, ḥirāba*)
- unlawful sexual intercourse (*zinā*)
- an unfounded accusation of unlawful sexual intercourse (slander, calumny, defamation) (*qadhf*)
- the drinking of alcohol (*shurb khamr*)
- apostasy (*ridda*) (according to most schools).

The principal purpose of the institution of *ḥadd* crimes is deterrence from acts that are harmful to humanity. In pursuance of this objective, fixed penalties must be carried out in public in order to deter others from committing the same offence. Expiation or purification from sin (*taṭhīr*) is only of secondary importance and does not extend to all cases in which fixed penalties are imposed, as these punishments also apply to non-Muslims, who cannot be purified from their sins. There is, however, a widespread conviction that a person who has been subjected to a fixed penalty will no longer be punished for the same offence in the Hereafter.

Since the objective of *ḥadd* penalties is to protect public interest, they are labelled as claims of God (*ḥuqūq Allāh*) and not claims of men, which apply to the interests of private persons. Legal proceedings against those who commit *ḥadd* crimes can be initiated by any Muslim, including the *qāḍī* himself. Moreover, once the procedure has been initiated, the victim cannot pardon the defendant, or conclude a settlement with him. Sentences for *ḥadd* crimes are regarded as fixed by God and therefore immutable. Unlike retaliation, they cannot be waived. Not even the head of state can commute them. The only exception, according to most jurists, is the *ḥadd* offence of *qadhf*, the unfounded accusation of unlawful intercourse, whose punishment is regarded as both a claim of God and a claim of men and whose prosecution depends primarily on a complaint by the victim. Some *ḥadd* offences, such as theft for instance, also infringe individual rights. However, punishment of theft is regarded by the Muslim jurists as required by public interest. The victims may get compensation for their losses through a civil procedure, although, as we shall see, the criminal proceedings may affect the admissibility of the claim for compensation.

A salient feature of the law of *ḥadd* crimes is that the doctrine has made it very difficult to obtain a conviction. This is achieved by (1) the strict rules of evidence for proving these crimes (see § 2.2.3.1); (2) the extensive opportunities to use the notion of uncertainty (*shubha*) (see § 2.3.2.2) as a defence; and (3) defining the crime very strictly, so that many similar acts fall outside the definition and cannot be punished with fixed penalties, but only at the *qāḍī*'s discretion.

In the Hanafite doctrine in particular, it is nearly impossible for a thief or fornicator to be sentenced, unless he wishes to do so and confesses. This occasionally happened, probably due to a need felt by the perpetrator to atone for his sins. This, at least, seems to have been the defendant's motive in the following judgment, given in a seventeenth-century Egyptian case:

A man voluntarily admitted having had sex at a time when he was unmarried (the exact time was not mentioned) and demanded to be punished. The *qāḍī* proceeded to investigate the man's mental health by questioning people who knew him. The mental capacity of the defendant was also tested by asking him simple questions, such as what day, month, and year it was. Finally, the *qāḍī* gave the man a chance to reconsider his claims. When he persisted, he was sentenced.[47]

[47] Galal H. El-Nahal, *The judicial administration of Ottoman Egypt in the seventeenth century* (Minneapolis etc.: Bibliotheca Islamica, 1979), p. 28.

In *zinā* cases, the court must of its own accord examine whether the accused can benefit from possible defences. This principle goes back to a *ḥadīth* about a man called Māʿiz, who confessed four times to the Prophet that he had had illegal sexual relations. The Prophet then questioned him in detail about possible defences that he might put forward:

When Māʿiz came to him to confess that he [had] committed *zinā* and repeated his confession, the Prophet asked whether he was insane or whether he had drunk wine, and ordered someone to smell his breath. Thereupon he questioned him about *zinā*, saying, 'Have you perhaps just kissed her or touched her?' In another version, 'Did you lie down with her?' He said, 'Yes.' Then [the Prophet] asked, 'Did your body touch hers?' He answered, 'Yes.' Then [the Prophet] asked, 'Did you have intercourse with her (*a-jāmaʿtahā*)?' He said, 'Yes.' In the *ḥadīth* of Ibn ʿAbbās [the Prophet asked], calling a spade a spade, 'Did you fuck her (*a-niktahā*)?' He said, 'Yes.' Then he asked, 'Did that thing of yours enter that thing of hers?' He answered, 'Yes.' He asked, 'Like the kohl stick disappears into the kohl container and the bucket into the well?' He answered, 'Yes.' Then he asked, 'Do you know what *zinā* means?' He said, 'Yes, I did with her unlawfully what a man does with his wife lawfully.' Then the Prophet said, 'What do you intend with these words?' He answered, 'That you purify me.' Then he ordered him to be stoned.[48]

There are several explanations for the paradoxical reluctance of the jurists to implement the serious *ḥadd* penalties. Muslim jurists themselves regard it as a consequence of the fact that *ḥadd* penalties are the claims of God: God is without needs and so sublime that it is not necessary that all of His claims be satisfied. In this the claims of God differ from those of men, which must always be fulfilled if they are not waived by the claimant. Others have argued that the laws of *ḥudūd,* and especially the rules regarding theft and unlawful intercourse, are meant as rhetorical devices: the severity of the punishments (stoning to death, amputation) serves in the first place as a warning to the public by emphasising the seriousness of the violation of property rights and of the rules for contact between men and women, in spite of the fact that they are usually punished, not with a fixed but with a discretionary penalty (*taʿzīr*).[49]

2.6.2 *Theft* (sariqa)

Unlawfully taking away property (*ghaṣb*) is essentially a tort with civil remedies: return of the stolen object or damages. In addition, the thief may

48 ʿAbd al-Qādīr ʿAwda, *al-Tashrīʿ al-jināʾī al-Islāmī muqāranan bi-l-qānūn al-waḍʿī*, 2 vols. (Cairo: Dār al-Turāth, n.d.), vol. II, pp. 433–4. For the basic version of this *ḥadīth*, see ʿAsqalānī, *Bulūgh*, no. 1033.

49 Leslie Peirce, *Morality tales: law and gender in the Ottoman court of Aintab* (Berkeley etc.: University of California Press, 2003), p. 333.

be sentenced to a discretionary punishment. Under very special circumstances, however, he may be sentenced to amputation of the right hand (or, according to the Shiites, of the four fingers of the right hand). This fixed penalty is based on K 5:38: 'As for the thief, both male and female, cut off their hands. It is the reward of their own deeds, an exemplary punishment from God.' In case of a second offence, the left foot is removed.

The jurists define the *ḥadd* crime of theft very narrowly. It contains the following elements:

- surreptitiously taking away
- of (movable) property with a certain minimum value (*niṣāb*)
- which is not partially owned by the perpetrator
- nor entrusted to him
- from a place which is locked or under guard (*ḥirz*).

The act must have been surreptitious: if someone steals goods from a market stall in broad daylight, the fixed penalty for theft cannot be imposed, because the goods were not stolen surreptitiously. Another restriction is that the value of the stolen goods must be at least 8.91 g of silver (3 silver dirhams of 2.97 g; see n. 45) or 1.06 g of gold (one-quarter of a gold dinar of 4.25 g; see n. 45, according to the Malikites and Shafiʿites), or 29.7 g of silver (10 dirhams, according to the Hanafites). The goods must be capable of being owned and have legal value: the kidnapping of a free person does not entail the fixed penalty for theft, since free persons cannot be owned. Some goods, such as wine and pigs, can be owned by non-Muslims but not by Muslims because they are impure and forbidden. As a consequence, the fixed punishment can only be imposed if such goods are stolen from a non-Muslim. A further requirement for the fixed punishment to apply is that the thief must not have the goods legally at his disposal or be a co-owner. For example, a shop assistant who takes away goods or money from the shop he attends to, or a person who steals state property, or a soldier who steals from the war booty that has not yet been divided cannot be punished with amputation. In Hanafite law, finally, taking away perishable foodstuffs cannot entail the fixed punishment. In order to emphasise the owner's responsibility in protecting his property, the fixed penalty cannot be applied if the stolen goods are not guarded or stored in an adequate place. Locked houses, shops, stables and coffers count as such places, taking into account the nature of the object. A stable, for instance, is a suitable place for cattle, but not for jewellery. The stealing of a donkey left in front of a mosque or of a thing found in a public bath does not qualify as legal theft, nor does embezzlement, i.e. the misappropriation of goods entrusted to the embezzler. The application of the fixed punishment for theft is further restricted by uncertainty (*shubha*) as to the unlawfulness of the act (see § 2.3.2.2). There is assumed to be uncertainty, for instance, if a person steals from his son or wife, or debtor.

Unlike homicide or bodily harm, the prosecution of theft is not a private matter. Once the case has been reported to the government (the *imām*) and the victim has demanded the application of the fixed penalty, he cannot pardon the defendant. But he can prevent the amputation of the thief's hand by other legal means, as for instance by donating the stolen property to him, in which case he can no longer reclaim it. The return of the stolen goods by the thief before the judgment has the same effect. The reason is that all schools but the Malikites require that the victim of the theft demand the application of the fixed penalty in addition to reclaiming the stolen property from the thief. If the stolen object does still exist, it must be given back to its rightful owner. But what if the object has been destroyed? According to the Hanafites, the victim can only demand damages or the application of the penalty of amputation but not both. The Shafiʿites hold that he can demand both, whereas the Malikite view is that the victim may demand damages in addition to the penalty if the thief is rich, but otherwise only the penalty.

2.6.3 Banditry or disturbance of the peace (ḥirāba *or* qaṭʿal-ṭarīq)

The rules governing banditry have their origins in K 5:33–4:

> The only reward (*jazāʾ*) of those who make war upon God and His messenger and strive after corruption in the land will be that they will be killed or crucified, or have their hands and feet on alternate sides cut off, or will be expelled out of the land. Such will be their degradation in the world, and in the Hereafter theirs will be an awful doom. Save those who repent before ye overpower them. For know that God is Forgiving, Merciful.

On the basis of this verse, Muslim jurists have developed a rather complex doctrine regarding banditry. The minimum element of this crime is a hold-up: the show of drawn weapons in order to frighten people travelling on a public road and to prevent them from continuing on their journey. It is essential that the assailants are superior in strength and that the victims cannot escape. Hanafite jurists assert that women cannot be convicted for this crime because of their physical weakness. According to all schools but the Malikites, the attackers must be armed and the hold-up must take place outside a city, on the presumption that in a city the public or the police will come to the aid of the victims. The Shafiʿites qualify this and hold that an attack in a city can constitute banditry if the Sultan does not have effective power. Aggravating circumstances consist in taking the property of the victims and/or killing them. Repentance by the bandits before capture precludes their prosecution for banditry (K 5:34), but does not exempt them from criminal responsibility for other crimes committed during the attack, such as homicide or wounding.

Koran 5:33 mentions four penalties: capital punishment, crucifixion, cross-amputation or banishment. The Shiites hold that the judge or head of state can impose, at his discretion, any of these punishments if someone has committed an armed hold-up, regardless of the aggravating circumstances. Malikite law is more specific: it prescribes minimum penalties in each case, and gives the judge the freedom to impose more serious punishments: if someone has been killed, the punishment must be the death penalty or crucifixion; if property of whatever value has been taken, the defendant(s) must be punished with at least cross-amputation; and if there has only been a hold-up, the defendants must be sentenced to banishment at least. According to the other Sunnite schools, there is a precise correspondence between the offences and the punishment. If the crime consisted only of a hold-up, the punishment is banishment, or, according to some, imprisonment until repentance; the culprit is to be punished by cross-amputation if he has taken property with a minimum value equal to that required for the punishment of theft (*niṣāb*) or, according to some Shafiʿites and Malikites, if he has raped or sexually abused one of the victims; if a person has been killed, then the killer is to be put to death; finally, if the robber has both plundered and killed, his punishment is death and crucifixion. The Hanafites, however, hold that in the last case the head of state may choose between amputation, capital punishment and capital punishment with crucifixion. The *ḥadd* penalties lapse, however, for those robbers who are closely related to one of the victims.

Banditry is envisioned as a collective crime, which means, in the opinion of all schools but the Shafiʿites, that if the aggravating act is committed by one of the robbers, all of them are liable for the consequences. Thus, all of the bandits must be sentenced to death if one of them has killed. According to the Hanafites, the reverse is also true: if one of the bandits is not legally responsible, for example because of insanity, none of them can be convicted of the *ḥadd* crime of banditry.

Some jurists discuss the very relevant problem of the relationship between the claims of God regarding *ḥadd* penalties and the claims of men resulting from homicide. Contrary to the general rule about the concurrence of penalties (see § 2.4), most schools hold with regard to banditry that God's claims precede the claims of men. That means that prosecution for banditry precludes proceedings introduced by the victim's next of kin based on retaliation. Only if God's claims lapse, e.g. because of the culprit's repentance (*tawba*) expressed before his arrest or because the robbers retract their confessions after their conviction, do the claims of man become enforceable. The Shafiʿite view, however, is that the claims of men have priority. That means that homicide committed during a hold-up must first be tried according to the rules for homicide. If, however, the heirs of the victim pardon the killer or accept bloodmoney, the bandit can be convicted for the *ḥadd* crime. Liability for bodily harm inflicted during a hold-up is not affected by the proceedings for banditry and, according to all schools except the Hanafites, actions arising from it can be initiated regardless of whether the proceedings for banditry have been started. The property that has been taken during the attack must be returned. As in the case of theft there is a difference of opinion on whether damages can be claimed if the goods are destroyed.

2.6.4 *Unlawful sexual intercourse* (zinā)

Under the Shariʿa, sexual intercourse is only permitted within a marriage or between a slave woman and her master. A man who engages in unlawful sexual intercourse commits a tort, regardless of whether or not the woman consented. If the woman is not married, the man is liable for the proper brideprice (*mahr al-mithl*, i.e. the average brideprice that a woman of the same age and social status would receive upon marriage in that region), for having enjoyed her sexual services. If she is a slave, the man has to pay damages to the owner. In addition it may be an offence punishable at the discretion of the *qāḍī*. The following case (from nineteenth-century Egypt) is typical, in the sense that the issue is both the financial liability and the discretionary punishment of the man:

A woman sued a man claiming that he had given her some sweets while they were in her father's house and that the sweets were drugged so that she had fainted after having eaten them. Then the man had taken her on a boat to a villa in the Gharbiyya Province. There he had deflowered her with his member, while she was still unconscious. The defendant admitted that he had deflowered her, but added that he had done so with his finger and not with his member. [This is also a standard phrase in admissions of illegal defloration, used so as to avert the application of the fixed punishment for unlawful sex, RP.] The plaintiff demanded 12,500 piasters from the defendant, the value of her proper brideprice, as an indemnity for the loss of her virginity. She claimed that her cousin had recently been married for the same amount. The defendant rebutted this claim arguing that this cousin was younger and more beautiful than the plaintiff. Finally the parties agreed on a compensation of 2,500 piasters. The settlement was then ratified by the *qāḍī*, who, in addition, sentenced the man to be flogged for his sinful behaviour. The flogging was carried out during the same session.[50]

Finally, under very special circumstances, persons who have had illegal sex can be punished with the fixed penalties of either 100 lashes or death by stoning, depending on their legal status. For proving this offence, very strict standards of evidence are applied: instead of the testimonies of two, those of four eyewitnesses are required and most schools hold that a confession must be made four times in four different court sessions (see § 2.2.3.1).

The offence is mentioned in the Koran, but only with flogging as the penalty: 'The adulterer and the adulteress, scourge ye each one of them [with] a hundred stripes. And let not pity for the twain withhold you from obedience to God, if ye believe in God and the Last Day. And let a party of believers witness their punishment' (K 24:2). The penalty of stoning is based on a *ḥadīth*, according to which the Prophet Mohammed imposed this on an adulteress:

A Bedouin came to the Prophet and said: 'O Messenger of God, I implore you by God to pass judgment on me in accordance with God's Book.' And his adversary, who was better versed in jurisprudence than he, said: 'Yes, pass judgment between us and allow me to speak.' The Prophet said: 'Talk.' He said: 'My son worked as a labourer for this man and then he fornicated with his wife. I was told that my son deserved to be stoned to death, so I ransomed him for one hundred sheep and a female slave. I then asked the people of knowledge and they informed me that my son deserved one hundred lashes and banishment for one year and that the woman deserved to be stoned to death.' The Prophet answered: 'By the One Who holds my soul in His hand, I shall certainly pass judgment between you in accordance with God's Book. As for the female slave and the sheep, they must be returned to you. Your son deserves one hundred lashes and banishment for a year. Go, Unays, to this man's wife and if she confesses, stone her to death.' Thereupon Unays went to the woman and she confessed. Then the Prophet ordered her to be stoned.[51]

On the basis of these texts, the jurists hold that the general punishment for those who have unlawful intercourse is 100 lashes if they are free and fifty if they are slaves, followed, according to all schools except the Hanafites, by banishment for the period of one year, both for men and women. As mentioned before, the Malikites only banish males, whereas the other

[50] Rudolph Peters, 'Islamic and secular criminal law in nineteenth century Egypt: the role and function of the *qāḍī*', *Islamic Law and Society* 4, 1 (1997), 85.
[51] 'Asqalānī, *Bulūgh*, no. 1031.

schools require that women who are banished be accompanied at their own expense by a close male relative to watch over them (see § 2.4.5). The Shiites impose, in addition, a degrading punishment for men: the shaving of their beards.

For a specific group of people, called *muḥṣan*, capital punishment by stoning applies. The Hanafites and Hanbalites even require that for the penalty of stoning to be applicable, both partners must have this status. As is clear from the quoted *ḥadīth*, this has something to do with being married. The legal theory gives a more precise meaning to the concept of *iḥṣān* (i.e. being a *muḥṣan*). In Sunnite law a *muḥṣan* is a person who is:

- adult
- free
- Muslim (except in Shafiʿi law, where a *dhimmī* can also be *muḥṣan*) and
- has previously enjoyed legitimate sexual relations in matrimony (regardless of whether the marriage still continues).

Shiite legal doctrine is different in this respect. It defines *muḥṣan* as an adult free Muslim who is in a position to have legal sexual intercourse and whose partner is actually available and not e.g. imprisoned or absent on a journey.

All Sunnite jurists agree that the essential element for the *ḥadd* crime of unlawful intercourse is actual penetration by the man into the vagina. The Hanbalites and Shiites, however, include also anal intercourse in the definition. For the latter, in addition, sexual acts without penetration (petting) are also regarded as *ḥadd* offences, to be punished with 100 lashes. For the Sunnites such acts are not *ḥadd* offences, but can be punished at the *qāḍī*'s discretion.

Homosexual intercourse (with penetration) is equated to unlawful heterosexual intercourse by most schools. However, there is a difference of opinion about the punishment. The Malikites, the Shiites and some Shafiʿites and Hanbalites are of the opinion that the penalty is death, either by stoning (Malikites), the sword (some Shafiʿites and Hanbalites) or, at the discretion of the court, by killing the culprit in the usual manner with a sword, stoning him, throwing him from a (high) wall or burning him (Shiites). Among the Shafiʿites and Hanbalites there are also scholars who hold that the death penalty by stoning applies only to the active partner or to those who are *muḥṣan*, and that otherwise the punishment is flogging in combination with banishment. The Hanafites, finally, do not put homosexual intercourse on a par with the *ḥadd* crime of unlawful intercourse. They hold that homosexual intercourse must be punished at the *qāḍī*'s discretion. The following *fatwā*, given by an Ottoman mufti in the sixteenth century, sets forth the Hanafite position and explains that capital punishment is not mandatory but may be imposed, even if the accused is not married (i.e. not *muḥṣan*):

Question: The military commander Zeyd sends 'Amr and Bekr to the beardless Beşīr, telling them to fetch him. The forenamed persons forcibly remove Beşir from his neighbour Halid's house, whither he has fled and hidden, and take him to Zeyd. If Zeyd were to take the beardless Beşir to the mountains, and – may God forbid – forcibly commit sodomy with him, what would his sentence be according to the Shari'a?
Answer: It is canonically possible to execute Zeyd, even if he is not married. If he is not executed, his sentence is a severe beating and long imprisonment, and he must be removed from his post. The authorities who connive in [carrying out] his command have no excuse or answer before God. 'Amr and Bekr's sentence is a severe chastisement and long imprisonment.[52]

All schools accept that a woman who has been raped (*mustakraha*) is not punishable, since she acted under duress. However, she may be confronted with some unfortunate consequences if she reports the case to the authorities and identifies the perpetrator but is unable to produce legal proof against him. In the first place, this could be regarded as a confession of having committed unlawful intercourse. Under the circumstances, it is unlikely that she will be punished with the fixed penalty, since her statement that she was raped produces *shubha*. A further obstacle, at least under Hanafite and Hanbalite law, is that a single confession does not suffice for a conviction, unless it is repeated four times. However, she may be punished at the *qāḍī*'s discretion on the strength of her confession. Moreover, she can be prosecuted for defamation (*qadhf*), since she accuses a person of having had illegal sexual intercourse without being able to prove it, which is punishable with eighty lashes (see § 2.6.5).

There are numerous circumstances that can be put forward as a defence of uncertainty (*shubha*) against an charge of unlawful intercourse and that prevent the application of the fixed punishment. Especially with regard to intercourse with female slaves we find many examples of such circumstances, e.g. the fact that one is a co-owner, that one has obtained the owner's consent or that the woman is the property of one's son. In the case of intercourse with free women, there is uncertainty, e.g. if both partners are married to each other, but the marriage contract is null and void; if the woman is hired for the purpose; or if the man is blind and thinks erroneously that the woman is his wife or slave.

52 Colin Imber, 'Zina in Ottoman law', in *Contributions à l'histoire économique et sociale de l'Empire Ottoman* (Leuven: Peeters, 1981), p. 82.

2.6.5 *Unfounded accusation of unlawful intercourse* (qadhf)

The legal definition of this offence is the allegation that someone has had unlawful intercourse of whatever kind, or the denial of a person's legitimate descent, at least if his or her mother is a Muslim and a free person. It is based on K 24:4–5: 'And those who accuse honourable women but bring not four witnesses, scourge them [with] eighty stripes and never [afterwards] accept their testimony – They indeed are evil-doers. Save those who afterward repent and make amends. [For such] Lo! God is forgiving, Merciful.' The penalty of eighty lashes for this offence is a powerful deterrent against rashly giving evidence in cases of illicit sex, since witnesses to acts of unlawful intercourse incur this punishment if their testimonies do not satisfy the legal requirements.

For the penalty to be applied, the victim must be *muḥṣan*, which here has a meaning slightly different from the one used in connection with unlawful intercourse. Instead of denoting a person who has previously enjoyed legitimate sexual relations in matrimony, *muḥṣan* here means a person who is chaste, i.e. who has never been convicted of unlawful sexual intercourse or been subjected to the *liʿān* procedure (a procedure by means of which a husband can deny the paternity of a child born during his marriage). The further conditions for being *muḥṣan* are the same as in the case of illicit sex: being adult (in Malikite law, a woman does not have to be adult, but must be capable of intercourse), free, and Muslim. Unlike the other schools, the Malikites also impose the fixed penalty if someone has used an indirect or metaphorical expression. For the other schools this would constitute uncertainty (*shubha*).

The punishment is eighty lashes and the removal of the right to testify until one repents, or, according or the Hanafite doctrine, forever. The punishment can be averted if the defendant produces four witnesses in support of his allegations. In Hanafite law this suffices, but the other schools require that their testimonies satisfy the conditions for evidence in cases of unlawful intercourse, otherwise they also will be guilty of *qadhf*.

Imposing the punishment for *qadhf* is both a claim of men and a claim of God. The schools differ as to which aspect has priority. Hanafite doctrine is that the claim of God is stronger. Therefore they hold that the injured party cannot withdraw his demand for the punishment of the perpetrator after he has reported the case to the authorities and that the right to demand punishment does not devolve to the injured party's heirs after his death. The Shafiʿite and Hanbalite view is that the claim of men has priority. Therefore they allow the injured party to pardon the culprit until the moment of punishment, and they hold that the right to demand punishment is inherited by the injured party's heirs. The Malikites take an intermediate position, allowing the injured party to withdraw his claim after the authorities have been notified, but only if he is motivated by the protection of his own reputation. After the victim's death, the heirs may demand punishment if the allegations also affect their honour.

2.6.6 Drinking alcoholic beverages

Drinking wine (*khamr*) is forbidden in K 5:90: 'O ye who believe! Wine and games of chance and idols and divining arrows are only an infamy of Satan's handiwork. Leave it aside in order that ye may succeed.'

The penalty, however, is based on a *ḥadīth*:

> Once a man who had drunk wine was brought before the Prophet. He then inflicted about forty strokes with two palm-leaf stalks on him. Abū Bakr did the same. But when ʿUmar came to power he consulted the people and then ʿAbd al-Raḥmān ibn ʿAwf said, 'The lightest of all fixed penalties is eighty [strokes].' Thereupon ʿUmar decreed this.[53]

The Shafiʿites follow the example of the Prophet and make drinking alcohol punishable with forty lashes. The other schools follow the example of ʿUmar, who increased the punishments to eighty lashes. For non-Muslims, drinking alcohol is no *ḥadd* offence. There is some controversy about drinking alcoholic beverages other than wine. Most schools put them on a par with wine and hold that their consumption in whatever quantities is punishable, but the Hanafites hold that if a person drinks these beverages, he will only be punished if he actually gets intoxicated.

2.6.7 Apostasy (ridda, irtidād)

Under the Shariʿa, it is a punishable offence for Muslims to renounce Islam publicly by words or conduct. This can be done expressly or implicitly. An express renunciation consists in abjuring Islam and/or being converted to another religion. Implicit renunciation occurs if one rejects axiomatic articles of faith (*mā ʿulima min al-dīn ḍarūratan*, i.e. the things that Muslims must necessarily know of their religion), e.g. by denying Mohammed's mission or asserting that ritual prayer (*ṣalāt*) or fasting during Ramadan is not obligatory. Examples of conduct entailing apostasy are disrespectful

[53] ʿAsqalānī, *Bulūgh*, no. 1061.

treatment of copies of the Koran, such as sitting or treading on them; or uttering words such as 'In the name of God' (*bismillāh*), while raising a glass of wine. Most books on *fiqh* give long lists of examples.

According to most schools, apostasy is a *ḥadd* crime, to be punished with death. This is based on the following words of the Prophet Mohammed: 'If someone changes his religion, then kill him.'[54] In order to dispel any uncertainty (*shubha*), the apostate is granted a delay of three days for reflection and repentance after his apostasy has been established in court. If he does not return to Islam, he is put to death. In Hanafite law, the delay for repentance is recommended and not obligatory. In Shiite law only an apostate who previously became a Muslim by conversion is entitled to this delay and to repentance, but not one who was born a Muslim. The latter cannot revoke his apostasy and must be put to death.

Unlike the other schools, the Hanafites and Shiites do not regard apostasy as a *ḥadd* offence. Further, they hold that only male apostates are to be executed, whereas female apostates must be imprisoned until they repent and be beaten at the hours of ritual prayer (according to the Shiites) or every third day (according to the Hanafites). Their justification for the death penalty is that apostates have become potential enemy combatants. Since during warfare women may not be killed, they exempt them from capital punishment.

If the apostasy consisted in insulting the Prophet (*sabb al-nabī*), according to most schools the apostate is not given an opportunity for repentance, but is killed immediately after the sentence. The same is true for the *zindīq*, an apostate who to all appearances continues to be a Muslim. Since there is no way to ascertain what he really believes, his repentance cannot be accepted.

2.7 DISCRETIONARY PUNISHMENT ON THE STRENGTH OF *TAʿZĪR* AND *SIYĀSA*

2.7.1 Taʿzīr

In principle all forbidden or sinful acts, even if they do not constitute *ḥadd* offences, homicide or bodily harm, are punishable under the Shariʿa. Executive officials and judges (and, with regard to slaves, their masters) may, at their discretion, impose corrective punishment on those who have committed such acts. This is called *taʿzīr*. In the legal handbooks it is

[54] Ibid., no. 1019.

discussed as a residual category of penalties. In practice, however, *ta'zīr* (together with *siyāsa*, see below) was the most important heading under which punishment was administered.

An important function of *ta'zīr* is to provide grounds for the punishment of those who have committed *ḥadd* crimes or crimes against persons but cannot be sentenced to the appropriate punishment for procedural reasons (e.g. because of uncertainty (*shubha*), or pardon by the victim's next of kin, or lack of legally required evidence) or for the punishment of those who have committed acts that resemble these crimes but do not fall under their legal definitions. Instances of such acts are illegal sexual acts not amounting to intercourse; misappropriation not amounting to theft, such as embezzlement; and defamation on other grounds than forbidden sexual intercourse. Moreover, discretionary punishment may be imposed on those who refuse to perform religious duties such as ritual prayer or fasting. The authorities imposing such punishments were hardly restricted by procedural restraints. With regard to accepting evidence, in particular, they had much latitude (see § 2.2.3.1).

The principal aim of discretionary punishment is to prevent the perpetrator from repeating the offence and, therefore, it has two aspects: it may be a punishment for conduct in the past, with the aim of reforming the perpetrator and restraining him from repeating the offence; or it may have the character of a coercive measure to force a person to carry out his duties, such as ritual prayer or fasting. Retribution and deterrence play a role in the selection of the appropriate punishment. It will be more severe if the accused is a repeat offender or if the offence is widespread and an example needs to be set. In addition, a very important factor in selecting the punishment is the personal situation of the offender. The crucial question in determining the type and severity of the penalty is a pragmatic one: is the chosen punishment suitable to prevent this individual culprit from repeating his sinful behaviour? The meting out of punishment, therefore, is individualised and people are not treated equally: status plays an important role, for it is assumed that the common people need more severe punishments in order to be disciplined than the elite, for whom a frown, a verbal reprimand, or harsh words often suffice for mending their ways.

The range of punishments that may be imposed as *ta'zīr* is almost unlimited, ranging from a reprimand to the death penalty. The most common ones were flogging, public rebuke, exposure to public scorn (*tashhīr*), banishment and imprisonment until repentance. Apart from flogging, no corporal punishments are allowed. The only exception is that the Malikites allow the amputation of the right hand of a person who has forged documents. During the course of history the jurists have tried to impose certain restrictions on the wide discretionary powers of *qāḍīs* and officials, but only a few have become generally accepted. The discussions among the jurists have left traces in the doctrine about the maximum number of lashes that may be inflicted on an offender as discretionary punishment.

The number of lashes that may be administered on the strength of *ta'zīr* is a matter of controversy. The Malikites do not fix a limit, and leave the number of lashes to the discretion of the official imposing the punishment. The other schools hold that this number may not exceed those for *ḥadd* offences. But there is disagreement about the exact implications. According to Abū Ḥanīfa the maximum is thirty-nine lashes (one less than the smallest number, i.e. the penalty for drinking alcohol committed by a slave), but according to Abū Yūsuf this is seventy-nine or seventy-five, since the normal situation of a person is that he is free and not a slave. Since according to Shafi'ite doctrine the punishment for drinking alcohol is forty lashes, some Shafi'ite scholars hold that the maximum is thirty-nine for free persons and nineteen for slaves. Other Shafi'ites and some Hanbalites argue that the maximum number is ten, on the strength of the *ḥadīth*: 'No one is to be flogged with more than ten lashes except in the case of *ḥadd* crimes.'[55] Finally, some Hanbalite and Shafi'ite jurists argue that the maximum number depends on the kind of offence: if it is an offence related to a *ḥadd* crime, the number of lashes must not exceed the number designated as the fixed penalty: not more than ninety-nine for sexual offences that cannot be punished with the fixed punishment for unlawful intercourse (e.g. sexual relations with a slave woman owned by one's wife); not more than seventy-nine for drinking alcohol or defamation. Another controversial aspect of the *ta'zīr* doctrine is the question of whether or not capital punishment is a lawful *ta'zīr* penalty. The issue was seriously debated but in the end all schools allowed it for repeated offenders and for serious crimes such as manslaughter (if no sentence of retaliation could be issued), spying for the enemy, spreading heresies, homosexual acts and sorcery.

2.7.2 Siyāsa

Ta'zīr and *siyāsa* both refer to the meting out of discretionary punishment on the basis of simple procedures without formal rules of evidence (see § 2.3.1) Although the terms are sometimes used as synonyms, they refer

[55] Ibid., no. 1072.

to different concepts. Whereas *taʿzīr* punishment can only be imposed for acts that are forbidden by the Shariʿa, *siyāsa* punishment may be administered for any act threatening public order, regardless of whether or not the perpetrator is to be blamed for it. This is justified by a precedent of Caliph ʿUmar, who banished a certain Naṣr b. Ḥajjāj from Medina because his beauty was a source of temptation for women. ʿUmar realised this when he had heard a woman recite:

> Is there a way to come by wine so that I can drink it?
> Or is there a way to meet Nasr b. Hajjaj?
> A youth of noble family, in the prime of life
> With a soft face, obliging and not obstinate.

When Naṣr remonstrated and asked what he had done to deserve punishment, ʿUmar is reported to have said: 'You have not committed a sin, but I would have committed one if I had not cleansed this town from you.'[56]

A further difference between the two concepts is found in the aims of punishment. For *taʿzīr* this is in the first place reform of the offender and in the second place deterrence. *Siyāsa* justice, on the other hand, is administered for the public interest, to protect society from persons whose acts constitute a danger to law and order (*fitna*). The most effective way to do so is to incapacitate such persons by executing them or imprisoning or banishing them for life. In Hanafite doctrine the most prominent form of *siyāsa* justice is the sentencing to death of habitual criminals for 'striving after corruption in the land', an expression taken from K 5:33.[57] *Siyāsa* punishment consisted very often in the death penalty, and in the Ottoman Empire *siyāsa* became synonymous with capital or severe corporal punishment. A final difference between *taʿzīr* and *siyāsa* punishment is that the former can be imposed by both the *qāḍī* and the executive authorities, whereas the latter is exclusively administered by the executive.

[56] Muḥammad al- Bābartī, *al-ʿInāya sharḥ al-hidāya*, 10 vols. (Cairo: Dār al-Fikr, n.d.), vol. V, p. 245.
[57] See n. 21.

CHAPTER 3

The implementation of Islamic criminal law in the pre-modern period: the Ottoman Empire

3.1 INTRODUCTION

In this chapter I will examine how, during the pre-modern period, the state punished criminals and what role the doctrine of the Shariʿa played in it.[1] Since there was a great deal of variation, both regional and temporal, I will focus, for the reasons I mentioned in the introduction, on the Ottoman Empire. Here a legal system developed on the basis of the Hanafite doctrine and supplemented by state legislation (*qānūn*). In § 3.2 I will discuss this specifically Ottoman legal system. According to the classical doctrine the enforcement of criminal law was the duty of both the *qāḍī* and the executive authorities. In order to understand a given system of criminal law in the world of Islam, it is important to examine the distribution of judicial powers between the *qāḍīs* and the state officials authorised to punish criminals. How these jurisdictions were defined in the Ottoman Empire is the subject of § 3.3. In the following section matters related to procedure, such as arrest, investigation of crimes and sentencing will be discussed. The last section of this chapter (§ 3.5) deals with substantive law as applied by the courts. Here I will examine the extent to which the Shariʿa was applied, the role of legislation and finally the range of punishments that were enforced.

Many European observers found that the Ottoman legal system with its swift justice compared favourably with European legal practice, characterised by long-drawn-out and costly procedures. Although some of them

[1] The principal sources for this chapter are: Uriel Heyd, *Studies in old Ottoman criminal law* (Oxford: Oxford University Press, 1973); Imber, *Ebu's-Suʿud*; Abülaziz Bayındır, *Islam muhakeme hukuku: Osmanlı devri uygulaması* (Istanbul: Islami Ilimler Araştırma Vakfi, 1986); Ebussuud and Düzdağ, *Fetvaları*; Boğaç Ergene, *Local court, provincial society and justice in the Ottoman Empire: legal practice and dispute resolution in Çankırı and Kastamonu (1652–1744)* (Leiden: Brill, 2003); Eyal Ginio, 'The administration of criminal justice in Ottoman Selanik (Salonica) during the eighteenth century', *Turcica* 30 (1998); 185–210; Ahmet Mumcu, *Osman devletinde siyaseten katl* (Ankara: Ankara Üniversitesi, Hukuk Fakültesi, 1963), Peirce, *Morality tales*; Richard Repp, 'Qānūn and Shariʿa in the Ottoman context', in *Islamic law: social and historical contexts*, ed. A. Al-Azmeh (London: Routledge, 1988), pp. 124–46.

criticised certain negative aspects of the Ottoman system, such as hasty capital sentences and, sometimes, cruel punishments, they were on the whole impressed by its efficiency, effectiveness, and even fairness. Moreover, they praised the low crime rates resulting from efficient police methods and the collective responsibility for tracing offenders.[2] Admittedly, we have to be careful in accepting the assessments of Western observers at their face value. They often had hidden agendas – for instance, a desire to criticise their own governments by pointing out the positive traits of the Ottoman Empire. However, in the light of recent studies of Ottoman administration of justice, it is plausible that these Western positive value judgements contained an element of truth.

The Ottoman legal system, as it emerged during the sixteenth century, was based on two pillars: Ottoman law and the Ottoman judicial institutions. Ottoman law was the result of the interaction between the Ottoman, Hanafite, jurists and state officials. This interaction produced its effects in two fields: the transformation of Hanafite legal discourse into a body of unambiguous and consistent legal rules and the creation of enacted laws (*qānūn*), supplementing the Shariʿa. As for the Ottoman judicial institutions, they were characterised by jurisdictions that were clearly defined by enacted laws. Their powers were distributed in such a way that the actors, i.e. the *qāḍī*s and the executive officials, kept one another in check. The local *qāḍī* occupied a key role: he monitored the lawfulness of the acts of other officials involved in criminal justice and thus ensured the legal basis of criminal proceedings, including interrogation and custody of suspects. For his part, the *qāḍī*'s conduct was checked by the local governor and the Sultan, who could open detailed investigations of a *qāḍī*'s dealings and, if necessary, dismiss and imprison him. An overall corrective to ensure the fair working of the system was the right of the people to submit petitions to the central government. As a rule these were taken seriously and could result in the sending of a commission of inquiry to examine alleged abuses.

A final characteristic of Ottoman Islamic law, which it probably shares with other pre-modern legal systems based on the Shariʿa, is the important role assigned to the local communities in criminal trials. By giving evidence about the character and reputation of a person, these communities had far-reaching powers over their members: their testimonies to the effect that the accused was a habitual offender could be the deciding factor for passing a death sentence or for a sentence banishing him from the neighbourhood or

[2] Heyd, *Studies*, p. 313.

village where he lived. This must have been an effective means in ensuring compliance with social and legal norms.

3.2 SHARIʿA AND *QĀNŪN*

In this section I will discuss the emergence of Ottoman law, based on a unique combination of Hanafite doctrine, transformed by the state into an unambiguous body of legal rules, and of state-enacted laws, the *qānūnnāmes*. When the Ottoman state emerged, the Hanafite school of jurisprudence, brought by the Saljuqs from Central Asia, was already well established in Anatolia. It was therefore the obvious choice for the Sultans to select the Hanafite school as the official one of the empire. Although there were many contradictory opinions within the Hanafite school, as within other schools, the Hanafite jurists had developed clear and formal criteria for determining which was the most authoritative view among those held by the founding fathers: an opinion of Abū Ḥanīfa would have precedence over those of the others, whereas, if no opinion of Abū Ḥanīfa was known, Abū Yūsuf's view had to be followed. Only if neither of them had had declared his view on the issue was the opinion of Muḥammad al-Shaybānī the authoritative one.[3] The Ottoman Sultans made use of this principle and directed the *qāḍīs* they appointed to apply the most authoritative Hanafite views. Since the state could delimit the *qāḍīs*' jurisdiction, this instruction implied that judgments passed according to other Hanafite or non-Hanafite views would be null and void and would not be enforceable. The standard formula used in the letters of appointment was that the *qāḍīs* were ordered

> to enforce the provisions of the laws of the Prophet and to apply the divine commands and interdictions without overstepping the boundaries of the true Shariʿa, to properly study the various opinions [transmitted] from Hanafite imams with regard to the questions that present itself, to determine the most authoritative one (*aṣaḥḥ-i aqwāl*) and to implement it.[4]

Sometimes, however, the most authoritative Hanafite opinion would be deemed not to be in the interests of the state or society. The Sultan could then decide to instruct the *qāḍīs* to follow – in certain cases – not the prevailing view, but another, less authoritative, opinion. In the sixteenth century, there were already thirty-two such orders. Many of these date from

[3] Rudolph Peters, 'What does it mean to be an official madhhab: Hanafism and the Ottoman Empire', in *The Islamic school of law: Evolution, devolution, and progress*, ed. P. Bearman, R. Peters and F. Vogel (Cambridge, MA: Harvard University Press, forthcoming).

[4] İsmail Hakkı Uzunçarşılı, *Osmanlı devletinin ilmiye teşkilâtı* (Ankara: Türk Tarih Kurumu Basımevi, 1988), p. 113.

the period of office of the famous Ottoman state mufti (*Şeyh ül-Islâm*) Ebu's-Su'ud (d. 1574). The following example, concerning the law of *qasāma* (see § 2.2.3.2), will clarify how this worked.

The Hanafite doctrine of *qasāma* provides that if a body with traces of violence is found on private property, the victim's next of kin may demand his bloodprice from the owners or users, after a special judicial procedure consisting in a formal complaint brought by the heirs of the victim against the owner or inhabitants of the property and fifty disculpatory oaths sworn by the defendants. However, there is a controversy about the persons that are liable: Abū Ḥanīfa and Muḥammad al-Shaybānī hold that the owner's solidarity group (*'āqila*) (see § 2.5.5.1) is liable, whereas according to Abū Yūsuf's view the actual occupants (whether owners or tenants) and not their solidarity groups must pay. Although the latter opinion was weaker according to the formal rules, the Sultan issued a decree directing the *qāḍīs* to follow it, as it was regarded to serve the public interest better. Because of the liability of the inhabitants themselves, rather than their solidarity groups, they would be stimulated to exercise greater vigilance and be more diligent in keeping their neighbourhoods safe.[5]

Thus, by using their power to delimit the *qāḍīs*' jurisdiction, the Ottoman Sultans, in cooperation with the jurists, created an Ottoman–Hanafite body of Shari'a law that was unequivocal and more predictable in its application, and therefore offered more legal security. The final stage of this development was reached in the nineteenth century when texts on certain topics were written that only contained the authoritative opinions, leaving out the rejected views. An example of these is the manual of the Islamic law of homicide and wounding by 'Ömer Ḥilmī.[6]

The other pillar of the Ottoman legal system was enacted law (*qānūn*). Enacted law also existed in other regions of the Islamic world, but in the Ottoman Empire it became a crucial feature of government. Ottoman *qānūn*s dealt with topics that were not covered in detail by the Shari'a, such as fiscal law, land law, organisation of the state and criminal law. They consisted of sultanic orders (*fermān*), given in individual cases, but made to apply in one region or in the entire empire. For practical purposes these orders were compiled in collections. In general they did not introduce change, but consolidated and further specified existing practices. Since under the Shari'a such orders were bound to the person of the ruler, they had to be reconfirmed whenever a new Sultan came to power. This often entailed

[5] Ebussuud and Düzdağ, *Fetvaları*, no. 767.

[6] 'Ömer Ḥilmī, *Mi'yār-i 'adālet* (Istanbul: Bosnawī Ḥajjī Muḥarrem Efendi, 1881–1882 (1301 H)).

a new drafting of the law, usually with changes on minor points. The Ottoman *qānūn* is a product of the centralised and bureaucratic character of the empire. It provided uniform standards of official conduct that were followed in all parts of the empire. Moreover, it was also a means to check and restrain the actions of the local officials and *qāḍī*s and to prevent oppression and arbitrary behaviour on their part.

The earliest Ottoman criminal legislation dates from the reign of Meḥmed II (1451–81). It was part of a more comprehensive statute that also included fiscal and other laws. It was revised and extended by his successor Bayezid II (1481–1512). Around 1534, during the reign of Süleyman the Magnificent (1520–66), a new *qānūnnāme* was promulgated, which was usually referred to as the *Qānūn-i ʿOsmānī*. The text included previous legislation with many new additions. Articles on criminal law are found in chapters 1, 2, 3 and 15 and represent only a smaller part of the law. The criminal provisions have been edited and translated by U. Heyd[7] and in the following I refer to this body of enacted criminal law as OCC (Ottoman Criminal Code), followed by the article numbers according to Heyd's numbering. Unless otherwise indicated, I have followed Heyd's translation. This law remained in force until the end of the seventeenth century, as it was adopted, sometimes with minor changes, by Süleyman's successors.

The OCC contains some rules of procedure, e.g. regarding the tracking down of suspects, custody during investigation and the duties of the *qāḍī*s and the executive officials during criminal proceedings. The bulk of its provisions, however, deal with substantive penal law. They list punishable offences and give an indication of their penalties. The chapters on criminal law deal with the following topics:

1. Chapter 1 'On illegal sexual intercourse (*zinā*) and other [offences]' (arts. 1–35) lists sexual offences and offences against gender segregation.
2. Chapter 2 'On mutual beating and abuse, killing and the fines for them' (arts. 36–60) contains provisions supplementing the Shariʿa law of homicide and wounding and a few injunctions regarding insult and defamation (arts. 54–56).
3. Chapter 3 'On fines, administrative (*siyāsa*) and other types of punishment for the drinking of wine, theft, usurpation of property, and [other] transgressions [of the rights of others]' (arts. 61–120) has provisions on a variety of subjects, including procedure.
4. Chapter 15 'On suspects and their connections' contains four articles on investigation and procedure.

7 Heyd, *Studies*, pp. 54–131.

5. Finally there are two articles, not included in a separate chapter, dealing with procedure.

In modern times the main function of penal legislation is to protect the rights of the citizens: citizens are not subjected to punishment unless they have committed an act that the law labels an offence and for which it specifies a punishment. Ottoman criminal law, like other pre-modern penal codes, is not based on this principle. Acts not mentioned in the criminal code can still be punished at the discretion of the *qāḍī* or the executive officials (*ta'zīr* or *siyāsa*). Moreover, the OCC does not exactly specify the punishment for each offence, but gives only an indication of the type of penalty incurred. Characteristic of Ottoman criminal *qānūn* is that many offences were 'fiscalised', i.e. in addition to the punishment (usually just globally defined as *ta'zīr*, meaning, in the Ottoman context, flogging or caning) a fine was imposed, the amount of which was made dependent on the number of strokes that were actually inflicted. The following article (art. 20) exemplifies this:

> If [a person] kisses [another] person's son or approaches him on his way and addresses [indecent words] to him, [the *qāḍī*] shall chastise [him] severely and a fine of one *akçe* shall be collected for each stroke.

Among historians of the Ottoman Empire, there is a difference of opinion on the relationship between the Shari'a and *qānūn*. According to some, *qānūn* was at points in conflict with the Shari'a and abolished certain of its provisions, whereas other scholars assert that this is not the case. I belong to the latter school of thought and believe that, at least in the field of criminal law, the provisions of the *qānūn* can only be construed as supplementing the Shari'a with the aim of giving the law-enforcement authorities specific instructions regarding cases on which the Shari'a doctrine is silent. That the provisions of the *qānūn* were subsidiary to the law of *ḥadd* is evident from the wording of provisions such as that found in article 67 OCC:

> If [a person] steals a purse or a turban or towels – unless his hand is to be cut off, the cadi shall chastise [him] and a fine of one *akçe* shall be collected for [every] stroke (or one *akçe* shall be collected for each stroke).

The purpose of this article is obviously to regulate a case in which a person has stolen, but cannot be sentenced to the fixed punishment for theft, e.g. because the act he committed does not include all elements of the strict Shari'a definition, or because the evidence against the defendant does not meet the standards required for the application of the fixed penalty. In this case, the law stipulates, the culprit must be punished with flogging as a discretionary punishment and a fine to be paid to the state, the amount of which depends on the number of strokes to which the *qāḍī* sentences the defendant. Another example of such a subsidiary penal provision is article 7, which penalises stealing between parents and children or between spouses. These are typically circumstances that constitute, according to Hanafite law, uncertainty (*shubha*) which prevents the application of the fixed penalty for theft. It is, in my view, unthinkable that the Ottoman Sultan, whose principal source of legitimacy was that he upheld God's law, would, even implicitly, abolish parts of the Shariʿa. That some fixed penalties were not or only rarely enforced does not mean that the provisions of the law of *ḥadd* offences had become obsolete, but only that these provisions were so strictly applied that the conditions for a conviction were rarely met.

3.3 THE ENFORCEMENT AGENCIES

The reconstruction of the Ottoman practice of criminal law suffers from a major drawback: the available records show only one facet of the legal process. What is left are the records of the *qāḍīs* – but not, if they ever existed, those of the executive officials, who, as we shall see, played a major role in dealing with crime. Since the latter in most cases imposed the punishment, we find few criminal sentences in the *qāḍīs*' records, a fact observed by many students of the Ottoman judicial records. There are, however, many entries in the registers that show the *qāḍīs*' involvement in criminal procedures. We find records of criminal investigations, depositions of witnesses for possible use in future criminal proceedings, records of settlements reached between the parties involved in a criminal trial, petitions forwarded by a *qāḍī* to the central government and requesting an investigation into the conduct of a local official. These entries can tell us something about the division of labour between the *qāḍī* and the other authorities, the *ehl-i ʿörf*[8] in Ottoman Turkish, in dealing with crime.

When Sultan Süleyman introduced his legal reforms, one of his objectives was to curtail the almost unlimited powers of the executive officials in criminal proceedings. He tried to achieve this by putting the *qāḍīs* in charge of monitoring the legality of the actions of the executive officials, giving permission for taking suspects into custody or torturing them in order to get confessions and of registering evidence. In a seventeenth-century *qānūn*

[8] In Ottoman Turkish, *ʿörf* (from Arabic *ʿurf*, custom) was used as a synonym of *siyāsa*.

the jurisdiction of the *qāḍī* as opposed to that of the executive was delimited as follows:

> The cadis are to carry out the laws of the Shariʿa . . . but are ordered to refer matters relating to public order (*nizām-i memleket*), the protection and defence of the subjects, and the capital or corporal severe punishment (*siyāsa*) [of criminals] to the [local] representatives of the Sultan (*vükelā-i devlet*), who are the governors in charge of military and serious penal affairs (*hükkām-i seyf ve siyāsa*).[9]

In practice this meant the following. If a crime was brought to the notice of the *qāḍī*, he would investigate the case. If he found that there was sufficient evidence against a suspect to impose punishment on the strength of the Shariʿa, he would register the depositions of the witnesses or the confession of the accused and his judgment that the person deserved to be punished, e.g. for manslaughter or defamation. Such sentences would conclude with a statement to the effect that the case is now brought to the attention of the executive for taking the necessary measures. A document (*iʿlām*) containing the judgment would then be handed over to the executive officials to whom the execution of such sentences was entrusted. If, on the other hand, the *qāḍī* was of the opinion that the evidence in the case was not sufficient for a Shariʿa sentence, but might result in the imposition of a *siyāsa* penalty, he would draw up a document (*ḥüccet*) containing the relevant statements and, without sentencing, hand the case over to the executive authorities. Article 88 OCC regulates this procedure:

> If according to administrative law [*ʿörf*, i.e. not according to the requirements of the Shariʿa, RP] it is proved and evident that a person has committed a crime, he who serves as cadi shall give a certificate (*ḥüccet*) [to that effect] to the executive officers (*ehl-i ʿörf*). In accordance with that certificate the executive officers shall hang the person who incurs hanging and cut off a limb of the person who incurs the cutting off of a limb. And the cadi shall not prevent this [but] let the punishment be carried out at the place where the crime was [committed].

The executive officials could not imprison a person without a previous investigation of the case by the *qāḍī*. This is clearly spelled out in article 116 OCC: 'The executive officials (*ehl-i ʿörf*) shall not imprison or injure a person except by [permission of] the cadi.' If persons were illegally detained, the *qāḍī* could order their release. A similar protective function was exercised by the *qāḍī* with regard to the reclaiming of fines that were illegally collected by executive officials (art. 116 OCC). By requiring the cooperation of the judges for imposing fines and giving them the power to order repayment, the *qānūn* intended to put an end to extortion by the executive officials:

9 Heyd, *Studies*, p. 209.

Officials may not interfere with a person or impose a fine with nothing being proved according to the Shariʿa and merely on suspicion of misconduct. If they do exact [a fine], the judge shall give an order and recover it (art. 115) . . . Officials shall impose a fine according to the offence a person has committed and take nothing more. If they do impose [too great a fine], the judge shall give an order regarding the excess and recover it (art. 116.2).

The executive authorities were entitled to torture persons in order to obtain a confession, but only if there were proven suspicions against him. In such cases, the *qāḍī* had to establish whether there were sufficient grounds for such a suspicion, such as a bad reputation, a previous conviction or enmity between him and the victim of the crime of which he was suspected. Article 43 OCC explains this for cases of grievous bodily harm:

If a wounded person states that a certain person has struck him, no regard is [to be paid to his allegation] unless that person is suspect (*müttehem*) or is someone who has openly been at enmity with the wounded person. [In that case, the assailant] is liable to torture (*ʿörf*) with the co-operation of the cadi.

People would often come to the *qāḍī*'s court proactively to establish certain facts and record the necessary depositions in order to strengthen their legal position in the event of criminal legal proceedings against them. The court registers contain records with the testimonies of persons concerning the good behaviour or the unlawful activities of certain persons, without mention of any legal consequences, recorded just for possible future use. A telling example is the deposition, recorded in the court of Salonika some time during the eighteenth century, of the elders of a village declaring that the behaviour of a certain Niko was irreproachable. This deposition was made at the request of this Niko, because he claimed that the local military chief was planning to accuse him of theft in order to extort a fine from him.[10] By anticipating the moves of the military chief, Niko tried to prevent being arrested on the charge of theft, since for such an arrest it was required to be established in court that the accused was a suspect person. For a powerful military officer, such testimonies would probably not be difficult to procure. Another example, also from Salonika, is a medical report concerning a man who had been wounded by a bullet, registered together with the victim's deposition that he held only a certain Albanian soldier responsible for his injuries, and not the Jews and the kettle makers working in the courtyard where he had been injured. The entries were made at the request of the Jews working in that courtyard, after an Albanian soldier, who was sitting in the courtyard and cleaning his rifle, had inadvertently

[10] Ginio, 'Criminal justice in Selanik', p. 204.

shot the victim. In this case, the Jews apparently feared that the victim would die and that his heirs would sue them and initiate the *qasāma* procedure, with the result that those who worked and lived in the courtyard would become liable for the bloodprice.[11]

The group collectively referred to as *ehl-i ʿörf* included a variety of officials. The highest in rank were the provincial and district governors (*beylerbeys* and *sancak beyis*). They presided over their own *dīvāns*, where they adjudicated cases, often in the presence of the *qāḍī*. Officials whose primary tasks were the maintenance of public order and punishing criminals were the police chief (*subaşı*) and the chief of the night watchmen (*ʿasesbaşı*), who fell under the command of the district governor. There were also market inspectors, *müṭtesibs*, who could carry out disciplinary corporal punishment for offenders caught *in flagrante delictu*, but had to report other crimes to the *qāḍīs*, to whom they were subordinate. In the countryside, fiefholders (*sipahi*) and the administrators of the imperial domains (*hāṣṣemīni*) could also play a role, especially since they were entitled to all or a part of the fines paid by criminal offenders living on the lands they administered.

The highest court in the empire was the Imperial Divan (*Dīvān-i Hümāyūn)*, presided over by the Grand Vizier. Among its members were the two *qāḍī-ʿaskers* of the empire, the chiefs of the judicial organisation. Every subject was entitled to bring his case before this council, and this frequently happened. Certain groups of subjects had the privilege of being tried only before this court. This applied to *qāḍīs* and teachers of religion (*müderris*), as well as to foreign residents if they had committed an offence against an Ottoman subject. These foreign residents could only be tried in the presence of a diplomatic representative. Finally, there was a special jurisdiction for the head of the guilds, who could punish members for violating their professional codes of behaviour.

However, not all offences were tried by the competent authorities. In many cases conflicts in the domain of criminal law were 'resolved' by the offended party and his family or clan, by taking justice in their own hands in the form of revenge or honour killings according to customary law. The family of a homicide victim would kill the murderer or a member of his family in retaliation, or the male relatives of a woman who had compromised family honour would kill her and/or the man who was involved. These incidents have left traces in the judicial records when those who killed in revenge were apprehended by the judicial authorities and brought to justice.

[11] Ibid., p. 192.

There were also cases that would be brought to the notice of the authorities and investigated, but did not end in criminal sentences. Settlement between the victim (or his heirs) and the culprit was a common phenomenon, which would stop the criminal prosecution. These settlements were as a rule duly recorded by the courts to prevent future disputes about the rights and obligations of the parties involved. There is abundant written evidence in the form of *fatwā*s and court records showing that such settlement contracts (*ṣulḥ*) were very common. As a rule the alleged perpetrator of the crime took it upon himself to pay a sum of money to the victim or his heirs – often, however, with the stipulation that this did not imply his guilt. It is not clear why, in such a situation, someone would be willing to pay the required sum. Heyd has suggested some possible answers. If the accused was guilty and the plaintiff could produce evidence, it is evident that the former would agree to pay money in order to save himself from prosecution by state officials. But even if the plaintiff did not have legal proof, it could be profitable for both parties to reach a settlement and exclude the risk of litigation: for the accused because he might fear that the plaintiff would concoct false evidence (or produce evidence that the defendant belonged to the people of corruption (*ehl-i fesād*), which might even result in a death sentence, as we shall see); and for the plaintiff because he was poor and wanted to see money immediately.[12] Settlements would usually be the result of mediation. Most entries in the records mention that the settlement was achieved through the offices of *muṣliḥūn*. These were not court officials but private persons asked by both parties to act as mediators.

Homicide cases would often end in a settlement, whereby the victim's next of kin would pardon the killer for a sum of money. Such settlements could be precarious since the executive officials might decide, in dealing with the case administratively (*siyāsat^{an}*), that the perpetrator still deserved the death penalty. Settlement agreements would therefore sometimes contain a stipulation that in such a case, the settlement agreement would be rescinded.

3.4 PROCEDURE

3.4.1 Initiation of the proceedings, arrest

Criminal proceedings would start with the notification of the authorities – either the executive officials, such as the police commander, or the *qāḍī*.

[12] Heyd, *Studies*, pp. 248–50.

This could be done by the victim of the crime or by witnesses. The victim could also submit a petition to a governor or to the Sultan requesting an order (*fermān* or *buyuruldu*) directing the *qāḍī* or the police to investigate a certain matter. If the request was granted, the results of the investigation had to be reported back. In order to discourage frivolous complaints, the *qānūn* provided that a complainant could be punished if it appeared that his complaint was unfounded (art. 55 OCC). With regard to 'victimless' crime, such as violations of public morality or irreligious behaviour, the complaint could also be lodged by the inhabitants of the culprit's neighbourhood, or by the nightwatchmen or police officers. In Istanbul, and probably in other cities too, there were special committees attached to mosques to supervise public morality and inform the authorities of any violations.[13] In some circumstances the enforcement of criminal law took place without a complaint: if police officers or the market inspector saw a person *in flagrante* and, if the offence was not too serious, they would punish him on the spot.

If the accused was known and refused to appear in court, the plaintiff could have him brought in by the police. For that, it sufficed that the plaintiff informed the competent authority that he had a complaint against a certain person. Bringing the accused to court would entail expenses, to be paid by the plaintiff. But even if the accused was known, he could not always be apprehended, since certain places offered asylum. This was the case with the workshops and markets of certain guilds, barracks of the Janissaries, mosques, public markets and the residences of notables. The state would respect this, unless public security was endangered, as in the case of disturbances.

If the accused could not be found, the authorities would hold his relatives – or, in the case of a slave, his master – responsible for producing him. But first they would ascertain whether the accused at some time in the past, had provided a guarantor (*kefīl*) to the authorities. This was often the case since in many situations officials would require that a person find a guarantor, who would be obliged to find him if the former (the *mekfūl*) did not comply with an official summons to appear. The appointment of guarantors would be registered at the *qāḍī*'s courts. Providing a guarantor was standard procedure when persons were released from prison after an acquittal or after the completion of their sentences or when criminal investigations were initiated against a suspect without remanding him into custody. Sometimes the *mekfūl* had fled and the guarantor had to leave the district in order to find him. Then he himself had to find two or three

[13] G. Jacob, 'Türkische Sittenpolizei im 16. Jahrhundert', *Der Islam* 11 (1921), 254–9.

guarantors to ensure his return. If a guarantor failed to produce his *mekfūl*, he would be held responsible in his stead.

A similar responsibility for producing an accused on the penalty of being held liable oneself could also arise from living in the vicinity of the scene of a crime. If a body was found with traces of violence in a town quarter or in or close to a village, the inhabitants must find the killer, or must to pay the bloodprice collectively (arts. 44, 76 OCC). Obviously, this is a practical elaboration of the *qasāma* procedure (see § 2.2.3.2). A similar collective obligation existed for the local inhabitants if goods were stolen within a village or closed town quarter or from a traveller halting near a village (arts. 78, 86 OCC). If goods were stolen in a caravan serail, those who stayed there must find the thief or were held liable, unless there were traces of burglary such as the piercing of one of the outer walls (arts. 83–6 OCC).

3.4.2 *Investigation and custody*

Once the accused was in court, or in the hands of executive officials, any further proceedings depended on his reputation and the available evidence. As we have seen, it was the duty of the *qāḍī* to investigate the alleged crime, establish the facts and establish the suspect's guilt or innocence. This might include collecting the necessary depositions, conducting an investigation at the place of the crime, establishing the identity and the reputation of the witnesses from other witnesses, or ordering an autopsy and taking the statement of a medical expert. Often he would instruct his deputy (*nā'ib*) to carry out specific tasks related to the investigation. After the investigation the *qāḍī* could issue a document summarising its results (*ḥüccet*) or order a trial session where the plaintiff presented his claim, the defendant had the opportunity to respond and the necessary witnesses would give their testimonies in the presence of the parties. After such a session the *qāḍī* would pass judgment (*ḥukm*) which would be recorded in a special document (*iʿlām*). Many cases would thus be dealt with solely by the *qāḍī*, assisted by his deputy, within one or two days, such as the case mentioned below (see § 3.4.3).

In complicated cases more time was needed to complete the investigation. Then the *qāḍī* had to decide whether the accused should be remanded into custody. If the accused was of good standing, he would remain at liberty during the investigation on condition that he produce a guarantor. However, if he had a dubious reputation or if there were clear indications suggesting his guilt, he would be imprisoned, while the plaintiff was granted a term of some weeks to find the necessary witnesses to prove his claim. Often the plaintiff would not succeed in producing conclusive evidence satisfying the requirements of the Shariʿa, although the accused's guilt would otherwise be clear. Then the *qāḍī* would issue a *ḥüccet* and hand the accused over to the executive officials so that the case could be dealt with according to *siyāsa*. These rules are summarised in the following *fatwā* given by the *Şeyh ül-Islâm* Ebu's-Suʿud:

The people of the *sharʿ* must arrest him [the accused] and bring him to the Shariʿa court. Then he must be handed over to a reliable guarantor [i.e. he will be released upon producing a guarantor]. However, if he has a bad reputation (*müttehem*) or if there is only one witness regarding the crime (*ẓulm ü ʿadāvet*) of which he is accused, he must be imprisoned until the investigation by the *qāḍī* is concluded . . . It is either [producing] a guarantor, or imprisonment and the executive officials must not interfere with this. Only when his crime has become clear, may he be handed over to the executive officials.[14]

Investigation by the executive officials routinely involved torture to extract confessions. This was regarded as lawful and had its basis in the *qānūn*. The OCC allowed the executive officials to use torture but only if the accused had a bad reputation and there were already indications of his guilt, such as when stolen goods were found in his house (art. 82 OCC), if he was accused of grievous bodily harm by the victim (art. 43 OCC) or if a criminal during investigation mentioned him as an accomplice (art. 90 OCC). Confessions obtained under torture could not be used as a ground for awarding punishment unless they were corroborated by circumstantial evidence, as stipulated in article 89 OCC: 'If a criminal confesses under torture and there are signs indicating [his guilt], then his confession is valid and he will be punished with *siyāsa* punishment.' The officials administering torture are admonished to take care not to kill the accused before the case is proven. However, if he does die, the torturer is not liable for the bloodprice (art. 82 OCC).

With regard to the lawfulness of torture, Ottoman Hanafite jurists show some ambivalence. In a procedure before the *qāḍī* a statement extracted under torture would not be admitted as evidence since it would have been obtained by coercion (*ikrāh*). This general principle is set out in the following *fatwā* given by the Ottoman *Şeyh ül-Islâm* Ebu's-Suʿud:

If someone confesses to something (*iqrār*) because he was intimidated by [people threatening him with] the words: 'Confess or we shall give you a severe beating,' and if he believed that if he would not confess they would carry out what they said, then his confession shall not be valid.[15]

[14] Ebussuud and Düzdağ, *Fetvaları*, no. 661. [15] Ibid., no. 662.

However, the Hanafite jurists disagreed on the validity of confessions extracted by torture in a *siyāsa* procedure. Some hesitantly accepted them, but many others did not. The following passage from an authoritative sixteenth-century Ottoman text asserts that the prevailing Hanafite opinion held that such confessions were invalid:

If [a thief] confesses [to theft] under coercion, [the confession] is not valid. However, some of the more recent jurists have issued *fatwās* to the effect that [such a confession] is valid and that beating is allowed. But this is not an authoritative opinion (*lā yuftā bihi*) because it is injustice. In the *Minaḥ* [probably *Minaḥ al-Ghaffār* by Timurtashi, d. 1595] [we find the following opinion]: 'If [the accused] is known for immoral behaviour that fits the accusation, then some jurists hold that the governor (*wālī*) or the *qāḍī* may beat him, whereas others maintain that only the governor may do so. But there are also jurists who hold that he [the accused] is not to be beaten. If [the accused's] circumstances are not known, he is to be imprisoned until the matter becomes clear. Some say that he must be imprisoned for a month and others that he may be imprisoned as long as the ruler (*walī al-amr*) thinks fit.'[16]

Ebu's-Suʿud, however, who was always keen to show the Islamic legality of Ottoman legal practice, followed the Hanafite minority opinion that executive officials were under certain circumstances allowed to use torture in order to find the truth.[17]

If torture under certain circumstances is lawful, the official administering it will not be liable for bloodmoney if the accused dies as a result of it. As we have seen above, the OCC confirms this (art. 82). There is, however, a *fatwā* by Ebu's-Suʿud that seems to give a contrary opinion:

Question: If Zeyd, whose goods have been stolen, hands over the suspect ʿAmr to the executive officials (*ehl-i ʿörf*) to have him tortured by them, and if ʿAmr dies during the torture, are then ʿAmr's heirs entitled to demand the bloodprice from Zeyd, who was the cause of his death, although he did not personally torture him? *Answer*: They can have him punished with severe beating and long imprisonment and demand the bloodprice from the person who tortured him.[18]

Since Ebu's-Suʿud as a rule endorsed Ottoman administrative practice, I think this *fatwā* is not an expression of a critical attitude vis-à-vis the practices of the executive officials, as Heyd believed it to be.[19] The difference between the ruling of the *fatwā* and the provision in the *qānūn* derives from the fact that they deal with different cases. Article 82 OCC speaks of torture applied with the *qāḍī*'s approval after he has established that stolen goods

[16] Shaykhzāde (d. 1667), *Majmaʿ al-anhur fī sharḥ multaqā al-abḥur (li-Ibrāhīm al-Ḥalabī, d. 1549)*, 2 vols. (Istanbul: Maṭab ʿa-yi ʿĀmira, 1883–4 (1301 H)), vol. II, p. 571.

[17] Imber, *Ebu's-Suʿud*, p. 224.

[18] Ebussuud and Düzdağ, *Fetvaları*, no. 666.

[19] Heyd, *Studies*, p. 252.

were found in the possession of the accused and that the accused has a bad reputation. That means that the use of torture is justified. The *fatwā*, on the other hand, discusses a situation where torture is applied without regard for the required legal procedure: the official applying torture does so, without permission of the *qāḍī*, but at the request of a private person who harbours suspicions against someone.

3.4.3 Trial and sentencing

If the investigation of a crime did not yield sufficient evidence against the accused, the *qāḍī* would investigate whether the suspect had a prior criminal record, or would have his neighbours questioned about his character and behaviour. If this was favourable for the accused, the *qāḍī*, at the request of the plaintiff, could allow him to swear a disculpatory oath and then release him, usually on condition that he find a guarantor.[20] But otherwise, depending on the available evidence, either the *qāḍī* or the executive officials would sentence the accused.

If there was sufficient proof under the Shariʿa, the *qāḍī* would try and sentence the accused. In simple cases the investigation was often conducted by the deputy *qāḍī* (*nāʾib*), and the sentencing would take place on the same day, as the following document, dating from 1764, shows:

> His Honour the *Qāḍī* is notified, after the case has been recorded at the request [of the plaintiff] **(1)** that a person named Ṣāliḥ b. Eyyüb, living in the village Bulgurlu. . . claimed during the session of the Shariʿa court in the presence of his adversary Halīl b. ʿAbdüllāh that the aforementioned Halīl on the day of this notification unlawfully slapped and punched him, tore his collar and offended his honour, and demanded what is due to him [according to the Shariʿa]; **(2)** that, after introducing his claim and the questioning and denial of the defendant, the aforementioned Ṣāliḥ was unable to substantiate his claim and demanded that the defendant be offered to swear a [disculpatory] oath; **(3)** that the aforementioned Halīl refused to swear the oath when it was offered to him; and **(4)** that as a consequence Halīl by law (*sharʿan*) must be punished with a discretionary punishment.[21]

The case shows that the imposition of the disculpatory oath on the defendant if there was no evidence was not just a formality. The punishment incurred by the defendant was entirely due to his refusal to state under oath that he was not guilty. Oaths were taken very seriously by those who had to swear them and, as appears from Ottoman judicial records, it frequently

[20] Ibid., pp. 250–2. [21] Bayındır, *Islam muhakeme hukuku*, pp. 22–3.

happened that the accused preferred being punished for the crime of which he was accused to swearing a false oath that might endanger his well-being in the Hereafter. For this reason, oaths were also used during the investigation by the executive officials, in order to test the veracity of the statements of the accused. Even in proceedings before the *qāḍī*, oaths were used on a larger scale than required by the Shariʿa: several Ottoman muftis ruled that *qāḍīs* could make witnesses swear an oath on their truthfulness, which is not mandatory under the Shariʿa.

Shariʿa sentences could only be passed after a trial during which the witnesses gave their testimonies in the presence of the parties. For these testimonies to be admitted as evidence, the witnesses' good reputation had to be established and could be challenged by the party against whom they testified. Much of the necessary preliminary work would have been done by the deputy, as we have seen before. With regard to serious offences the accused was first interrogated by the executive officials. Most sentences would stipulate that the accused deserved to be punished at the *qāḍī*'s discretion (*taʿzir)*, without further specification. In cases of homicide or wounding the *qāḍī* would award retaliation or bloodprice. Occasionally the *qāḍī* would impose a fixed punishment for defamation or drinking alcohol, rarely or never for the other *ḥadd* offences. The documents containing the sentences are called notifications (*iʿlam*) because they end with a statement that the facts of the case and the sentence have been passed to the executive authorities so that they can issue the necessary instructions.

In serious cases the trial would take place in the presence of high executive officials such as the governor, other notables and prominent men of religion. The following trial, of a case of homosexual gang rape, belonged to that category.[22] It took place in May 1713 in the northern Anatolian town of Çankırı. The proceedings illustrate that the rules of the Shariʿa were meticulously followed. In Hanafite legal theory, homosexual acts, if committed by habitual offenders, are punishable with the death penalty. During the trial it was not only proven that the defendants had raped the youth, but also that they were known for committing such acts.

The case was introduced by the victim, a beardless youth (*ṣābb-ı emred*) named Muṣṭafā b. el-Ḥācc Meḥmed, who sued four men, Muṣṭafā b. Meḥmed, Ḥasan b. Maḥmūd Kethudā, Ibrāhīm b. Solak ʿAlī and Aḥmed b. Aḥmed, and presented the following claim:

[22] Ergene, *Local court*, pp. 172–3.

On the night of the thirteenth day of *Rebi'ülahir*, I left my house to check on our horse in the village of Balınedik. On the way, the defendants – who are currently present in the court and the stepbrother of the aforementioned Ibrahim, Ahmed, who is currently absent – caught me in the vicinity of the village of Aynaç. They beat me up, and each and every one of them raped me. I demand that the defendants be interrogated and what is required according to the holy law be executed.

When questioned, the aforementioned Muṣṭafā, Ḥasan, Ibrāhīm and Aḥmed all confessed that they went after and caught the plaintiff at the time and the place that he mentioned. Subsequently, Muṣṭafā acknowledged that he was the first to rape the plaintiff. Then Ḥasan, Ibrāhīm and Aḥmed all confirmed that they too had raped him. Afterwards all four of them stated three times in the noble court that the other Aḥmed, who was absent at the time of the legal proceeding, also had raped the plaintiff.

Since this was a trial that could end in a death sentence, the *qāḍī* convened a new session so that the final sentence would be pronounced in the presence of a large number of dignitaries. The court was set up in the presence of the governor of Kengiri, his excellency Can Arslan Paşazade Ḥüseyin Paşa, with the participation of the religious scholars, the righteous people, the notables of the sub-province and other impartial Muslims. Here, the plaintiff re-stated his accusations and the defendants confessed once again without being subjected to any external pressure or coercion.

At this point the plaintiff presented a *fatwā* from the mufti of Kengiri in which it was stated that it is lawful to execute Zeyd, if he rapes a minor, 'Amr, and if it is also proven that Zeyd is a 'spreader of corruption' (*sā'ī bi'l-fesād*). In order to prove this last point, the plaintiff Muṣṭafā asked the court to investigate the reputation of the defendants by taking the testimonies of those who knew them well, and to award the punishment that corresponds to their crimes. Prayer leader (*imām*) 'Abdüllāh Halīfe, Ḥāccı Mūsā b. Ḥāccı Mūsā, etc. (more than twenty names follow) all testified in the court that sodomy (*livāṭa*) was a common habit (*'ādet-i müstemirreleri*) of the defendants. After these testimonies the court decided to sentence the defendants in accordance with the *fatwā*. This meant that the culprits were handed over to the governor, whose final approval was needed for their execution.

Sentences passed by *qāḍī*s were executed by the executive officials. *Ta'zīr* sentences were usually carried out immediately. Although the records do not specify the details of the discretionary punishment incurred by the accused, it seems that the *qāḍī* determined the number of strokes to be administered. The executive officials would then collect the fine, which was usually proportional to the number of strokes. Capital sentences needed the approval of the Sultan or the Grand Vizier, although in practice this was also given by the governors.

If no specific offence could be proven against a person, but his neighbours considered him a criminal or a person of easy virtue, they could lodge a complaint with the *qāḍī* and bring witnesses to testify that they considered the accused unfit to live among them because of his criminal behaviour or bad morals. On the ground of such testimonies the *qāḍī* could order the accused to be expelled from the village or neighbourhood as stipulated in article 124 OCC:

> Furthermore, if the community of his (or her) [town-]quarter or of his (or her) village complains that a person is a criminal or a harlot, saying: 'He (or she) is not fit [to live with] us', rejects him or her, and if that person has in fact a notoriously bad reputation among the people, he (or she) shall be banished, i.e. ejected from his (or her) quarter or village. And if he (or she) is not accepted also in the place to which he (or she) moves, he (or she) shall be expelled from the town [altogether]. But action shall be suspended [for] a few days [to see how things turn out]: If that person repents his (or her) former misdeeds and henceforth leads a righteous life, very well. If not, he (or she) shall be expelled from there too and be definitively expelled; he (or she) shall leave the town and go away.

The procedure in such cases would be conducted before the *qāḍī* and in the presence of the defendant. The *qāḍī* had to be satisfied by the testimonies of a number of persons from the neighbourhood, usually including the religious officials of the local mosque, that all the inhabitants felt that the defendant could no longer be tolerated in the neighbourhood. Grounds for expulsion, as found in the records, were for example that the defendant's 'wife always hurts [our] feelings by obscene insults addressed to all of us and to our wives and that her aforementioned husband [i.e. the defendant] . . . is unable to restrain her', or that 'they could no longer bear with the defendant's behaviour, because he used to address obscene insults to his neighbours and disturb the peace (*ifsād*) by bringing strange people to his house and publicly behaving in a dissolute way'. Sometimes, if the neighbours were convinced that someone who had been expelled had mended his ways and repented, they would take him back, as appears from a nineteenth-century formulary for the *qāḍī* that contains several examples of documents in connection with the expulsion of persons from their neighbourhoods.[23] The documents carefully specify that the defendant lived in the neighbourhood in a rented home, since if the alleged troublemaker owned property in the neighbourhood, forced expulsion was unlawful under the Shariʿa. In that case he would have had to be disciplined by means of corporal punishment and imprisonment.[24] The right to expel someone from a neighbourhood was often resorted to until well into the nineteenth century.

If there were indications of the accused's guilt that did not amount to full Shariʿa evidence, or if it was otherwise a case for *siyāsa* punishment, the *qāḍī* could not conclude the case with a sentence. Instead he would draw up a document (*ḥüccet*) recording the available evidence and submit the case to the executive officials so that they could deal further with it. The following case, taken from the records of a Shariʿa court in the northern Anatolian town of Kastamonu, shows the different stages in the procedure.[25]

The case began as a regular Shariʿa lawsuit in March 1736, when the legal representative (*vekīl*) of Havvā bt. ʿAlī Çelebi accused Ḥüseyin b. Meḥmed and his wife ʿĀʾişe bt. Muṣṭafā of stealing her money, jewellery and belongings from her house thirteen months earlier. The plaintiff asked the court to question the defendants and punish them according to the law since some of the stolen items had been found in the couple's house. The defendants denied the charge and claimed that the goods were their property. The plaintiff then produced two witnesses who testified saying: 'We do not know whether it was the aforementioned Hüseyin and his wife ʿAʾişe who robbed the house of the aforementioned Havvā. Yet we can testify that the items that were found in the house of the defendants are among the belongings of Havvā that had been stolen from her house thirteen months ago.' The court then ordered the defendants to return the goods to Havvā without awarding punishment, as it had not been proven that they had stolen the goods.

At that point a new charge was brought against the defendants. The legal agent (*vekīl*) of two other people, Ḥüseyin Çelebi b. Meḥmed and his wife ʿAtīqe, accused the same defendants of stealing their money, jewellery and belongings six months earlier. Again some of the stolen items had been found in the house of the defendants, and the plaintiffs requested therefore that the defendants be questioned and punished according to law. Once again the defendants denied that the items found in their house belonged

[23] Ahmet Akgündüz et al., *Şerʿiye sicilleri. C. 1: Mahiyeti, toplu kataloğu ve seçme hükümler. C. 2: Seçme hükümler* (Istanbul: Türk Dünyası Araştırmaları Vakfı, 1988–9), vol. II, pp. 139–40; Meḥmed ʿAzīz Çavuşzāde, *Dürr al-ṣukūk*, 2 vols. (Istanbul: Maṭbaʿa-yi ʿĀmira, 1871–2 (1288 H)), vol. I, pp. 113–14.

[24] Ebussuud and Düzdağ, *Fetvaları*, no. 678.

[25] Ergene, *Local court*, pp. 155–6.

to Hüseyin Çelebi and ʿAtīqe, and alleged that they had in fact bought them from someone else about five months before the hearing. When the plaintiffs were asked to submit evidence, they produced two witnesses who stated in court: 'We do not know whether it was the aforementioned Hüseyin who robbed the house of Hüseyin Çelebi and his wife ʿAtīqe. Yet we testify that the items found in his house are among the belongings of Hüseyin Çelebi and ʿAtīqe, which were stolen before.' The court then ordered the defendants to return the goods to Hüseyin Çelebi, the plaintiff.

On the strength of the presence of stolen goods in the defendants' home the *qāḍī* could not award punishment. Since, apparently, conclusive proof according to the Shariʿa could not be furnished, the *qāḍī* decided to hand over the defendants to the executive officials. This, however, could only be done, according to art. 82 OCC (see above), after the bad reputation of the defendants had been established in court. To this end character witnesses were called. Seven individuals came to the court and testified as follows regarding the reputations of the defendants:

> The aforementioned Hüseyin is a troublemaker and a bandit. Previously he assaulted a woman in our neighbourhood and stole her money and forcefully took her silver hair-band from her head. Also he was planning [*sic*] to assault some virtuous women in the aforementioned neighbourhood in order to rape them. He is a corrupter and a bandit and his wife too is a troublemaker. We are not safe from them and we would not stand surety for them.

The last stage of the proceedings was initiated with a *fatwā*. At the request of both plaintiffs, the mufti of Kastamonu had given the following *fatwā*, which the plaintiffs now submitted to the court:

> What should be done to ʿAmr if the stolen belongings of Zeyd are found in his [ʿAmr's] possession and the witnesses testify that those items belong to Zeyd although they cannot be sure about the fact that it was ʿAmr who committed the crime? [Also, take into consideration the fact that] some individuals report that ʿAmr robbed Hind a year ago. The answer is that the found items should be returned to Zeyd, and ʿAmr should be imprisoned and interrogated according to law.

At this point the court ordered the implementation of the *fatwā*, which means that the suspects were handed over to the executive officials. Unfortunately, the records do not inform us about the actual outcome of the investigation and the punishment imposed on the accused. The case is interesting because it shows that the provisions of the *qānūn* were meticulously followed and that the trial in the *qāḍī*'s court was well prepared. The two plaintiffs came to the same session; witnesses had been found and instructed; a *fatwā* had been obtained. All this required a great deal of coordination. The documents do not give any clue as to who had been in charge of the investigation and the preparation of the trial. It is plausible, however, that this was the police officer (*subaşı*) in close cooperation with the *qāḍī*.

If a plaintiff could not produce conclusive evidence against a defendant, but the *qāḍī* had reason to believe that the accused was a dangerous criminal against whom society should be protected, he could ask the plaintiff to bring character witnesses to prove that the accused was a serious or habitual criminal. If the plaintiff could substantiate this, the *qāḍī* would draw up a *ḥüccet* and hand the accused over to the governor so that the *siyāsa* punishment (usually the death penalty) could be inflicted on him. This is based on article 125 OCC, which reads:

> If a person is a threat to public order [*ehl-i fesād*] and is constantly engaged in mischievous acts, and if Muslims declare in his presence that they do not find him a law-abiding person, the judge and the police chief shall withdraw [from the proceedings against him]. The person in whose hands has been placed the authority to inflict capital or severe corporal punishment [*siyāsa ve yasak*] shall punish him.

The grounds for being regarded a threat to public order could be specific, such as spying, rebellion, *lèse-majesté* and counterfeiting coins.[26] But there was also a very general one: being a habitual offender. That a person has the continuous habit (*ʿādet-i müstemirre*) of criminal behaviour must be established by the testimonies of a group of unbiased Muslim witnesses.[27] This seems to be the most frequently mentioned justification for *siyāsa* capital punishment. Ottoman muftis regarded this practice as being in accordance with the Shariʿa, as demonstrated by the following *fatwā* issued by the seventeenth-century *Şeyh ül-Islâm* ʿAlī Efendi. By denying the heirs of an executed robber the right to claim the bloodprice, the mufti in this case asserted by implication that the execution was lawful:

> The robber Zeyd is a spreader of corruption (*sāʿī bi-l-fesād*) because he, as the headman of a [band of] robbers, has unjustly taken and caused [his men] to take the properties of Muslims in Muslim countries and because this type of oppressive and unlawful behaviour has become his continuous habit. If Zeyd is caught and the *qāḍī* issues a document that he must be killed in order to get rid of his evil, and if the governor ʿAmr kills him, can [in that case] Zeyd's heirs claim anything by way of bloodmoney (*diyet*)? Answer: No.[28]

26 Mumcu, *Osman devletinde siyaseten katl*, pp. 52–3, 131–3.

27 Paul Horster, *Zur Anwendung des islamischen Rechts im 16. Jahrhundert: die juridischen Dar legungen* (maʿruzat) *des Schejch ül-Islam Ebu Su'ud* (Stuttgart: Kohlhammer, 1935), pp. 32, 74.

28 ʿAlī Efendi, *Fatāwā ʿAlī Efendi*, 2 vols. (Istanbul: n. p., n.d.), vol. I, pp. 205–6.

Labelling a person a 'spreader of corruption' was a legal remedy that was often used to sentence people for a crime that could not be proven. If a number of people from the community would testify that the suspect was a repeat offender, his fate would be sealed. It was a simple but effective way to get rid of criminal suspects or unwanted persons, as the following case illustrates.

In 1667 Receb b. Şa'bān came to the court of Çankırı and claimed that two brothers, Meḥmed and Muṣṭafā, had forcefully entered his house some time before and had stolen his property. After the defendants had denied this claim in court, the plaintiff was asked to substantiate his accusations. However, instead of bringing witnesses to corroborate his claims, the plaintiff alleged that the defendants were regarded as 'spreaders of corruption' in their own village and asked the court to investigate their reputation by hearing the testimonies of 'those who knew them well'. Thereupon certain unidentified members of the community bore witness to the evil character of the defendants, declaring that Meḥmed and Muṣṭafā were 'not good people; they do not abstain from such actions'. The court then ordered that the defendants be punished in proportion to their crime.[29]

This case also shows the power of the community: if some members would testify that a certain person was a 'spreader of corruption' he would be in for severe *siyāsa* punishment. This must have been a very efficacious means to ensure conformist behaviour. Once you were for whatever reason at odds with the majority of the neighbourhood's inhabitants, the sword of Damocles was suspended over your head and could descend on it at any moment the community wanted to get rid of you.

From the cases presented here, it is evident that *fatwā*s were very important during the procedure. In serious cases where the death penalty could be imposed, such *fatwā*s were even mandatory. They could be solicited by the parties (plaintiff and defendant) and by the *qāḍī*. The typical Ottoman *fatwā* is highly formulaic and consists of a question, which mentions the relevant facts and refers to people with standard names (Zeyd, 'Amr, Hind etc., like John Doe and Richard Roe), and a short answer, often just yes (*olur*) or no (*olmaz*). In *siyāsa* procedures, especially if capital sentences were pronounced, *fatwā*s were also used in order to underline the Islamic legality of *siyāsa* justice and the unity of the legal system.

There was no formal system of appeal in the Ottoman legal system, but sentences, barring those given by the Sultan himself, were not unassailable. Capital sentences would routinely be reviewed by the Sultan or the governor

[29] Ergene, *Local court*, pp. 154–5.

before giving their order of execution. In order to appeal against a sentence the aggrieved party could send a petition to the Sultan or the Divan of the Grand Vizier requesting the revision of the sentence. If this request was granted, a *fermān* would appoint a special investigator (*müfettiş*) to examine the matter and issue a new decision or instruct a *qāḍī* to retry the case. Sentences could be revoked for mistrial, e.g. because the *qāḍī* or the executive official who imposed the penalty was bribed or because the outcome was based on false testimonies.

Criminal trials of military fiefholders and members of the imperial household (together constituting the military or *ʿaskerī* class in the Ottoman Empire) did not follow this pattern. They would be tried by special committees, sometimes in the presence of the Grand Vizier or Sultan. After the examination of the case, the Sultan would give a sentence by *fermān*, often supported by a *fatwā*. If the case was investigated and tried by others, e.g. a provincial governor, the Sultan had to approve the sentence, before it could be executed. Often they would merely investigate the case and leave the final decision to the Sultan. Sometimes members of this class were executed or otherwise punished without any investigation, just by order of the Sultan. Since they were regarded as the Sultan's personal slaves (*kullar*), the Sultan had an absolute right of life and death over them.

3.5 SUBSTANTIVE LAW

3.5.1 Criminal offences

As we have seen in the previous section, the Ottoman *qāḍī* would in the first place apply Islamic criminal law, i.e. the law of homicide and wounding, the law regarding the *ḥadd* offences and the rules of *taʿzīr*. In all these fields Shariʿa criminal law was actually applied. The judicial records, the *fatwā* collections and the legal formularies abound with cases in which *qāḍī* courts awarded retaliation for homicide or wounding and the payment of bloodmoney, which invariably was to be paid by the perpetrator and not by his solidarity group (*ʿāqila*). In one of his *fatwā*s the *Şeyh ül-Islâm* Ebu's-Suʿud stated apodictically: 'There is no *ʿāqila* in these lands.'[30] The Hanafite *qasāma* procedure, mentioned in the *qānūn* and addressed in many *fatwā*s, was regularly applied whenever bodies with traces of violence were found. With regard to fixed penalties, the *qāḍī* would regularly impose those consisting in flogging. Amputation, at least in the eighteenth century,

[30] Imber, *Ebu's-Suʿud*, p. 247.

was rarely practised as a fixed penalty for theft.[31] Stoning to death was also extremely rare. The only instance that I have come across took place in 1680, when a woman was stoned to death for having an affair with a Jew. The sentence was executed in the Hippodrome in Istanbul, in the presence of Sultan Meḥmed IV. The case was regarded as so exceptional that it was recorded in the chronicles.[32] In view of the threat they posed to law and order, brigands, as a rule, would be punished with *siyāsa* punishment (which could involve amputation as prescribed in the Shariʿa) and not with the fixed penalties for banditry (*qaṭʿ al-ṭarīq*). The awarding of discretionary punishment by the *qāḍī*s is also well attested, but the sentences never specify the penalties that are imposed.

Now, what was the relationship between the *qāḍī* and the *qānūn*? Did the *qānūn* address the *qāḍī* and was he bound by it? I think this question cannot simply be answered with yes or no. With regard to procedural questions, the *qāḍī* followed the provisions of the *qānūn*, as we have seen in the cases presented earlier (see § 3.4.3). Such provisions, dealing with procedure, investigation and jurisdiction, represent about 25 per cent of the total body of rules, which is a considerable part of the OCC. They delimited the *qāḍī*'s jurisdiction vis-à-vis the executive officials and mentioned the facts that had to be established before the case was submitted to the latter. However, in the field of substantive law, the *qānūn* did not address the *qāḍī*. The *qāḍī* was not bound by the definitions of the offences that the law offered. He had the power – and actually used it – to punish at his discretion acts that were not listed in the *qānūn*. The only function of the *qānūn* with regard to the *qāḍī* was that it showed him what acts the state wanted punished, but since the *qāḍī* did not play an active part in the prosecution of crime, this was of no great concern to him, as long as the offences listed in the *qānūn* were also punishable under the Shariʿa.

The *qānūn* was primarily meant for the executive officials, and this for two reasons. First, because the OCC was just as much a tax law as a criminal code. It fiscalised crime by providing that culprits, in addition to their punishments, also had to pay a crime tax. The *qānūn* specified for what offences tax could be levied and fixed the amount, often in relation to the number of strokes the culprit would receive as punishment. With very few exceptions (e.g. art. 108 OCC) the number of strokes is not specified, and left to the discretion of the *qāḍī*. The second reason is that if penalties other

[31] Heyd, *Studies*, pp. 265–6; Ignace Mouradgea d'Ohsson, *Tableau général de l'empire othoman*, 3 vols. (Paris: Imprimerie F. Didot, 1788–1820), vol. III, p. 266.

[32] Ahmet Gökçen, *Tanzimat dönemi Osmanlı ceza kanunları ve bu kanunlardaki ceza müeyyidleri* (Istanbul: Ahmet Gökçen, 1989), p. 68; d'Ohsson, *Tableau général*, vol. III, p. 241.

than flogging are mentioned (e.g. castration, branding, amputation), the instructions are not addressed to the *qāḍī* but to the executive officials, as such punishments are *siyāsa* punishments.

The criminal provisions of the OCC are arranged in four chapters (1 to 3 and 15). In addition there are two separate articles not included in a chapter. The arrangement of the articles is that offences resembling one crime according to the strict Shariʿa penal laws are placed together, although there are some discrepancies, especially in chapter 3. A global survey shows that the major concerns of the legislators were very similar to those of Shariʿa criminal law in general: the protection of social order by enforcing strict sexual morals (28 per cent of all articles); the maintenance of economic order by protecting property rights (23 per cent); and the protection of life, body and honour (20 per cent).

The first chapter ('On unlawful sexual intercourse and other matters') contains offences against sexual morality. The first nine articles of this chapter deal with unlawful sexual intercourse itself if the fixed penalty of stoning to death cannot be imposed. In that case the culprit must pay a fine in addition to being subjected to corporal punishment. The amount of the fine depends on legal status (being married or not, being a slave or free, and religion – non-Muslims pay only half of the fine imposed on Muslims, art. 31) and on the culprit's financial means. The rich pay more than the poor. Being in another (married) person's house without his consent is construed as an attempt to have sexual relations with the person's wife or female slaves, and is punished with the same penalties as actual unlawful sexual intercourse (art. 9). The same is true if there are rumours about a man and a woman having an illicit relationship and they are seen together at a secluded place (art. 17). The other articles in this chapter deal mainly with sexually improper acts such as kissing another man's wife, female relatives or slaves or addressing indecent words to them, with abduction, pimping, homosexual acts and bestiality. With two exceptions (amputation of the male member or branding a woman's vulva for abduction and willingly accepting being abducted, arts. 10 and 11), the penalties for these acts are flogging (*taʿzir*) and fining.

The second chapter ('On fighting, abuse and killing and their fines') deals with public acts of aggression. It is clear that the provisions of this chapter were complementary to the Shariʿa rules for killing and wounding, to which some of these articles refer. Central to the chapter is the ordinary quarrel: 'If two persons scuffle and tear each other's collars, the cadi shall chastise [i.e. impose discretionary punishment on] them both, but no fine shall be collected' (art. 36). Such quarrels may result in wounding or in the violation of a person's honour by abusive acts or language. If someone attacks another and breaks his arm or leg, or knocks out an eye or a tooth, and the *qāḍī* cannot impose retaliation, the attacker must pay both compensation (*diya*) and a fine (arts. 41, 50). If two persons tear each other's beards, then they also have to pay a fine in addition to being subjected to discretionary punishment (arts. 37, 39), no doubt justified by the fact that tearing a person's beard is more insulting than just pulling at his clothes. Other articles deal with assaults and wounding by means of arrows or knives. For some offences the culprit is to be paraded through his town or village with the weapon thrust through his arm or ear (arts. 48, 49). Article 41 deals with killing and, in its relation to strict Islamic criminal law, closely resembles the articles on unlawful intercourse: if no retaliation can be carried out, the perpetrator must pay a fine commensurate with his financial means. The amounts are identical to those for illegal intercourse, with the same reductions for slaves and non-Muslims (art. 51). Article 54 lays down that if the fixed penalty for an 'unfounded accusation of unlawful sexual intercourse (*qadhf*)' is imposed, the defendant shall in addition pay a fine, which is twice as much as the fine to be paid for the same offence, if not the fixed punishment but only discretionary punishment can be awarded. The following article, 55, makes punishable any form of defamation.

The third chapter ('On fines and *siyāsa* punishment for drinking wine, theft, usurpation of property, and [other] transgressions') contains injunctions on a variety of topics. It is difficult to detect a rationale in the arrangement of the articles. Most of them are related to the rules of investigation and criminal procedure. Theft is ranked second in importance. Many of the provisions on theft clearly indicate that they were subsidiary, to be applied if the culprit was not punished with the amputation of his right hand (arts. 66–8, 71). The articles provide that the stealing of livestock, agricultural produce and tools must be punished at the *qāḍī*'s discretion, and that the culprit must pay a fine. Two other articles make punishable thefts for which, according to Hanafite doctrine, no fixed penalty can be imposed: the stealing from close relatives and the theft of persons (slaves, prisoners of war, young children) (arts. 72, 73). The latter offence is a capital crime and, in the same article, put on a par with burglary and being a habitual thief. The other offences mentioned in this chapter are drinking, producing and selling wine and attending wine parties. There are a number of injunctions in connection with religious laxness in praying and fasting (arts. 101, 102) and with public morality: article 113 for example forbids disreputable men from coming to places where women and boys go to fetch water and to wash clothes, and article 114 mentions a form of disguised prostitution through spurious sales of slave women. Article 95 forbids lepers from living among other people, whereas the following article makes it possible to expel gypsies. The remaining provisions deal with all types of infractions of personal rights: arson; damage caused by one's animals; mutilation or killing of another person's animals; ways to proceed with lost and found goods; the giving of false testimony; the forging of documents; counterfeiting; falsely informing against a person; marrying a woman before the expiration of her waiting period; and forbidden loan transactions.

Chapter 15 ('On suspects and their connections') deals mainly with procedure. Articles 124 and 125 describe the procedure for the banishment of persons from a neighbourhood or village at the request of the inhabitants and the one for dealing with serious or habitual criminals.

3.5.2 The penalties

From isolated formulae in *qānūn*s and court records one can form an idea of what the Ottoman elite regarded as the justifications for judicial punishment. These notions are very global, and we do not find detailed expositions that relate specific forms of punishment with the goals to be realised. One aim is rehabilitation or reform of the soul (*iṣlāḥ-i nefs*). This appears from the way imprisonment was enforced: an offender was not released after a period fixed by the court or the executive officials, but would be kept in prison until his repentance and rehabilitation was evident. Rehabilitation and reform is also the main objective of *taʿzir* punishment, as explained in the classical doctrine of the *fiqh*: such punishments must prevent offenders from recidivism by disciplining them. Deterrence and incapacitation were the principal aims of *siyāsa* punishment, which usually consisted in capital punishment or severe corporal punishment such as mutilation. The application of *siyāsa* punishment was as a rule justified with the formulae 'as an example for others' (*sāyirlere mūcib-i ʿibret, ʿibrat^{an} li-l-sāʾirīn*) and 'in order to provide safety to the people and to cleanse the country' (*teʾmīn-i ʿibād ve taṭhīr-i bilād*). In addition, public order or state interest (*niẓām-i memleket içün*) were invoked when *siyāsa* punishment was imposed. Retribution had an important place in the penal system, since it was at the basis of the law of wounding and killing, as we have seen before. It is also occasionally referred to in other contexts, for instance when the *qāḍī* requests from the executive officials that an accused be punished in proportion with the seriousness of his crime.

Our knowledge about the types of punishments that were actually applied is unfortunately incomplete. Administering punishment and carrying out penal sentences were the tasks of the chief of police (*subaşı*). Unfortunately, these officials did not leave records. Moreover, the Shariʿa court records do not mention the punishments that were actually inflicted, except in the case of the fixed penalties and retaliation. Usually the *qāḍī* would content himself with stating, without further specification, that the defendant deserved to be punished with *taʿzir*, which, in the Ottoman context is identical with flogging or caning. Our main sources of knowledge about the penal system are the *qānūn*s and *fermān*s and the reports of Western travellers in the Ottoman Empire.

In the following I will give a survey of the punishments that were applied in practice.

3.5.2.1 Reprimand

In the previous chapter it was mentioned that in classical *fiqh* the principal aim of *taʿzir* punishment was to prevent the individual perpetrator from committing criminal offences again and that the punishment therefore could vary according to the culprit's status and class (see § 2.7.1). This principle has found its way into Ottoman *qānūn*, witness article 123 OCC, which stipulates that religious officials with imperial appointments are not to be chastised by flogging or beating and that it is sufficient for them that the *qāḍī* tells them harshly not to commit such an act again.

3.5.2.2 Fines

Although fining was a controversial punishment among the jurists (see § 2.4.3), it became a prominent feature of the Ottoman penal system. One of the functions of Ottoman *qānūn* was to regulate this type of punishment. Offenders who were to be punished with flogging or beating by way of *taʿzir* usually had to pay a fine in addition, the amount of which, as a rule, depended on the number of strokes that the *qāḍī* ordered to be inflicted. For some offences, such as unlawful sexual intercourse, killing or wounding, fines had to be paid if the proper Shariʿa penalty could not be enforced. Fines were treated like taxes and collected by those entitled to the other taxes of the region. In the cities, the police and nightwatchmen would receive them. In the countryside, the fines would accrue to those entitled to the land tax, such as the fief (*timar*) holder or trustee of the imperial domains. Fines were often collected by tax-farmers, who paid a fixed sum for the right to collect them in a certain village or town. It was one of the duties of the *qāḍī*s to deal with complaints about excessive or unjustified fines and instruct the officials involved to pay them back (see arts. 115 and 116 OCC).

3.5.2.3 Confiscation of property

Confiscation of all property was a common complementary punishment for those who were sentenced to death by way of *siyāsa*. If the convict was a member of the imperial household (*kul*), confiscation was a standard measure because both they and their property were regarded as belonging to the Sultan. Since they would not be very much inclined to hand their movable property over, they were sometimes tortured before their execution in order to discover where they had hidden their riches.[33]

3.5.2.4 Public exposure to scorn (tashhīr, tajrīs)

Exposure to public scorn was a common punishment, often imposed in combination with other penalties. The OCC lays down that a person who has wounded someone is to be led through the streets with an arrow or a knife thrust through their arm. Other decrees mention that someone who has stolen a chicken is to be paraded with the stolen chicken hanging from his neck and a person who has thrown carcasses in the street, in spite of warnings from the environmental police (*çöplük subaşısı*), must go around the town with a carcass's head hanging from his neck. In cases of violations of market regulations, an offender was sometimes led around with his faulty goods hanging from his nose, which was first pierced for the purpose, or with his head put through a very heavy wooden board to which a small placard was affixed and on which his defective commodities were placed. Sometimes such offenders had their ears nailed to the doorposts of their shops with their feet hardly touching the ground and were left there for some time.[34]

3.5.2.5 Banishment (nafy, taghrīb)

Banishment is mentioned in several articles of the OCC as a punishment for those who unintentionally set fire to houses, for negligent watchmen who fail to prevent arson, gypsies, lepers and irreligious or immoral people. The latter, as we have seen above (§ 3.4.3), could be banished at the instigation of the inhabitants of their quarters or villages (arts. 92–6, 124 OCC).

3.5.2.6 Imprisonment (ḥabs)

Imprisonment was an important element of the penal system, but not necessarily as punishment. More important was imprisonment during

33 Mumcu, *Osman devletinde siyaseten katl*, p. 146; d'Ohsson, *Tableau général*, vol. III, p. 241.
34 D'Ohsson, *Tableau général*, vol. II, p. 112.

investigation or awaiting the execution of corporal punishment or the death penalty. Although Ottoman muftis frequently mention imprisonment as a punishment, usually in combination with flogging – the common expression being severe beating and long imprisonment (*taʿzīr-i şedīd ve ḥabs-i medīd*) – it is hardly mentioned in the OCC. Prison sentences did usually not specify a term but stipulated that the prisoner would be released when it had become clear that he had mended his ways and sincerely repented of his crimes. In the course of the sixteenth century, as a result of the growing need for oarsmen in the navy, penal servitude on the galleys (called *kürek*, i.e. oar) became a common punishment, to which people were sentenced for a great variety of offences, ranging from capital ones (such as apostasy and homosexual intercourse) to trivial ones (such as drunkenness, gambling and swearing at a muezzin). The average time spent on the galleys was eight years. In the eighteenth century, when sailing galleons were taking the place of oar-driven galleys, the need for oarsmen decreased. From that time prisoners were sent to arsenals and fortresses to serve their sentences.[35]

3.5.2.7 Flogging (jald)

Flogging and caning were the most common form of punishment. The strokes were usually applied on the back or on the soles of the feet. The latter punishment was known as *falaqa*. Sentences of flogging pronounced by the *qāḍī* were carried out in the courtroom immediately. The number of strokes, to be fixed by the *qāḍī*, varied with the seriousness of the offence. Although a *fatwā* exists stating that the state is liable for half the bloodprice if a person dies after receiving more than one hundred strokes (which implies that the executioner had acted unlawfully), Western travellers report that in some cases offenders received several hundred strokes. The *mühtesib* and the executive officials also had the power to administer this form of punishment. The former would do so if he caught someone *in flagrante*. The latter often did so immediately after the arrest of the suspect, partly as a first instalment of his punishment and partly in order to intimidate him and make him confess.[36]

3.5.2.8 Amputation (qaṭʿ) of the right hand or of the right hand and left foot

Ottoman criminal *qānūn*, as we have seen, imposes amputation of the right hand as a punishment for those who habitually cut other people's purses or attack them with a knife. In addition, it is the prescribed penalty for

[35] Mehmet Ipşirli, 'XVI. Asrının ikinci yarısında kürek cezasi ili ilgili hükümler', *Tarih Enstitüsü Dergisi* 12 (1982), 204–48.

[36] Heyd, *Studies*, pp. 271–5; d'Ohsson, *Tableau général*, vol. I, pp. 274–5, vol. II, p. 112.

forgers of decrees and documents and counterfeiters (arts. 49, 98, OCC). We do not know whether this punishment was often applied. It is likely that from the second half of the sixteenth century offenders were sent to the galleys rather than being subjected to amputation. Amputation as a fixed punishment for theft is hardly mentioned in published court records[37] and Ottoman *fatwā* collections, which is an indication that it was not a frequently applied penalty. This is corroborated by an eighteenth-century observer.[38] According to some *fermāns*, cross-amputation was imposed as a penalty in the Ottoman Empire, but as *siyāsa* punishment and not as a fixed penalty.

3.5.2.9 The infliction of injuries by way of retaliation

The OCC mentions retaliation for the loss of eyes and teeth (art. 50 OCC). These are parts of the body that can be removed or put out of action with relatively few medical risks. The only instances of retaliation for wounding I found in the Ottoman *fatwā* collections were those for knocking out teeth and for the cutting off of fingers. It is likely that in many cases where retaliation might have been possible, a financial settlement was reached between the parties. The executive officials must have encouraged such settlements since they were more profitable for them than retaliation: according to article 50 OCC they could collect a fine from the culprit in such cases only if no retaliation had taken place. The following *fatwā* discusses a case in which such a settlement was reached under strong pressure of these officials:

> *Question*: After Zeyd has wilfully hit ʿAmr's mouth with his fist and knocked out two teeth and retaliation became [legally] possible, it was said to Zeyd: 'Let there be a settlement (*ṣulḥ*) to the effect that you pay a certain amount of *akçe* and the retaliation will be dropped.' With the help of the executive officials considerable pressure was put on him and a settlement was reached by coercion. Now, has the right to demand retaliation from Zeyd been forfeited?
> *Answer*: Yes.
> *In this case*: Is ʿAmr entitled on the strength of the aforementioned settlement to demand from Zeyd the amount of *akçe*?
> *Answer*: No.[39]

The reason that Zeyd is not obliged to pay and that ʿAmr has forfeited his right to retaliation is that Zeyd's obligation is based on coercion, whereas ʿAmr's abandonment of his right to retaliation is based on his declaration that he pardons Zeyd. Such a declaration is valid regardless of whether or not it was willed, such as for example repudiation in family law (*ṭalāq*).

[37] E.g. Akgündüz et al., *Şerʿiye sicilleri*. [38] D'Ohsson, *Tableau général*, vol. III, p. 266.
[39] Meḥmed b. Aḥmad al- Kudūsī, *Natījat al-fatāwā*, 2nd edn. (Istanbul: n. p., 1848–9), pp. 569–70.

3.5.2.10 Other forms of corporal punishment

The OCC mentions amputation of the male member as a punishment for abduction and the branding of the vulva as a penalty for women who agreed to be abducted (arts. 10, 11 OCC). The branding of the forehead is mentioned as the punishment of procurers and forgers (arts. 75, 98 OCC). Finally there are *fermāns* prescribing the slitting of noses and the cutting of ears as the punishment of army deserters, if it is the first offence. However, these provisions were later abolished, probably as the result of the emergence of penal servitude on the galleys.

3.5.2.11 The death penalty

Death sentences and executions are intimately linked to the authority of the head of state. In the Ottoman Empire death sentences had to be approved by the Sultan or high-ranking representatives, such as governors. The link between the executions and imperial power was physically symbolised by placing the heads of executed offenders in front of the palace gate in Istanbul, with placards indicating the grounds for the execution. At times, hundreds of heads were exhibited outside the palace. These included the heads of all those who were put to death in the capital and those of brigands, rebels and officials executed in the provinces, and whose heads were sent to Istanbul so that the authorities in the capital could ascertain that their orders had been obeyed. During transport the heads coming from the provinces were filled with straw, preserved in brine or contained in sacks filled with honey in order to keep them from decaying.

The ordinary methods of execution were hanging and beheading with a scimitar or an axe. But other methods were used too. High officials, military officers and high-ranking *'ulamā'*(in the rare cases that *'ulamā'* were sentenced to death) were usually executed by strangling them with a bowstring. This goes back to an old Turkish–Mongol taboo on the shedding of the blood of members of the dynasty and high servants of the state by the sovereign. As there existed a similar taboo on the shedding of the blood of women, they were usually drowned, after first having been sewn into a sack. In order to enhance deterrence, brigands, rebels or those executed for political reasons were executed in ways that prolonged their suffering and agony: the sources mention for instance impaling (a favourite method of the Ottomans); throwing on sharp hooks attached to a wall or on pointed stakes; pounding to death in a mortar; sawing or hacking in two; and flaying alive.

Deterrence was also achieved by staging spectacles around executions. Often such a spectacle consisted in parading those sentenced to death through the streets in a humiliating manner: manacled and half-clad they were forced to shout out loudly what crimes they had committed or were accompanied by a crier doing the same. After the sentence had been carried out, the bodies were left for some time at the place of the execution, Muslims lying on the backs with their heads under their arms, Christians on the face, with their heads placed on their buttocks. The executioner was entitled to all personal belongings of the convict, with the exception of jewellery, and to the body. The next of kin had to pay him to hand over the body so it could be buried.[40]

[40] Mumcu, *Osman devletinde siyaseten katl*, pp. 116–24, 131–41, d'Ohsson, *Tableau général*, vol. III, pp. 59, 241.

CHAPTER 4

The eclipse of Islamic criminal law

4.1 INTRODUCTION

In this chapter I will discuss the reform and subsequent eclipse of Islamic criminal law as a result of the modernisation and Westernisation of the Muslim world. From the late eighteenth century, Western powers extended their influence into the Islamic world. This resulted in the colonial conquest of Indonesia, India, North Africa and Central Asia, accompanied by a sharp increase in Western political and economic influence in countries that did not lose their independence. A few regions, such as the Arabian Peninsula, escaped Western expansion, because Western powers regarded them as devoid of economic or strategic interests. In those countries where Western dominance, political or otherwise, did establish itself, state and society were affected in many ways. One of the areas to change was that of the law. The nineteenth century was a period of drastic law reform in the Muslim world, due to two global factors. One was the aforementioned Westernisation of state and society, which entailed the adoption of Western laws. The other was indigenous: the emergence of modernising states with centralised bureaucracies, both in the colonies and in the countries that had kept their independence. Such states needed new legal systems, and especially new systems of criminal law.

A centralising and modernising state requires effective and rational tools for disciplining its subjects, tools that are applied by a rational bureaucracy (in the Weberian sense) through impersonal procedures. The jurisdictions and powers of the various bureaucratic and judicial organs must be clearly delimited, so that the same procedures will be followed throughout the state without room for the personal discretion of officials. The law must be enforced impartially, without regard to persons. All subjects should be treated on an equal footing before the law (except, of course, that in the colonies there was a fundamental legal distinction between coloniser and colonised, to whom different laws were applied). In the field of criminal law, this would mean that deterrence based on arbitrary public spectacles of corporal punishment and painful executions would make way for deterrence founded on a greater chance of being caught due to more efficient policing methods, and the certainty of punishment imposed in accordance with the law. Moreover, legal certainty, i.e. predictability of the outcome of legal proceedings, was a major objective of law reform and did play an important role in the reform of criminal law.

Colonial administrators as well as indigenous officials regarded Islamic criminal law as wanting in this respect. It was thought to be arbitrary, since in the field of *taʿzīr* and *siyāsa* there were no clear definitions of offences and no fixed relations between crime and punishment. Moreover, it was not impersonal, since the punishment for murder – and, in practice, for many other offences where victim and perpetrator could agree to a financial settlement – depended not on the court, but on the will of the victim's heirs. This was not only seen as arbitrary justice, but also as undermining the power of deterrence of the punishment for manslaughter. In addition, Islamic law did not treat persons equally, since for example religion – both of the perpetrator and of the victim or his heirs (at least in cases of homicide and wounding) – could result in impunity or in different punishments for the same offence. Finally, cultural sensitivities played a role. In Western states there was a growing aversion to corporal punishment, especially to mutilating penalties such as amputation, and to painful methods of execution such as stoning and impaling. This aversion found its way to the modernising elites in independent Muslim countries.

In the Islamic world, reform of criminal law during the nineteenth century took three forms: complete abolition of Islamic criminal law; reform of Islamic criminal law; and reform of *siyāsa* justice. The first was followed in most colonial states. Here Islamic criminal law was simply abolished and replaced by enacted Western statute law. This was for instance done by the French in North Africa. The French penal code, with some changes to adapt it to the colonial situation, was introduced in the Muslim territories over which they had acquired control. This process, however, falls outside the scope of this book. Here I will focus on the countries where Islamic criminal law was not immediately abolished.

The second type of reform is the one followed by the British, both in India and, a century later, in Northern Nigeria. Here, Islamic criminal law continued to be applied but was subjected to a gradual process of change, until, in the end, it was abolished and replaced by statute law. This was part of British colonial policy, which laid great stress on ruling through the existing power structures and preserving, under British control, indigenous law. In the process, Islamic law was stripped of those traits that specifically offended Western ideas of justice, or that were felt to be obstacles to the enforcement of law and order. As a result, a type of criminal law emerged that was Islamic only in name. In both countries it was in the end replaced by Western-inspired penal codes.

The third method, finally, is the one chosen by independent Muslim countries with modernising elites, notably the Ottoman Empire and Egypt. Here, the states focused on the reform of *siyāsa* justice and subjected it to some form of the rule of law by codifying it and by creating specialised courts to apply it, whereas Islamic criminal law, without modifications, continued to be implemented through the Shariʿa courts. This dual system of criminal law enforcement came to an end in Egypt in 1883 with the wholesale introduction of French law and the creation of a new national court system, and in the Ottoman Empire in 1917, when the new Code of Shariʿa Procedure of 1917 removed the jurisdiction over homicide and wounding from Shariʿa courts.[1]

However, the legal system was not reformed everywhere in the Muslim world: in independent Muslim states that fell outside the Western sphere of influence or where the central government was very weak, a traditional system of Islamic justice continued to function for a long time – sometimes, as in Saudi Arabia and Yemen, until today. In Iran and Afghanistan, the traditional system was, at least partially, replaced in 1924, when in both countries penal codes were introduced. These codes, however, preserved the jurisdiction of the religious courts to try *ḥadd* offences. The Afghan code resembles classical *qānūn* in that it only contains provisions based on *taʿzīr* and does not specify the punishment for the offences that are defined in the code.[2] This chapter will not deal with these countries, but in the following chapter I will briefly discuss the criminal law of Saudi Arabia.

I will begin by presenting two episodes that illustrate the different concepts of Islamic criminal law held by British and Egyptian administrators in their colonies (in this example in India) and local, Muslim officials in Islamic countries (in our example in Egypt).

On 10 March 1771, Rous [a young East India Company official, appointed 'supervisor'] again strongly recommended the infliction of capital punishment

[1] M. J. L. Hardy, *Blood feuds and the payment of bloodmoney in the Middle East* (Beirut: Catholic Press, 1963), p. 58.

[2] Mahmoud Akhoundi, *De l'influence de la tradition religieuse sur le droit pénal de l'Iran* (Teheran: Imprimerie de l'Université Téhéran, 1961); S. Beck (tr.), 'Das afghanische Strafgesetzbuch vom Jahre 1924. Aus dem persischen übersetzt und mit einer allgemeinen Einleitung in die afghanische Strafgesetzgebung versehen', *Die Welt des Islams* 11 (1928), 67–157.

in a case of wilful murder tried in the Bhaturia 'Adalat [court of justice] in which a man had cleft off with a hatchet the head of his six-month-old daughter. The culprit Alauddin repeatedly confessed that he had done so in a fit of despair and brought it [the child's head] to Nator to strengthen his complaint against the Qazi [*qāḍī*] who by delaying his marriage had caused him to perpetrate this barbarous act. The Quran laid down death for such a crime, but some later commentators regarded the destruction of a grown-up person as a punishment more than adequate to the death of a child. The Qazi therefore declined to inflict the death sentence. The peculiar circumstances of this barbarity induced Rous to recommend a severe punishment and as a consequence the Naib Nazim [official with judicial powers, in this case acting on appeal] went in some degree beyond the letter of the Mahomedan law, tho' not so far as immediately to affect the life of the culprit.[3]

This confrontation between the Englishman Rous and the Muslim judge's Islamic criminal law shows the deep divide between British and Muslim cultural assumptions and notions of justice. Although the East India Company had acquired sovereign rights in large parts of the country, in theory the Mughal regime continued to exist and Islamic law, both civil and criminal, remained the law of the land. Rous was shocked by the inability of Islamic criminal law to punish such a heinous crime, of which he seemed unable to gauge the cultural motives: although the details of the case are unclear, it seems that the accused killed his baby daughter as a means of exerting pressure on the *qāḍī*, after having warned him that he would do so if the latter did not accede to his request. This was a not unusual course of action for Indians. Moreover, the Englishman was only superficially acquainted with Islamic criminal law, as shown by the explanation why capital punishment could not be imposed. For the reason was not that the victim's value was less than the perpetrator's, but the fact that the killer was the child's father.

British officials were baffled by the leniency of Islamic criminal law and by the loopholes that often precluded the infliction of what they saw as adequate punishment for serious criminals. Application of unmodified Islamic criminal law, they believed, stood in the way of maintaining law and order. On the other hand, they were reluctant to allow *siyāsa* sentences, which they regarded as arbitrary and opposed to the notion of the rule of law. The British, then, saw no other way than to gradually modify strict Islamic criminal law, by putting it on the Procrustean bed of British notions of justice and law and order.

[3] Tapas Kumar Banerjee, *Background to Indian criminal law*, repr. edn. (Calcutta: R. Cambray, 1990), p. 73.

Now let us compare this intercultural clash that occurred in late eighteenth-century India with the following episode that took place in Egypt, four decades later.

In 1812, a gang of thieves were apprehended in Cairo and brought before the chief *qāḍī*. They confessed to having committed many thefts, yet the *qāḍī* could not sentence them to the fixed punishment for theft since, in their confessions, they used not the phrase 'we have stolen', but the words 'we have taken'. Under the Shariʿa, this constitutes uncertainty (*shubha*) which precludes the application of such a punishment. The *qāḍī* then wrote a report to the *kethüda* [the governor of Cairo] and entrusted the matter to him for further disposal. The latter, after some reflection, sentenced them to amputation of their right hands on the strength of his authority to impose *siyāsa* punishments.[4]

In this case the Ottoman procedure was duly followed: if a *qāḍī* cannot reach a verdict in a criminal case, he draws up a document recording the relevant depositions and submits the case to the executive officials. Unlike the British official Rous, the governor of Cairo, apparently, was not unduly worried about the loopholes of the law. He knew that he had the discretionary power to impose exemplary punishment on the basis of *siyāsa* if the strict rules of the Shariʿa would prevent the *qāḍī* from awarding a fitting punishment for a proven crime. For him *siyāsa* was part of the legal order. However, later Egyptian and Ottoman administrators regarded these almost unlimited powers to inflict *siyāsa* punishment as inexpedient and their reforms were aimed at restricting these powers.

These different episodes illustrate why the path of modernisation of Islamic criminal law in early British India was so different from that followed in the Ottoman Empire and Egypt. In the Ottoman Empire and Egypt, modernisation of criminal justice was realised by introducing statute law and setting up special courts to regulate the exercise of *siyāsa* justice, whereas Shariʿa criminal justice remained relatively free from state interference. The British, on the other hand, were reluctant to administer *siyāsa* justice, which offended their sense of what law should be. Therefore, they had no other choice than to transform strict Islamic criminal law. Yet the results of reform in India, the Ottoman Empire and Egypt were, in spite of their different forms of legal modernisation, in the end, similar: the emergence of a body of authoritative and unambiguously formulated criminal law. In India this was achieved by adapting Islamic criminal law, in the other states by enacting penal codes to regulate the exercise of *siyāsa* justice.

4 ʿAbd al-Raḥmān al-Jabartī, *ʿAjāʾib al-āthār fī al-tarājim wa-l-akhbār*, 4 vols. (Bulaq: n.p., 1879–80), vol. IV, p. 144.

The reason that the ultimate results were to some extent similar is that in all three countries the state was in the process of becoming centralised and modernised. Part of this process was that arbitrariness should make place for government by law, that procedures ought to be orderly and predictable, and that the bureaucracy and the courts should treat all subjects on an equal footing, regardless of privileges conferred by, for example, social status and religion. An essential step to achieve this was the enactment of well-defined laws – and especially penal laws specifying each offence and its punishment – as well as the creation of courts with clearly demarcated jurisdictions. This forced officials and judges to treat persons impartially and equally before the law and to act according to the provisions of the law instead of using their own discretion.

Another development connected with the centralisation of state power is that the state takes an active part in the prosecution of crime. Unlike under classical Islamic law, e.g. in the Ottoman Empire, where the prosecution of crime was essentially left to the victim, the state begins to take a more active part and, ultimately, introduces the office of public prosecutor, thereby underlining the public aspect of punishing crime. This means that a prosecution can no longer be stopped at the will of the victim and that settlements between perpetrators and victims cannot take the place of punishment imposed by the state. This had important effects, especially in the law of homicide and wounding.

Criminal law reform was also informed by cultural assumptions. British aversion to the mutilating penalties of Islamic criminal law led to their abolition in India. Although initially Hastings (Governor-General, 1774–85) confirmed sentences of amputation, this punishment was soon abolished by introducing the practice of automatically commuting such sentences into hard labour, whereby each limb counted for seven years. The British were very outspoken in their opposition to mutilating penalties. Paradoxically, they seemed to value limbs more than lives, as they attached great value to capital punishment as a deterrent, introduced it for a variety of offences and applied it widely.[5]

In Egypt and the Ottoman Empire, the severe fixed punishments of amputation and stoning to death became obsolete without any express government decree. This happened during the first half of the nineteenth century. Documentary evidence with regard to Egypt shows that, even if

[5] J. Fisch, *Cheap lives and dear limbs: the British transformation of the Bengal criminal law 1769–1817* (Wiesbaden: Steiner, 1983).

lower *qāḍīs* felt that they had to sentence a defendant to such penalties, which occasionally happened, muftis and higher courts would find grounds to reverse such sentences.[6] They were never officially abolished since that would have been regarded as cancelling God's law, which would have met with strong religious opposition. Apparently these considerations did not exist with regard to doing away with flogging and caning: these punishments were abolished by decree, in the Ottoman Empire in 1858 and in Egypt in 1861.[7] It is difficult to ascertain the motives for the abolition of corporal punishment in Egypt and the Ottoman Empire. Plausible reasons are that the rehabilitating effect of prison sentences came to be regarded as more important than the deterrence produced by the severe fixed penalties and that the reformers in the bureaucratic elite felt that such punishments were signs of backwardness and would mar the image of modernity that they wanted to present to the West.

4.2 ANGLO-MUḤAMMADAN CRIMINAL LAW AND ITS DEMISE

4.2.1 India[8]

After the British East India Company, in 1765, had acquired the authority over the department of finances of Bengal, it gradually extended its control over other branches of government. One of these was the administration of criminal justice. Since Bengal was part of the Mughal Empire, the legal system was essentially Islamic and based, as far as penal law is concerned, on Hanafite law. Constitutionally, the British could not change that. However, they reformed the judiciary in such a way that the Muslim judicial officials were subordinated to British judges. Moreover, since they regarded Islamic criminal law as inconsistent and too lenient, they began to remedy those doctrines that they regarded as obstacles to the maintenance of law and order and as repugnant to natural justice. The main objection of the British to Islamic criminal law as administered in northern India was that it restricted the power of the courts to hand down capital sentences. Under Islamic criminal law, as compared to contemporary British law, there were relatively few capital offences and, in addition, there were so many defences available that convictions for such capital offences were difficult to obtain. On the

6 Peters, 'Islamic and secular criminal law', 86–7.

7 Rudolph Peters, 'Egypt and the age of the triumphant prison: judicial punishment in nineteenth century Egypt', *Annales Islamologiques* 36 (2002), 253–85.

8 For this section I have relied mostly on Fisch, *Cheap lives and dear limbs* and Banerjee, *Background*.

other hand, the British were reluctant to use the discretionary powers of *siyāsa* for pronouncing death sentences, although they were aware that this might help them to circumvent the restrictive provisions of the Sharīʿa. Apparently they regarded it as arbitrary justice which offended their idea of rule of law. Therefore they only rarely had recourse to it in their regulations. The following provision is one of the exceptional instances that I have come across: 'but leaders and heinous offenders [in connection with gang robberies] may be adjudged to death (if deemed deserving of it by the Nizamut Adawlut [Niẓāmat ʿAdālat]) if convicted of repetition, or of such a degree of cruelty, as may be punishable by death under the discretion allowed by Seeasut [i.e. *siyāsa*; RP]'.[9]

In general, the British modified Islamic criminal law proper rather than circumventing it by using the extensive discretionary powers of *siyāsa*. The process of reform initiated by the British had far-reaching consequences and totally altered the nature of the law applied in the Indian courts. However, the fiction that the system of criminal law was Islamic was maintained until 1861 when the Indian Penal Code of 1860 came into force.

The first task the British wanted to complete was the reform of the judiciary. On 3 December 1790 Cornwallis (Governor-General, 1786–93) enacted a regulation (re-enacted in greater detail by Regulation 9 of 1793) that introduced a new court system in Bengal, which was, as British power expanded, later imposed on other parts of India. There was to be a three-tiered court system staffed by British judges, assisted by Islamic jurisprudents called law officers. The latter were to expound the rules of the Sharīʿa applicable to the circumstances of the cases tried by the courts. The highest criminal court (Ṣadr Niẓāmat ʿAdālat or, as the British spelled it, Sudder Nizamut Adawlut) constituted the governor-general and his council,[10] assisted by the chief *qāḍī* of the district and two muftis. On the circuit courts in each division two British judges served, assisted by a *qāḍī* and a mufti, all appointed by the Governor-General. At the bottom of the hierarchy there were the magistrates' courts in the districts, with single judges who had jurisdiction in cases of petty crime. The courts were instructed, in the absence of applicable legislation ('regulations'), to apply Islamic law as communicated to them through the *fatwā*s of their law officers, at least

9 Regulation 1803/53 § 4, C 2, in James Edward Colebrooke, *Digest of the regulations and laws, enacted by the Governor-General in Council for the civil government of the territories under the Presidency of Bengal arranged in alphabetical order*, 2 vols. (Calcutta: n.p., 1807), vol. I, p. 537.

10 In 1801 the offices of Governor-General and President of the High Court were separated. The Nīẓāmat ʿAdālat consisted from that time of a President, who had to be a member of the government, and two British puisne judges. Regulation 1801/2 § 10, in ibid., vol. I, p. 516.

'if it appeared to be consonant with natural justice'.[11] If a court of circuit disagreed with a *fatwā*, the trial had to be referred to the Niẓāmat ʿAdālat, which was also bound by the *fatwā*s, but could propose legislation for future cases. The only possibility for the courts to deviate from the *fatwā*s was by mitigating the proposed penalty. Not until 1817 was the binding character of the *fatwā*s of the law officers repealed. A regulation issued in that year gave British judges the power to overrule or enhance these *fatwā*s.[12]

The British used two different methods to reform criminal law. In order to define offences and their punishment under *taʿzīr*, they promulgated criminal provisions for specific offences (regulations). In the domain of strict Islamic criminal law (*ḥadd* crimes and retaliation), which they did not want to alter, they issued binding instructions to the law officers of the courts ordering them to give their *fatwā*s in certain cases on the basis of certain hypothetical assumptions. In cases of manslaughter, for instance, the legal officers were ordered to give their *fatwā*s as if all heirs had demanded retaliation, regardless of whether or not this was the case. For the Muslim jurists this was not at all problematical: muftis, according to Islamic legal theory, expound the law on the basis of the facts that have been presented to them without examining their truth. Therefore, their *fatwā*s are not binding. The British, however, erroneously thought they were and regarded them as justification for the harsher sentences desired by them. It is likely that the introduction of this method of using legal fictions, which could not be challenged, in order to reform the law was influenced by eighteenth-century English legal culture. In common law, fictions were frequently used in order to adapt the limited number of available writs to new circumstances. By allowing fictitious details to be added to the facts of a case, the working of a writ would be expanded, without formally changing the law. British lawyers working in India at that time apparently compared the Shariʿa with common law, and had recourse to legal fictions in order to introduce reform.

As a result a strange and confusing mixture of Islamic laws and statute was applied. The following case may illustrate this: the accusation was death by poisoning, a problematic issue, since in Abū Ḥanīfa's doctrine this did not count as intentional homicide (see § 2.5.3). The law officers faithfully expounded the Hanafite doctrine on this point and suggested that the death penalty be awarded as a discretionary *siyāsa* punishment. But the court in

[11] Regulation 1793/9 § 47, in ibid., vol. II, p. 879.
[12] Fisch, *Cheap lives and dear limbs*, p. 82.

the end applied a regulation of 1799 that expanded the notion of wilful homicide far beyond the definition of the Shariʿa:[13]

The accused, Joorah Shah, a forty year old cultivator, had a quarrel with a certain Chunchul Shah with regard to the right to administer a *takiyya* [a sufi centre] in Behar, to which some *waqf* land was attached. After Chunchul Shah had ousted Joorah Shah from the office of administrator of the *takiyya* the latter wanted revenge and hoped that by killing Chunchul Shah he might regain control over the *takiyya*. Joorah Shah then poisoned Chunchul Shah, which was easy since they lived in the same house. The body was thrown in a well where it was later discovered. During the trial before the court of circuit, he withdrew his previous confession, claiming that it had been extorted from him by violence. However, several witnesses could testify to his having confessed. The law officer of the court of circuit pronounced the accused to be fully convicted of the murder of Chunchul Shah. He at the same time stated that, as the deceased had taken the poison without compulsion, the prisoner was liable to *diya*, on the claim of the heir, but for the ends of public justice, was liable to severe punishment at discretion. The law officers of the Court of Niẓāmat ʿAdālat, declared the accused liable to exemplary punishment (*siyāsa*) of death. Since the accused appeared fully convicted of the murder of Chunchul Shah, the court, in pursuance of the above fatwa, as well as under the provisions made by the regulation for the punishment of wilful murder by poison, sentenced the prisoner to suffer death.[14]

British reform affected both procedure and substantive law. With regard to procedure, they found that the Islamic law of evidence was too strict and often prevented the conviction of a person for a crime he had indeed committed. That the victim of a crime, or his heirs in murder cases, could prevent the punishment of a culprit by agreeing to a settlement with the perpetrator was another outrage for the British sense of justice, which they eliminated. Finally they modified the substantive law of homicide and the law of *ḥadd* offences on many points.

In a regulation issued in 1803, the British stipulated that convictions should be based on solid evidence, 'but in cases of strong suspicion, though not amounting to conviction, or of bad character, the Court may order the prisoner's detention, till he give security for further good behaviour and appearance when required'.[15] This seems to be a continuation of Mughal

[13] 'The Nizamut Adawlut shall sentence to death persons committing murder by drowning or poisoning, if the intention be evident, whatever may be the Futwa [i.e. *fatwā*] of the law officers; unless they be deemed proper objects for mercy; and shall not adhere to the distinctions made in murders, by the Muhamedan law, as to the mode and instrument of perpetration.' Regulation 1799/8 § 5, in Colebrooke, *Digest*, vol. I, p. 534.

[14] Niẓāmat ʿAdālat (1805), trial 69, 10 Sept. 1805. Court of Nizamut Adawlut, *Reports of criminal cases, 1805 [–11]* (n.p.: n.p., n.d.), pp. 64–6.

[15] Regulation 1803/53 § 2 C 6, in Colebrooke, *Digest*, vol, I, pp. 535–6.

practice, and compares with the Ottoman rules concerning people of bad reputation. The solidity of evidence required for a conviction was to be measured according to British standards and not necessarily by the criteria of strict Islamic criminal law. This is illustrated by the following trial that took place in 1805:

> Balik Ram, a thirty year old man, was charged with the murder of Ramhurry, brother to the prosecutor [i.e. the heir of the murder victim]. The following circumstances appeared on the trial from the concurrent testimony of several witnesses. For nearly a year an unlawful sexual relation had existed between the accused and Meghee, the victim's sister. In consequence of the prisoner's [i.e. the accused, RP] bad character, Meghee repeatedly endeavoured to break off the connection with him, but he persisted in visiting her. One night the prisoner went to the house of Meghee, and tapped at the window. She remonstrated with him and refused to admit him, saying that her brothers were at home and that they would be angry with her if he did not go away. Upon this, the accused left her, uttering threats of revenge against her and her brothers. Anxious that he might execute his threats, Meghee called some of the neighbours, who, on entering the house, found the deceased with his throat cut, but still alive. He told them, in a low voice, that the prisoner had wounded him. They also observed the accused with a knife in his hand running out of the room in which the deceased was lying. The deceased died the same night and the accused was apprehended the next day. The law officer of the court of circuit declared him liable to suffer death on the legal demand of retaliation. The law officers of the Nizamat ʿAdalat declared the prisoner to be convicted of murder on strong presumptive evidence of his guilt, and liable to suffer death, or other discretionary punishment, on the principle of *siyasa*. The Court of Nizamat ʿAdalat, considering the prisoner fully convicted of the crime with which he was charged, sentenced him to the death penalty.[16]

Although the circuit court had pronounced a sentence of retaliation for manslaughter, the law officers of the Niẓāmat ʿAdālat realised that the evidence did not satisfy the requirements of the Shariʿa. As there was no doubt as to the guilt of the accused, they proposed to sentence him to death on the strength of *siyāsa*. The British judges, however, were in general loath to use their *siyāsa* discretion. To solve the dilemma they applied English standards of evidence, instead of the Islamic rules.

Under the Shariʿa, the court could only admit testimonies given by Muslim eyewitnesses of good reputation. In a country where the majority of the population were Hindus, the British regarded this rule as 'an odious distinction, the absurdity and injustice of which are too glaring to require comment'.[17] This 'absurdity' was remedied in 1793 when a regulation was

[16] Niẓāmat ʿAdālat (1805), trial 34, 9 May 1805. Court of Nizamut Adawlut, *Reports*, pp. 30–1.
[17] Fisch, *Cheap lives and dear limbs*, pp. 47, quoting a British judge in the Niẓāmat ʿAdālat.

enacted that stipulated that the law officers had to prepare their opinions assuming that the witnesses were Muslims of good reputation.[18] In 1817 other restrictions imposed by the Islamic law of evidence were removed: if Islamic law declared the evidence of a witness inadmissible on grounds which might appear to the British judge 'unreasonable and insufficient', this was no longer to be respected. Law officers had to give their *fatwās* under the assumption that there had been no objections against the witness. Being of good reputation (*'adl*) did not matter any more. Since according to many Hanafite jurists government officials were not of good reputation, the new regulation removed the incapacity of police officers to testify in the cases they had investigated.

Another prominent procedural stumbling block for the British was the fact that in homicide cases, as well as some other offences, prosecution was a private affair and dependent on the wish of the victim or his heirs. At any stage of the proceedings, they could pardon the accused, whether or not against a financial consideration. This was hard to accept for the British, for whom the main function of punishing criminals was deterrence. They regarded punishing crime as a duty of the state indispensable for the maintenance of law and order. For Cornwallis, putting an end to this was a crucial element of his reform proposals: 'To take away the discretion of the relations, seems absolutely requisite to secure an equal administration of justice, and will constitute a strong additional check on the commission of murder, and other crimes, which are now no doubt often perpetrated, under the idea of an easy escape through the notorious defect of the existing law.'[19] One of the first criminal regulations issued by the British instructed the law officers to give their *fatwās* in homicide cases on the assumption that the heirs demanded retaliation.[20] Rape, too, was often not prosecuted under Islamic law because the victim (or her family) would often withdraw the charges in exchange for the perpetrator's promise to marry his victim. For a family this was, of course, a much better strategy for salvaging family honour than a public trial where all the painful details of the case would be made public. The British, however, wanted to put an end to the possibility of settlements in criminal cases. In order to underline the public interest in prosecuting and punishing crime, the British established the office of

[18] 'The law officer shall declare what would have been the Futwa if the witnesses had been Muhamedans' (Regulation 1793/9 § 56), in Colebrooke, *Digest*, vol. I, p. 529.

[19] Charles Grant, *Observations on the state of society among the Asiatic subjects of Great Britain with respect to morals and on the means of approving it. Written chiefly in 1792* ([London]: House of Commons, 1813), p. 35.

[20] Banerjee, *Background*, pp. 72–3. The instruction was repeated in a more detailed form in Regulation 1793/9 § 55, 76 and Regulation 1797/4 § 3, 4, in Colebrooke, *Digest*, vol. I, pp. 526, 534.

public prosecutor, who would instigate criminal proceedings regardless of the wishes of the victim or his heirs.

British interference was not restricted to procedure, but extended also to substantive law. Reforms were introduced to modify the law of homicide and of *ḥadd* offences. They were aimed in the first place at abolishing the penalties that the British considered unacceptable – amputation and stoning to death – and, second, at closing the loopholes that, in British eyes, thwarted the infliction of the punishment that criminals deserved.

A 1790 regulation instructed the courts to follow the opinion of Muḥammad al-Shaybānī and Abū Yūsuf with regard to the criterion for determining whether or not a killing had been wilful.[21] They held that criminal intent is assumed to exist if the perpetrator used a weapon or instrument that is usually fatal, whereas, according to Abū Ḥanīfa, this is only the case if a sharp weapon or object or fire was used (see § 2.5.3). That meant that killing a person with a large stone or by drowning him would not be regarded as wilful according to Abū Ḥanīfa. For the British, this was, evidently, an irrational doctrine that stood in the way of punishing murderers adequately.

In 1799 most other defences against a charge of homicide were eliminated: henceforth, there was no bar for capital punishment on 'any ground of personal distinction'. This included the circumstances that the victim was the perpetrator's descendant, one of the perpetrator's heirs, or the culprit's slave. Moreover, the fact that one of the accomplices was not liable for retaliation would no longer protect the others from the death penalty. The regulation also provided that criminal intent alone (i.e. the intent to kill) was the determining factor for allowing a sentence of retaliation and that the mode of killing or the instrument used were not the only grounds for establishing this intent. Poisoning and drowning were put on the same footing as other ways of killing in this respect.[22] Under the Mughals, as in the Ottoman Empire, murderers who killed using these means would be put to death by *siyāsa*. The British, having an aversion to *siyāsa* justice, wanted to uphold their notion of the rule of law by changing the law of retaliation, rather than relying on *siyāsa* sentences.

A last doctrinal obstacle to imposing the death penalty for wilful homicide was removed in 1801. The British were puzzled by the rule that accidental homicide in Islamic criminal law included those cases in which a person who planned to murder someone mistakenly killed someone else.

[21] Banerjee, *Background*, pp. 72–3. It was repeated in Regulation 1793/9 § 75, in Colebrooke, *Digest*, vol. I, p. 533.

[22] Regulation 1799/8 §§ 2–5, in Colebrooke, *Digest*, vol. I, p. 534.

Under the Shariʿa such a person could not be sentenced to death, on the grounds that he lacked the intent to kill the victim. Therefore the British enacted a provision saying that 'if a person intending to kill one individual, should accidentally kill another, the law officers shall declare what would have been the Futwa [*fatwā*] in case he had committed the murder intended'.

Curiously, the British had little difficulty with the impunity of the perpetrator of a *crime passionnel.* Under Islamic law (see § 2.3.3) a killer can validly plead that he has killed his wife or close female relative and/or her paramour because he found them engaged in act of unlawful sexual intercourse. The following case makes it clear that the British fully accepted such a plea, but on a totally different ground:

Gopeenath, a thirty year old peasant, was charged with the murder of Huree Kishn, who, although being warned by Gopeenath, had an illicit sexual relation with the latter's sister. Gopeenath had strangled his victim one day when he came home and had found his sister in bed with him. The body was thrown into a pond where it was found by the victim's brother. The latter immediately went to Gopeenath's house knowing the victim had intended to go there. Gopeenath's sister told him what had happened and he reported the case to the police. Gopeenath confessed during the interrogation, but withdrew his confession during the session before the Court of Circuit and pleaded not guilty. Nevertheless the law officer of the court of circuit issued a *fatwā* to the effect that wilful homicide had been proven against Gopeenath and that he deserved to be sentenced to death by way of retaliation. Upon review by the Nizamat ʿAdalat, the law officers of this court gave as their opinion that the circumstances stated in the confession of Gopeenath were such as to justify the homicide; and that, as there was no other evidence, he should be discharged. The Nizamat ʿAdalat upheld this decision, but justified the acquittal on the ground of 'the sudden irritation of mind, in which the homicide appeared to have been committed, on the deceased being unexpectedly found with the sister of the prisoner, after the caution given to him'.[23]

For the British judges, apparently, this defence was construed as provocation removing the *mens rea*, whereas, under Islamic law, the act is justified (and even commendable), for lack of *actus reus*; for homicide under such circumstances is regarded as necessary to put an end to a crime in progress (see § 2.3.3). The defence was not abolished until 1822, when a regulation instructed the law officers to issue their *fatwā*s as if such a plea had not been made by the accused.[24]

[23] Niẓāmat ʿAdālat (1805), trial 83, 29 Oct. 1805. Court of Nizamut Adawlut, *Reports*, pp. 80–2.

[24] Regulation 1822/4 § 7, in Fulwar Skipwith, *The magistrate's guide; being an abridgment of the criminal regulations and acts of the circular orders and constructions; and of the cases decided and reported by the Court of Nizamut Adawlut, under the Presidency of Fort William, in Bengal* (Calcutta: G. H. Huttman, Bengal Military Orphan Press, 1843), p. 69.

A final aspect of the law of homicide that offended the British notions of public justice was the rule that accidental death was regarded as a tort entailing the payment of financial compensation. The British were appalled by the fact that the heirs were the recipients of the 'fine', as they called the *diya*. They interpreted this as a kind of monetary expiation, expressing the idea that human lives could be bought for money. In 1797 the British laid down that 'no sentence of pecuniary compensation or damages, adjudged to or recoverable by individuals, shall be given on any criminal prosecution, nor any sentence of fine except to the use of Government'. If the law officers awarded *diya* in their *fatwās*, this should be commuted to imprisonment.[25] In 1801 the rule was formulated more precisely. Thenceforth, the commutation of bloodprice into imprisonment was not applicable in cases of wilful homicide, or in cases of 'homicides by real misadventure, in the prosecution of a lawful act, and without any malignant intention', even if the *fatwā* of the law officers should award bloodprice.[26] There are several decisions of the Niẓāmat ʿAdālat acquitting defendants who had accidentally killed persons while aiming at animals, although the *fatwās* of the law officers held them liable for bloodprice.[27] None of the regulations refers to the liability of the *ʿāqila* (which would have seriously offended British ideas of criminal justice), probably because it did not play a role in pre-colonial Mughal legal practice.[28]

Retaliation in the event of wounding does not appear to have been common before British rule was established, and the British did not issue special legislation in this respect. The regulation providing that sentences of amputation were to be commuted to imprisonment issued with respect to fixed penalties (see below) might be used in the unlikely case that the law officers would adjudge retaliation for bodily harm. With regard to the awarding of bloodprice in favour of a wounded person, the British issued legislation similar to the provisions on homicide: the courts of circuit were instructed to 'commute, for an adequate period of imprisonment, Futwas of their law officers awarding Deyut [*diya*] or pecuniary fines for any acts other than homicide'.[29]

With regard to the law of *ḥadd* offences, the first substantive criminal regulation of 1793 confirmed the already existing practice of commuting

[25] Regulation 1797/14 § 3, in Colebrooke, *Digest*, vol. II, p. 881.
[26] Regulation 1801/8 § 6, in ibid., vol. II, p. 882.
[27] Skipwith, *The magistrate's guide*, p. 70.
[28] The *ʿāqila* was probably of no practical importance in India. See John Herbert Harington, *An analysis of the laws and regulations enacted by the Governor General in Council, at Fort William, in Bengal, for the civil government of the British territories under that Presidency* (London: A. J. Valpy, 1821), p. 258.
[29] Regulation 1797/14 § 4, in Colebrooke, *Digest*, vol. II, p. 882.

the penalty of mutilation into imprisonment and hard labour 'of seven years for each limb'.[30] Ten years later a regulation was issued depriving the *ḥadd* doctrine of its special defences, such as *shubha*, and the strict rules of evidence. The pertinent section stipulated that if, in the absence of legislative provisions,

the crime be liable to a specific penalty [i.e. fixed penalty] by the Muhamedan law on full conviction, and the Futwa (*fatwā*) should award discretionary punishment in consequence of the conviction not being complete according to the Muhamedan law, the Court, if satisfied of the prisoner's guilt, shall require a second Futwa specifying the specific penalty on full conviction, and shall sentence the prisoner according to such second Futwa.

The same would apply 'if the specific penalty of the Muhamedan law be barred by some special exception not affecting the criminality of the offence and repugnant to general justice'.[31] This meant that if someone was accused of theft, for which there was evidence, but not sufficient for a sentence to a fixed penalty, or if the evidence was sufficient but the accused had stolen from his child, he would nevertheless, in the second instance, be sentenced to the fixed punishment for theft, which the British would commute to a long term of imprisonment. The same regulation specified this principle in detail with regard to armed robbery. The fixed punishment for banditry would not be barred

by any of the gang being under age, or a lunatic, or a relation to the person robbed, or by his having a joint interest in the property plundered, or by the person robbed not being a fixed resident under permanent protection, or by the property not being in custody with respect to any one of the robbers, or by the share of each robber not amounting to the specified value of ten Derhems.[32]

With regard to offences punishable with *ta'zīr* the law officers would state the grounds for discretionary punishment in their *fatwā*s, but leave the measure of it to the court. The upper limits of discretionary punishment were for the courts of circuit thirty-nine lashes ('stripes') or seven years' imprisonment and for the Niẓāmat 'Adālat any punishment but death. The latter court was instructed 'to provide for the case in the future', i.e. to enact legislation covering the offence.[33] One of the first examples of such legislation can be found in the regulation of 1797, which made punishable by *ta'zīr* the offence of perjury. The accused could be punished by public

30 Regulation 1793/9 § 51, in ibid., vol. II, p. 879.
31 Regulation 1803/53 § 2, C 3– 5, in ibid., vol. II, p. 884.
32 Regulation 1803/53 § 1, in ibid., vol. I, p. 536.
33 Regulation 1803/53 § 2, C 7, § 7, C 1, 3, in ibid., vol. I, p. 534, vol. II, pp. 462, 878.

exposure (*tashhīr*), or corporal punishment, or both. In particular cases, the culprit's forehead could be marked (branded) 'by the process termed Godena'.[34]

Thus, between 1790 and 1807 the British transformed Islamic criminal law totally and beyond recognition. Private prosecution was replaced with prosecution by the state. Anybody who had committed an act of wilful homicide could be sentenced to death, regardless of the circumstances. The heirs of the victim in cases of homicide, and the victim himself in cases of wounding, could no longer claim bloodmoney. Culpable homicide and wounding would be punished with imprisonment, whereas in those cases where, under Islamic law, there was a liability for the bloodprice even though the killer had acted without fault, there would be neither compensation nor imprisonment. The penalties of amputation and stoning to death were abolished and the numerous defences in *ḥadd* cases, based on the strict rules of evidence and the notion of doubt (*shubha*), were repealed. Although the law officers continued to function until 1864, the criminal law applied in the Indian courts had entirely lost its Islamic character except in name. However, the criminal law that was thus created was only formally abolished when in 1861 a new Indian Penal Code was promulgated.

4.2.2 *Nigeria*[35]

One century later, the British followed a similar course in Northern Nigeria. They allowed Islamic criminal law, like many other systems of local law, to continue to be applied, and interfered with and influenced its application on those issues that they regarded as being repugnant to 'natural justice'. In the process, Islamic law was 'domesticated' and made to conform to Western – and especially British – notions of criminal justice. The implementation of Islamic criminal law came to an end in 1960 with the introduction of the 1959 Penal Code for Northern Nigeria.

The institutional framework in which Islamic criminal law was applied differed from the one introduced previously in British India: whereas in India Islamic criminal law was applied by British judges, the Nigerian Islamic courts were staffed by Muslim judges only. However, British colonial

[34] Regulation 1797/17 § 2, in ibid., vol. II, p. 882.

[35] My principal sources for this section were J. N. D. Anderson, *Islamic law in Africa* (London: HMSO, 1954), pp. 195–204; A. G. Karibi-Whyte, *History and sources of Nigerian criminal law* (Ibadan: Spectrum Law Publishers, 1993); E. A. Keay and S. S. Richardson, *The native and customary courts of Nigeria* (London etc.: Sweet & Maxwell, 1966); and Abdulmalik Bappa Mahmud, *A brief history of Shari'ah in the defunct Northern Nigeria* (n.p.: n.p., 1988).

officials supervised the Islamic judiciary, in order to secure that no sentences were pronounced that involved mutilation or torture or that were repugnant to 'natural justice, equity and good conscience'. The result was similar to what happened in India. However, beyond that, interference in Northern Nigeria was much more restricted than in India. This was partly due to institutional factors: in India Islamic criminal law was applied by British judges, whereas in Northern Nigeria this was done by Islamic courts. But more important was the change in thinking about criminal law that in the mean time had occurred in England. In the late eighteenth century, the British administrators in India had wanted to reform Islamic criminal law because they found it too lenient and full of loopholes and, therefore, an unsuitable instrument for enforcing law and order. A century later, the British colonial officials in Northern Nigeria appear to have been more concerned with harmonising the application of Islamic criminal law by the Islamic courts with the legal practice of the other courts, based on the 1904 Criminal Code, especially in the field of homicide. Instead of furthering the infliction of capital punishment, as the British had done in India, they restricted the power of the Islamic courts to pass death sentences and allowed this only in cases in which this was lawful under the 1904 Criminal Code.

When the British, around 1900, occupied Northern Nigeria they left the local Emirs in their positions of power, intending to exert control through the existing administrative and judicial structures. The Native Courts Proclamation of 1900 was based on this principle: the British Resident (i.e. the provincial governor) could establish, with the consent of the Emir (the local ruler), native courts with full jurisdiction in civil and criminal matters over the native population. The British used this power to confer official status on to the existing courts of the Emirs and the *alkalis* (Islamic judge, from Arabic *al-qāḍī*). The judges, who were to apply Malikite Islamic law qua native law and custom, were appointed by the Emirs, with the approval of the Residents. They could award any type of punishment, except mutilation and torture or such punishments that were repugnant to humanity and natural justice. The British Resident had extensive powers to supervise and control the courts: he could enter and inspect the courts, suspend, reduce and modify sentences or order a rehearing of a trial before another native court or a transfer to a provincial court (i.e. a court applying English common law). In an address given in the Northern town of Sokoto in 1902, the British Governor-General Lord Lugard described his policy as follows:

The alkalis and emirs will hold the Law Courts as of old, but bribes are forbidden, and mutilation and confinement of men in inhuman prisons are not lawful . . . Sentences of death will not be carried out without the consent of the Resident . . . Every person has the right to appeal to the Resident who will, however, endeavour to uphold the power of the Native courts to deal with native cases according to the law and the custom of the country.[36]

From the beginning the native courts had full jurisdiction in criminal cases. However, capital sentences, which could only be pronounced by the Emir's courts, being the highest in the hierarchy, had to be approved by the Governor-General after review by the Resident. When in 1904 a Criminal Code based on English law was introduced in Northern Nigeria, Shari'a criminal law was not abolished. Section 4 of this code stipulated: 'No person shall be liable to be tried or punished in any court in Nigeria, other than a native tribunal, for an offence except under the express provisions of the Code or some other Ordinance or some law.' This section exempted the native courts from the principle that criminal sentences had to be founded on statute law and allowed them to try acts under Islamic law (qua native law), regardless of whether or not they were punishable under the Criminal Code and even in the case that the offence was not known under the Criminal Code. Therefore, they could convict persons for illegal sexual intercourse (*zinā*), which is an offence under Islamic law, but not under the 1904 Criminal Code.

The application of Islamic law by the native courts in the north extended to the courts' practice and procedure. The British authorities gave these courts much latitude. In a 1930 decision the West African Court of Appeal, the highest appeal court for the British colonies in West Africa, recognised the Malikite *qasāma* procedure, on the strength of which a suspect against whom there is some evidence – which is, however, not sufficient for a conviction – can be sentenced to death if the victim's male next of kin swear fifty oaths against him (see § 2.2.3.2). The Emir of Katsina's court had found a certain Abdullahi Kogi guilty of wilful homicide, although there was no admission nor any eyewitnesses, nor other legal evidence that could show that he had committed the offence. There was, however, circumstantial evidence (*lawth*) to support the conviction. The West African Court of Appeal did not uphold the sentence, but sent the case back and instructed the Emir's court to look for the victim's relatives to swear a *qasāma* oath,

[36] Karibi-Whyte, *History*, p. 177.

in order to make the sentence lawful. The Court of Appeal explained its position as follows:

There is no desire to interfere with decisions which are in accordance with native law, the principle has been that the verdict and sentence of a Native Court which is an integral part of our judicial system carried out in accordance with procedure enjoined by native law and not obviously inequitable will be accepted even though the procedure is widely different from the practice of English Criminal Courts.[37]

I have found only one decision in the field of criminal procedure in which a Shari'a provision was declared to be repugnant to natural justice, equity and good conscience. This was the rule that in the trial of *ḥadd* crimes, if the plaintiff produces full evidence, the defendant is not permitted to put forward a defence (except producing evidence to impugn the testimonies against him). In this case the Emir of Hadejia's court found a man called Guri guilty of homicide while attempting to rob and therefore sentenced him to death. On appeal, the Federal Supreme Court annulled the judgment on the grounds that the appellant was not allowed to defend himself. This is because according to the Islamic law of evidence, an accused is not allowed to give evidence on his own behalf, while under English law he can do so, but in a witness box. The court held that this rule of procedure and evidence of Islamic law was repugnant to natural justice, equity and good conscience.[38]

The Malikite law of homicide and wounding was fully applied. In order to make sure that murderers would be sentenced to death, the Emirs' courts would, if possible, classify the killing as 'heinous murder' (*qatl ghīla*; see § 2.5.3) or banditry (*ḥirāba*; see § 2.6.3), since then a death sentence could be pronounced without regard to the position of the victim's next of kin. If this was impossible, and the accused in a case of wilful killing could not be sentenced to death because the next of kin pardoned him or for some other reason, the punishment would be, as stated in Malikite doctrine, one year's imprisonment and 100 lashes, in addition to the payment of the bloodprice. The amount of the full bloodprice varied regionally and was quite low: it ranged from £12 to £60. In cases of wounding no sentences of retaliation would be imposed, usually with the argument that such wounds could not be inflicted without endangering the life of the convict. Instead

37 *Abdullahi Kogi and Others* v. *Katsina Native Authority* (1930) 14 NLR 49 as quoted in ibid., pp. 162–4. See also Mahmud, *A brief history*, p. 18.

38 2. *Guri* v. *Hadejia Native Authority* (1959) 4 FSC 44, discussed and criticised in M. Tabi'u, 'The impact of the repugnancy test on the application of Islamic law in Nigeria', *Journal of Islamic and Comparative Law* (Zaria), 18 (1991), 53–76.

the culprit would be sentenced to pay financial compensation (*diya, arsh ḥukūma*) and, in addition, to imprisonment or a fine.

The laws of *ḥadd* were faithfully enforced, except, as we have seen, that crucifixion, stoning to death or amputation would not be carried out but would be commuted into imprisonment. Caning and flogging were also lawful punishments, but sentences imposing these penalties had to be confirmed by the Emir or the District Officer.[39] There were different kinds of flogging. Apart from ordinary flogging there was flogging imposed as a fixed punishment ('*haddi* lashing'). This had to be administered with a cowhide whip, by someone holding some object under his arm, so as to prevent the use of his full strength. The punishment consisted in the disgrace rather than in the physical suffering.[40] The British objected to women being flogged: if they were sentenced to be flogged, the sentence would be commuted to imprisonment or a fine.

As a result of the restrictions on inflicting fixed punishment, the distinction between *ḥadd* offences and similar non-*ḥadd* crimes to be punished by *taʿzīr* had become obliterated, since now they all entailed imprisonment as a punishment. With regard to illicit sexual relations, there was not much difference in punishment for those who were *muḥṣan* and those who were not. The former would now be given a prison sentence, whereas the latter would be sentenced to 100 lashes and imprisonment if the accused was a man, and to imprisonment or a fine (in the place of the flogging) in the case of a woman. With regard to evidence, the Malikite rule was applied that women could be convicted on the basis of extramarital pregnancy (unless such a woman could prove that she had been raped). For banditry (*ḥirāba*) the same applied as for theft, except in the event that someone had been killed during the assault, in which case the Emir's court could sentence the accused to death, applying the pertinent rules of the Shariʿa. Unfounded allegation of illegal sexual intercourse (*qadhf*) and drinking alcohol (*shurb al-khamr*) were usually punished with eighty lashes or a fine.

An amendment in the Criminal Code heralded a gradual modification in the implementation of the Malikite law of homicide. In 1933 the relationship between the 1904 Criminal Code and the law applied by the native courts changed when section 4 of the Criminal Code was amended. The phrase 'other than a native tribunal', which gave the native courts the jurisdiction to try under native law offences that were not included in the Criminal Code, was deleted and the wording became: 'No person shall be liable to

39 Native Courts Ordinance 1933, § 16.

40 Alan Gledhill, *The penal codes of Northern Nigeria and the Sudan* (London: Sweet & Maxwell, 1963), pp. 768–9.

be tried or punished in any court in Nigeria for an offence except under the express provisions of the Code or some other Ordinance or some law.'

Initially judicial practice did not change. The common interpretation of 'some other Ordinance' was that it referred to the Native Courts Ordinance, which expressly permitted the native courts to impose punishment under native law and custom, and thus under Islamic law.[41] However, in 1947 the West African Court of Appeal interpreted the amendment differently. The court of the Emir of Gwandu had sentenced a man to death for having killed his wife's lover. The accused had pleaded that the homicide had been justified because of the affair between his wife and the victim. The court, however, had not accepted the defence, arguing that under Islamic law such a defence would only be admitted if his life had been threatened. On appeal the sentence was quashed. The Court of Appeal ruled that the accused had acted under provocation and that his act was therefore to be qualified not as murder, but as wilful homicide, which under the Criminal Code is not a capital offence. Therefore a death sentence could not be passed, although under Islamic law it was justified.[42]

This decision gave rise to much confusion. A common interpretation of it was that the native courts in the North could apply Islamic criminal law only if there was no specific provision in the Criminal Code, and that otherwise the native courts had to pass sentence on the basis of the Criminal Code. In 1948, after Islamic judges had protested against what they regarded as an unwarranted intrusion upon their jurisdiction, the Native Courts Ordinance was amended. The new text of the law stipulated that where an act constituted an offence under both a written and a customary law, the maximum punishment that could be given in a trial by a native court was the one prescribed by the written law. The basic principle applied here was that for such offences guilt would be established under native law and that subsequently the court should turn to the Criminal Code for guidance on the sentence.

The application of the new principle led to complications with regard to the trial and punishment of homicide. The main problem was that under Islamic criminal law homicide (wilful killing) is a capital offence, whereas under the 1904 Criminal Code killing incurred the death penalty

[41] Section 10 (2) of the Native Courts Ordinance of 1933 reads: 'Native courts . . . may impose a fine or imprisonment . . . or may inflict any punishment authorised by native law or custom provided it does not involve mutilation or torture, and is not repugnant to natural justice and humanity.'

[42] *Tsofo Gunna* v. *Gwandu Native Authority* (1947) 12 WACA 141, discussed in Mahmud, *A brief history*, pp. 17–18, and Muḥammad Tabi'u, 'Constraints in the application of Islamic law in Nigeria', in *Islamic law in Nigeria: application and teaching*, ed. S. Khalid Rashid (Lagos etc.: Islamic Publications Bureau, 1986), pp. 75–85.

only if classified as murder, i.e. premeditated homicide. Under the amended Ordinance, capital sentences for homicide without premeditation issued by an Emir's court could be quashed for being in conflict with the 1904 Criminal Code. A second complication was the idea of private prosecution and the notion that retaliation was only lawful if the victim's bloodprice was equal to or higher than the killer's. The pardon of the next of kin or the fact that the victim was a Christian would prevent the awarding of retaliation under Malikite law, even if the homicide had been committed with premeditation. In such cases the Shariʿa court could, under Malikite law, sentence the murderer only to 100 lashes and one year's imprisonment. After the Native Courts Ordinance had been amended, the punishment would be given according to statute law, once an Islamic court had established the facts of the case and the accused's guilt.

The controlled and restricted application of Islamic criminal law by Islamic courts came to an end in 1960 when the new Penal Code for the Northern Region 1959 came into force. Based on the 1861 Indian and the 1899 Sudanese Penal Codes, this code was essentially an English code. However, here and there special provisions were included derived from Shariʿa criminal law. Thus, illegal sexual intercourse (ss. 387–8) and drinking alcohol (s. 403) remained punishable by law, but only for Muslims. Moreover, Muslim offenders could be sentenced, in addition to the penalties prescribed by the law, to '*haddi* lashing' (see above), for the *ḥadd* offences of unlawful sexual intercourse, defamation (if constituting the *ḥadd* offence of *qadhf*) and drinking alcohol (s. 68(2)). This type of corporal punishment was intended to deter by the public disgrace involved, rather than by the pain. The 1959 Penal Code is still in force for non-Muslims in the north. For Muslims it has been replaced by the various Shariʿa penal codes enacted by the northern states from 2000.

4.3 LEGAL DUALISM: THE SEPARATION BETWEEN THE DOMAINS OF SHARIʿA AND *SIYĀSA*

Let us go back to a case I presented in the introduction to this chapter, the trial of the Cairo robbers in 1812. The governor of Cairo used his discretionary powers of *siyāsa* to punish with amputation three robbers, whose charges had been established in a Shariʿa court, but not according to the strict rules of evidence required for the infliction of a fixed penalty. Under Ottoman law – Egypt was still part of the Ottoman Empire – there was nothing extraordinary in the procedure. However, from the 1830s onward, opposition to the unbridled application of *siyāsa* punishment increased and reform was introduced, both in Egypt and in the Ottoman Empire. Unlike in India and Nigeria, where the reforms affected the application of Islamic criminal law, here reform was brought about by putting a check on *siyāsa* justice and removing the arbitrariness from it: it was to be administered by newly created courts, according to enacted laws that specified the punishments to be inflicted for each offence. These courts, applying the newly enacted codes, did not infringe on the criminal jurisdiction of the Shariʿa courts. They continued to hear criminal cases, but mainly in order to deal with private claims, including retaliation.

The motives for the process of establishing the new courts and enacting the new penal codes changed over time. It began as a measure of centralisation in order to give the rulers more control over their officials, but gradually it also became a way of streamlining the bureaucracy and applying rules impartially to all subjects. As a result the subjects, within certain limits, could assert their rights against government officials. Especially in the Ottoman Empire, where Western political pressure was more acute, reform of criminal law was also a means to present a modern image to the Western powers, by stressing equal treatment of Muslims and non-Muslims and the principle that punishment would be imposed only according to the law.

In the course of the nineteenth century the new court system developed into a multi-tiered judiciary with clearly defined jurisdictions which administered justice on the basis of written laws. At the same time the Shariʿa court system became more uniform and bureaucratised. With regard to criminal cases the jurisdictions of both types of courts often overlapped, but there was a relatively clear division of labour: the Shariʿa courts would consider private claims (including those related to homicide), whereas the new courts would deal with the offence from the point of view of law and order and public interest. The result was a dual system of criminal justice in which crimes would often be tried twice.

The new penal codes emphasised the notion of impartiality. The law must be applied to people of high and low status alike. The preamble of the 1840 Ottoman Penal Code states: 'Supposing that a shepherd's life is taken wilfully by a vizier, then retaliation according to the Shariʿa shall take place with regard to that vizier.' Many of the articles emphasise the principle that the provisions apply to everybody, whatever their status or class. Moreover, in the newly created councils, Muslims and Christians had the same standing.

In the following sections I will examine how this developed in the Ottoman Empire and Egypt. Although Egypt was technically still an

Ottoman province, it had become autonomous during the reign of Meḥmed ʿAlī (r. 1805–48) and had set up its own court system and enacted its own laws. As a result the legal reforms in the two countries followed separate but nevertheless more or less parallel paths.

4.3.1 The central Ottoman Empire[43]

Reform of criminal law in the Ottoman Empire was heralded by the 1839 Gülhane Decree, which declared that for good administration of the empire it was 'necessary and important that new laws be enacted and that the main subject-matters of these necessary laws be security of life and protection of virtue, honour and property'. This resulted in the promulgation of a Penal Code in 1840.[44] The most important feature of this new law was the principle of legality: art. 12 (2) stipulates that punishment shall be inflicted only according to the law and that persons against whom nothing has been proven during a trial shall not be punished. Apart from manslaughter, the law lists only one capital offence, 'spreading corruption on earth', which was defined as high treason or rebellion (art. 2 (2)). General confiscation of the property of offenders was abolished. At the same time, torture during investigation was explicitly forbidden.[45] The aim of the law was to restrict the arbitrariness of *siyāset* justice. Thenceforth *siyāset* punishment was no longer left to the discretion of the Sultan or high officials, but had to be awarded by administrative councils in accordance with the law.

Offences listed in the Penal Code, if committed in Istanbul, were to be tried by the Supreme Judicial Council (the Meclis-i Vālā-yi Aḥkām-i ʿAdliye) created in 1838, and otherwise before the provincial councils (*taşra mecalisi* or *memleket meclisleri*), established in 1840 as bodies with mainly administrative duties. That the provincial *qāḍī*s and muftis served on them shows that the judicial tasks of these councils were not seen as being in conflict with Shariʿa justice. The district councils (*sancak meclisi*) would try less serious offences but their sentences had to be reviewed by the provincial council.[46] The new code continued the dual system of *siyāset* and Shariʿa justice: some offences were to be adjudicated according to the

[43] The history of nineteenth-century Ottoman criminal law remains to be written. This section is mainly based on the texts of the pertinent penal codes, some studies of nineteenth-century legal reforms and a nineteenth-century formulary for *qāḍī*s, Çavuşzāde, *Dürr al-ṣukūk*.

[44] Text in Ahmet Akgündüz, *Mukayeseli Islam ve Osmanlı Hukuku külliyatı* (Diyarbakır: Dicle Üniversitesi Hukuk Fakültesi Yayınları, 1986), pp. 811–19.

[45] Taşra mecālisine verilen taʿlīmāt (Instructions issued to the provincial councils), art. 37. Text in *Düstur*, 2nd edn. ([Istanbul]: Maṭbaʿa-yi ʿĀmira, 1866 (1282 H)), vol. I, pp. 870–84.

[46] Ibid.

code, some according to the Shari'a (of which only a few were listed in the code) and some to both. Homicide and wounding were to be tried by the Shari'a authorities according to the Shari'a and by executive officials according to *siyāset*, as specified by the law. In Istanbul this was done by the Supreme Judicial Council in the presence of the state mufti, the *Şeyh ül-Islâm*. In the provinces such trials were to take place before the provincial council in the presence of the *qāḍī* and the mufti (Penal Code 1840, ch. 1, art. 3; Penal Code 1850, ch. 1, arts. 2 and 3). Both the Shari'a and the *siyāset* sentences had to be sent to the *Şeyh ül-Islâm* for review.

No code of criminal procedure was enacted along with the 1840 Penal Code. Therefore many Shari'a rules were applied by the administrative councils. This put non-Muslims at a disadvantage, especially as their testimonies against Muslims were not admitted. In order to remedy this and to implement the principle of religious equality proclaimed in the Gülhane Decree, the Ottoman government created mixed criminal courts. They dealt with crimes in which foreigners or non-Muslim Ottoman subjects were involved. The most important innovations were that non-Muslim judges could sit on these courts and that non-Muslim witnesses could be heard. If the defendant was a foreigner, half of the judges were also foreigners, appointed by the embassies. The courts had jurisdiction in all crimes, except homicide. In homicide cases the courts would only conduct the investigation, whereas the verdict was to be pronounced by the Supreme Judicial Council. The first courts of this type were the police courts, established in Istanbul in 1847. Similar courts (called *meclis-i taḥqīq*) were created outside Istanbul.[47]

These mixed courts must be regarded as the precursors of the secular courts (Niẓāmiye courts) established in 1864, after the introduction of the new French-inspired Penal Code of 1858. They also consisted of Muslims and non-Muslims and had jurisdiction in cases governed by the Penal Code of 1858 and in civil litigation between non-Muslims. For trade disputes there were specialised commercial courts. The Niẓāmiye courts had three levels coinciding with the newly introduced administrative divisions of *vilāyet* (province), *livā* (district) and *qażā* (subdistrict).[48] The same structure was introduced in Istanbul, abolishing a slightly different system that had been

[47] F. Eichmann, *Die Reformen des osmanischen Reiches mit besonderer Berücksichigung des Verhältnisses der Christen des Orients zur türkischen Herrschaft* (Berlin: Verlag der Nicolaischen Buchhandlung, 1858), pp. 217–24, 426–32; A. Heidborn, *Droit public et administratif de l'Empire Ottoman* (Leipzig: C. W. Stern, 1908–9), vol. I, pp. 219–20.

[48] See the Vilāyet Niẓāmnāmesi, enacted on 7 Jumāda II 1281 (1864), sections 18–23, 44, 55. Text in *Düstur*, vol. I, pp. 517–36.

introduced immediately after the promulgation of the new Penal Code of 1858.[49] Thus a four-tiered judiciary was created, with the Supreme Judicial Council functioning as the supreme court. The jurisdiction and procedure of these councils were governed by administrative laws dealing with local government.

The 1879 Code of Criminal Procedure introduced a number of reforms. One of the most important of these was the creation of the office of public prosecutor. The introduction of this office had already been announced in the 1876 Constitution (art. 91). Previously, there had been no clear separation of the roles of prosecutor and judge in the new courts. The police would prepare the case, after which the courts would deal with it on the basis of the written report. The office of public prosecutor symbolised a new attitude by the state towards punishment. It showed that punishing offences was in the first instance the responsibility of the state and could no longer be left to the victims, who, until then, in many cases could end criminal prosecution or reduce the punishment by concluding a settlement with the culprit.

The introduction of the penal codes and the creation of secular courts of law did not result in the gradual abolition of the Shariʿa courts. On the contrary, the latter continued to occupy an essential place in the Ottoman legal system and were also subjected to a process of modernising bureaucratic reform aimed at making them more efficient. Many decrees were issued during the nineteenth century, regulating the appointment of *qāḍī*s, their terms of service, the administrative aspects of the courts, the keeping of court records, court fees, the jurisdiction of the various classes of *qāḍī*s and the possibility of appeal. Special schools were founded for the training of Shariʿa judges. Shariʿa justice fell under the authority of the *Şeyh ül-Islâm*.

The new councils and courts applied successively the Penal Codes of 1840, 1850 and 1858. These did not abolish the enforcement of Islamic criminal law by Shariʿa courts, although in practice, its scope became limited. The first two codes fitted entirely into the dual system of *siyāsa* and Shariʿa justice and closely resemble the older Ottoman *qānūnnāme*s. However, they differed in an important aspect: the specification of the penalty for each offence. Ottoman *qānūn* usually did not go further than laying down that a certain offence was to be punished by *taʿzīr*, whereas the new penal codes specified the number of stripes and the type and length of detention.

49 Heidborn, *Droit public et administratif*, vol. I, p. 224.

The 1840 Penal Code[50] in forty-two sections is not systematic. Its main topics are the conduct of officials (eighteen sections) and state security and public order (fifteen sections). In addition we find some sections on the jurisdiction of the newly created judicial councils. Apart from two capital offences (manslaughter and 'spreading corruption on earth', i.e. rebellion and high treason), the offences mentioned in the code were punishable with banishment, forced labour, detention, caning and reprimand. The code apparently was not meant to give a complete list of punishable offences. For two offences the code provides that they must be tried according to the Shariʿa: homicide and public insult and fighting.

The 1850 Penal Code (called Qānūn-i Cedīd, the New Code),[51] containing forty-three articles, is more systematic. Its organisation in three chapters dealing respectively with offences against life, against honour and against property, echoes the 1839 Gülhane Decree which promised the protection of life, honour and property. The new code defines a wider range of offences than its predecessor. Like the latter, its main focus is official crime and the protection of state security and public order, typically the classical domain of *siyaset* justice. The law and procedure in cases of homicide (including manslaughter committed by officials) are expounded in some detail in chapter 1. Homicide cases are tried twice, by the *qāḍī* and the judicial councils, usually in one session. The code lays down that the state can punish a killer, even if the heirs have pardoned him or demand only bloodmoney. In addition, this chapter defines crimes against the security of the state and highway robbery. Chapter 2 (on the protection of honour) defines offences such as those against a person's honour; petty fighting; quarrelling; the relationship between soldiers and policemen on the one hand and civilians on the other; abduction; and public drunkenness. The last chapter (on the protection of property) deals with theft; embezzlement; forgery; fraudulent trading by shopkeepers; and tax evasion. A sizeable proportion of it is concerned with crime against property committed by officials. Article 13 of this chapter contains the old Ottoman rule according to which the inhabitants of a village or quarter may demand the removal and punishment of troublemakers and immoral people (see § 3.4.3). At various places in this code we find rules concerning the jurisdiction of the various courts and references to Shariʿa justice.

Whereas the Penal Codes of 1840 and 1850 were very much a continuation of traditional Ottoman legislation in criminal matters, the 1858 Penal Code

50 Text in Akgündüz, *Mukayeseli Islam*, pp. 811–19.

51 Text in ibid., pp. 821–3. For an analysis of its penalties, see Gökçen, *Tanzimat dönemi Osmanlı ceza kanunları*.

was different;[52] it was clearly of French inspiration, especially in its structure, system and general notions. Moreover, many sections dealing with the specific offences are translations of the French Penal Code of 1810. The introduction of the code was motivated by political considerations: the Ottoman government wanted to implement the provisions of the Reform Decree (Iṣlāḥāt Fermanı) of 1856 and show that the Ottoman legal system complied with Western standards, hoping – in vain, as appeared later – that the Western powers would agree to abolish the capitulations, by virtue of which foreigners in many cases fell outside the jurisdiction of the Ottoman courts of law.[53]

In spite of its Western origins, however, its introduction did not entail a clean break with the past, as for example the 1883 introduction of French law in Egypt did. The code can be regarded as a legislation of *taʿzīr* and *siyāsa* within the context of an Islamic legal system, especially since it refers the adjudication of private rights arising from homicide and wounding to Shariʿa justice. Article 1 of this code reads:

> This Code contains and guarantees the measure of punishment for *taʿzīr* offences, the defining and enforcement of which belongs, according to the Shariʿa, to the political authorities (*ūlū al-amr*). The reason is that offences committed against private persons are violations of the public order, and that, therefore, it is the duty of the state to punish them in the same way as the punishment of offences committed directly against the state. *However, this Code will under no circumstances infringe upon individual rights acknowledged by the Shariʿa.* [Emphasis mine, RP]

Several articles of the code (arts. 171, 177, 180–3, 192) stipulate that retaliation or bloodmoney (including the bloodprice for a foetus in the case of accidental miscarriage provoked during a fight with a pregnant woman (art. 192)) may be demanded in cases of wilful and accidental homicide and wounding. Such an offence would first be tried by a secular court and then by a Shariʿa court. This meant that a person accused of homicide or wounding could be sentenced both to a penalty consisting e.g. of imprisonment or banishment, and to payment of financial compensation by way of bloodprice. Occasionally it occurred in cases of wilful homicide that the accused was sentenced to imprisonment by the secular court and then to death by the Shariʿa court. Since capital sentences had to be approved both by the *Şeyh ül-Islâm* and the Sultan in order to be executed,[54] it was not unknown in such cases for the Sultan to issue a decree to the heirs

[52] Text in *Düstur*, vol. I, pp. 400–68. German tr. in E. Nord, *Das Türkische Strafgesetzbuch vom 28. Zilhidje 1274 (9. August 1858)* (Berlin: Guttentag, 1912).

[53] Nord, *Das Türkische Strafgesetzbuch*, p. x.

[54] Ḥilmī, *Miʿyāri ʿadālet*, p. 77.

ordering them to waive their claim and demand the bloodprice.[55] With regard to retaliation for wounding, which at any rate would be only rarely awarded, this was standard practice.[56]

In order to assist the *qāḍīs* in finding the law, at least two compilations of the law of homicide and wounding were published during the second half of the nineteenth century.[57] In the 1880s the value of the full bloodprice (that of a free Muslim male) was set at 1,333 $\frac{1}{4}$ silver *mecidiye* (of 83 per cent silver), 1 *guruş* and 20 *para* or 26,666 *guruş* and 20 *para*.[58] During the nineteenth century, the Sultans continued to issue decrees instructing judges to follow specific Hanafite opinions with regard to the law of homicide. Only in 1917 was jurisdiction in matters of retaliation and bloodmoney removed from the Shariʿa courts, but the substantive law was not formally abolished. As a result, the institution of bloodmoney continued to play a role in the law of torts in Syria and Lebanon after 1917. Shariʿa rules were used to determine the amount of damages in cases of accidental homicide. However, under the influence of French legal doctrine, the liability for bloodmoney was linked to fault or negligence, contrary to the Shariʿa doctrine which only required causation.[59]

The Ottoman Shariʿa courts did not only deal with cases of homicide and wounding: other parts of Islamic criminal law were also implemented. This is corroborated by an analysis of the formulary for Ottoman *qāḍīs* compiled by Çavuşzāde and printed in 1871. The composer published the book to inform the *qāḍīs* of the new rules for drafting documents and sentences that had been recently introduced.[60] We may assume, therefore, that the sentences presented in the book are real ones and reflect standard practice at the time of publication. Thirty-one pages of the book are devoted to documents related to criminal law. Of these twenty-one pages deal with homicide and wounding, five with *ḥadd* crimes and another five with *taʿzīr*. None of the sentences found in these documents in relation to *ḥadd* imposes a punishment other than flogging. Most of these are cases of drinking alcohol or of allegations of unlawful sexual intercourse (*qadhf*). Of the four documents related to unlawful intercourse, two ended in an acquittal (on the grounds of lack of proof and of prescription), one in a settlement and payment of damages (in this case a free male servant had deflowered his

55 Hardy, *Blood feuds*, p. 52.

56 Ḥilmī, *Miʿyār-i ʿadālet*, p. 65; Nord, *Das Türkische Strafgesetzbuch*, pp. 52–3.

57 Ahmed Reşīd Qırımīzāde Efendi, *Mesāʾili cināyete mütaʿalliq Qırımīzāde mecmuʿası* (Istanbul: n.p., 1288 [1871]); Ḥilmī, *Miʿyār-i ʿadālet*.

58 Ḥilmī, *Miʿyāri ʿadālet*, p. 71.

59 J. el- Hakim, *Le dommage de source delictuelle en droit musulman: survivance en droit syrien et libanais* (Paris: Librairie générale de droit et de jurisprudence, 1971); Hardy, *Blood feuds*, pp. 56–61.

60 Çavuşzāde, *Dürr al-ṣukūk*, vol. I, p. 1.

mistress's slave girl) and one in a sentence of 100 lashes, the fixed penalty for a person who is not a *muḥṣan*. The only document with regard to theft is a statement of the *qāḍī* that the accused cannot be sentenced to amputation, but has previous convictions (implying that a discretionary punishment should be inflicted). Finally there is a document containing the death sentence of an Armenian convert to Islam for apostasy. However, it is doubtful whether the sentence was ever executed since, as a result of Western pressure, death sentences for apostasy ceased to be carried out after 1844, when the Sultan formally pledged to the British envoy not to execute Muslim converts to Christianity.[61] As in the pre-modern times, *taʿzīr* sentences do not specify the actual punishment that was inflicted. They are awarded for offences like public abuse, quarrelling and beating, and indecent assault on a woman. From these documents it is clear that theoretically the whole domain of Islamic criminal law was applied by the nineteenth-century Ottoman *qāḍīs*, but that they would not sentence offenders to the severe fixed penalties such as amputation or stoning to death, rather making use of the possibilities offered by the Hanafite doctrine for averting those penalties. They did so, no doubt, because they were aware that the executive powers would not execute such judgments.

The application of Islamic criminal law by the Shariʿa courts ended in 1917, when a new law of Shariʿa procedure restricted their jurisdiction. They could no longer adjudicate in criminal matters. In 1924, after the downfall of the Ottoman Empire and the foundation of the Turkish republic, the Shariʿa courts were abolished by Atatürk as a part of his policy of Westernisation and secularisation.

4.3.2 *Egypt*[62]

Legal reform in Egypt began during the rule of Meḥmed ʿAlī (r. 1805–48), when, in 1829, a short penal code was promulgated defining some serious

61 Rudolph Peters and Gert J. J. de Vries, 'Apostasy in Islam', *Die Welt des Islams* 17 (1976–7), 1–25, at p. 13.

62 This section is based on G. Baer, 'Tanzimat in Egypt – the penal code', *Bulletin of the school of Oriental and African Studies* 26 (1963), 29–49; G. Baer, 'The transition from traditional to Western criminal law in Turkey and Egypt', *Studia Islamica* 45 (1977), 139–58; Rudolph Peters, 'Murder on the Nile: homicide trials in 19th century Egyptian Shariʿa courts', *Die Welt des Islams* 30 (1990), 95–115; Rudolph Peters, 'The codification of criminal law in 19th century Egypt: tradition or modernization?', in *Law, society, and national identity in Africa*, ed. J. M. Abun-Nasr et al. (Hamburg: Buske, 1991), pp. 211–25; Peters, 'Islamic and secular criminal law'; Rudolph Peters, 'Administrators and magistrates: the development of a secular judiciary in Egypt, 1842–1871', *Die Welt des Islams* 39 (1999), 378–97; Rudolph Peters, '"For his correction and as a deterrent example for others": Meḥmed ʿAlī's first criminal legislation (1829–1830)', *Islamic law and Society* 6 (1999), 164–93; and Peters, 'Egypt and the age of the triumphant prison'.

offences to be punished with *siyāsa*. This code, however, did not introduce any change in the procedure of trying crime. During the first decades of the nineteenth century, *siyāsa* justice was administered by executive officials or councils. Serious offences such as murder, high treason or theft were tried centrally in Cairo by state councils, i.e. the Khedival Council (al-Dīwān al-Khedīwī) and the Supreme Civil Council (al-Majlis al-ʿĀlī al-Mulkī). These were executive councils, and the trial of crimes was only a part of their duties. Less serious offences committed in Cairo were dealt with by police officers at the police station or by the government department where the perpetrator was employed. Outside Cairo local executive officials tried and punished petty criminals.

This state of affairs changed when in 1842 al-Jamʿiyya al-Ḥaqqāniyya, a specialised judicial council, was created in Cairo. In addition to trying serious offences in the first instance, this council also acted as a court of appeal from the decisions of lower authorities. In 1849 it was replaced by the Egyptian Supreme Judicial Council (Majlis al-Aḥkām), which had exactly the same jurisdiction and remained in existence, with the exception of two short intervals, until 1889. These new councils had to send their decisions to the Khedive for final approval and execution. Less serious crime was still tried by the police in the cities and the governors and district commissioners in the countryside. In the early 1850s lower regional councils were created to relieve the Supreme Judicial Council by trying serious offences in the first instance. The sentences of the councils were to be reviewed by the Supreme Judicial Council. Its decisions were then submitted to the Viceregal Cabinet (al-Maʿiyya al-Saniyya) for ratification and execution. In 1865, a new tier was created between the Supreme Judicial Council and the regional councils by the establishment of two courts of appeal (*majlis al-istiʾnāf*), one in Cairo and one in Alexandria. Six years later, in 1871, three more courts of appeal were set up. In the same year the base of the judicial pyramid was expanded by the creation of local councils in small towns. Thus a system of four tiers came into being with, at the top, the Supreme Judicial Council, acting as a supreme court that checked whether the lower councils applied the laws correctly. But this newly created hierarchical judiciary remained subordinated to the Khedive. It was abolished in 1883 (1889 in Upper Egypt), when the national courts were set up to implement the newly introduced French-inspired codes.

The procedure before the judicial councils was bureaucratic and very similar to those followed in other branches of the administration. Cases would be decided on the basis of written reports, without a session in which the accused could defend himself. The way they operated was very different from that prescribed by the Shariʿa and in order to emphasise that, these bodies were called council (*majlis*) rather than court (*maḥkama*). The main difference with Shariʿa procedure was that their proceedings were inquisitorial and not adversarial, as trials before a *qāḍī* are. The accused was not a party in litigation, but the object of investigation by the council. In the early years, the accused had no right at all to be heard, but was interrogated only if the council found this necessary in order to clarify certain points. Moreover, the trial was held in camera, usually in the absence of the accused and on the basis of the reports prepared by the police. If the council found it necessary to hear witnesses, it could do so, but it could also restrict itself to relying on the written depositions. The accused had no right to legal assistance. The councils were not bound by the strict Shariʿa rules of evidence and could find an accused guilty on the basis of suspicions. Since they were part of a bureaucratic structure, their decisions, before being carried out, were reviewed by higher instances. Capital and other severe sentences had to be approved by the Khedive.

As in the central Ottoman Empire, the creation of this secular judiciary did not replace the Shariʿa courts. In fact, the Shariʿa court system was strengthened and, like the other elements of the judiciary, subjected to a process of bureaucratisation. The jurisdiction of the *qāḍīs*' courts became more precisely defined and a hierarchy was imposed on them with the possibility of appeal. This development began in 1856, when the Shariʿa judiciary in Egypt became independent from the Ottoman Empire and the first *qāḍīs*' Ordinance was issued. These measures indicate that before 1883, when French-inspired legal codes were introduced in Egypt, there was no trend towards restricting the application of Islamic law. On the contrary, the government seems to have been keen on ensuring the correct application of Hanafite law. To achieve this, it organised and improved the Shariʿa judiciary and appointed official muftis to check the decisions of the *qāḍīs*.

The Egyptian Khedives, like the Ottoman Sultans, issued instructions to the *qāḍīs* to apply certain less authoritative opinions of Hanafite jurisprudents. As in the Ottoman Empire the state fixed the amount of the blood-money of a Muslim man. In 1858 the Supreme Judicial Council specified that the amount was 15,093.75 piastres for payment in silver and 40,762 piastres for payment in gold and stipulated, conform the classical doctrine, that the choice was the defendant's. In the previous chapter we have seen that the opinion of Abū Ḥanīfa with regard to determining whether or not a person had been killed with criminal intent (see § 2.5.3), was the authoritative one in the Ottoman Empire. That meant that killers who had used a stick or poison could not be sentenced to retaliation in a Shariʿa court. In the pre-modern Ottoman context, this was not felt to be a serious deficiency of the legal system, since a killer who had used these means could be sentenced to death under *siyāsa*. In nineteenth-century Egypt this possibility no longer existed: by mid-century, capital punishment had become rare and the death penalty was handed down only on the basis of a Shariʿa sentence on the grounds of retaliation or banditry. Now the flaws of the Hanafite opinion began to be felt, since murderers who had used sticks or large stones to kill their victims would escape the death penalty. In order to remedy this, the Khedive issued a decree in 1858, directing the *qādī*s to follow the opinion of Abū Yūsuf according to which the determining factor is whether or not the weapon or instrument used for killing is in general fatal.

Whereas the Shariʿa courts applied Islamic criminal law, the judicial councils enforced enacted laws. Between 1829 and 1858 five penal codes were enacted in Egypt:

1. The Penal Decree of 1829 concerning murder, highway robbery, counterfeiting, extortion by officials, theft and embezzlement.[63]
2. *Qānūn al-Filāḥa* (the Code of Agriculture) of 1830, dealing mainly with crimes and offences connected with agriculture and village life and aimed at disciplining the rural population and officials serving in rural areas.[64]
3. The Qānūn al-Muntakhabāt of 1848. This code is a compilation of a number of criminal laws issued between 1830 and 1844, dealing with both general offences and specific ones, such as those connected with the maintenance of dams and dykes and offences committed by officials. Among the articles dealing with general offences, arts. 122–94 are rather clumsy translations from the French *Code Pénal* of 1810, arranged in a different order with little apparent system.[65]
4. The Penal Code of 1849 containing ninety articles mostly taken from the Qānūn al-Muntakhabāt.[66]
5. Al-Qānūnnāme al-Sulṭānī (Sultanic Code), also called al-Qānūnnāme al-Humāyūnī (Imperial Code),[67] promulgated in the first half of the 1850s. The introduction of this new code was the result of negotiations

63 Text and analysis in Peters, '"For his Correction"'.

64 Text in *Lāyiḥat zirāʿat al-fallāḥ wa-tadbīr aḥkām al-falāḥ*, 2nd edn. (Bulaq: Dār al-Ṭibāʿa al-ʿĀmira al-Mīriyya, 1840–1).

65 Text in Aḥmad Fatḥī Zaghlūl, *al-Muḥāmāh* (Cairo: Maṭbaʿat al-Maʿārif, 1900), app., pp. 100–55; and Fīlīb Jallād, *Qāmūs al-idāra wa-l-qaḍāʾ*, 4 vols. (Alexandria: al-Maṭbaʿa al-Bukhāriyya, 1890–2), vol. III, pp. 51–78.

66 *Qānūn al-ʿUqūbāt (8 Rajab 1265 [30 May 1849])* (Bulaq: Dār al-Ṭibāʿa al-ʿĀmira al-Mīriyya, 1849).

67 Text in Zaghlūl, *al-Muḥāmāh*, app., pp. 156–78; and Jallād, *Qāmūs al-idāra*, vol. II, pp. 90–102.

between Egypt and the Ottoman government about the application in Egypt of Ottoman legislation. The first three chapters are largely identical with the Ottoman Penal Code of 1850 (see § 4.3.1). To these, two chapters were added containing provisions taken from previous Egyptian penal legislation: chapter 4, dealing with agricultural offences, such as theft of land or cattle, damage caused by cattle and offences related to irrigation; and chapter 5, listing offences committed by officials. In 1858 the code was amended by a decree of the Supreme Judicial Council.[68] It remained in force until 1883, when the French-inspired penal code was promulgated.

Criminal proceedings would typically begin with a complaint or notification to the police (*ḍabṭiyya*) in the cities or the local administration in the countryside. They would initiate the investigation, arrest suspects, trace witnesses and prepare the trial. Initially, physical pressure and torture were both lawful and customary during police investigations. However, from 1850 certain restrictions were imposed and in 1861 both torture and corporal punishment were made unlawful. If, for some reason, the investigation was not satisfactory for the complainant, he could submit a petition to the Khedive, asking him to order a new investigation. Such petitions were taken seriously and worked as a corrective for bureaucratic or other obstacles. The dossier prepared by the police would be submitted to the competent council (the jurisdiction of these councils varied over the years), which would deal with the case on the basis of this dossier, without a trial session. If the report lacked necessary information or needed clarification on certain points the council could question the accused or witnesses. Only in the 1870s was the accused given the right to be heard before being sentenced. On the information thus gathered, the council or the official would issue a sentence. Certain offences, such as homicide, wounding, sexual offences, defamation and abuse, also needed to be tried by a *qāḍī*. The Shariʿa case would also be prepared by the police or the administrative authorities in the countryside. The most important of these offences entailing a double trial was homicide. The following case, which was tried in Alexandria in 1860, shows how the proceedings before the *qāḍī* were embedded in those of the councils:

Three girls were on their way home after having picked beans and grains. When they passed the timber yard of a foreign merchant called Loria, they saw an ostrich walking there. One of the girls, ʿĀyida, age ten, went to the ostrich and touched it

[68] Decree of the Majlis al-Aḥkām ('Egypt, institutions: Supreme Judicial Council (*Majlis al-Aḥkām*)'), dated 25 Muḥarram 1275 (4 September 1858), text in Amīn Sāmī, *Taqwīm al-Nīl*, 3 vols. (Cairo: Maṭbaʿat al-Kutub al-Miṣriyya, 1928–36), vol. III/1, pp. 294–7.

to feel its feathers. At that moment a Nubian appeared and took hold of the girl. He beat her up and hit her in her stomach until she fell down. Thereupon he left. One of the girls stayed with her, while the other went to fetch her mother. The mother found the girl still alive and took her in her arms, but then the girl died. She brought the body to the police station. An officer went with the girls to the timber yard, where they found the Nubian, who, however, denied any responsibility for the death of the girl. Nevertheless he was arrested. The post mortem at the hospital showed that the victim had died as a result of the blows she had received. The mother sued the Nubian before the *qāḍī* demanding the death penalty, but she was not able to prove her claim since no adult witnesses had been present. Therefore the *qāḍī* had to dismiss the case. The case was then heard by the Diwan of the Governorate (*Muḥāfaẓa*), where the Nubian was convicted to three years forced labour in the Alexandria Arsenal Prison (*līmān Iskandariyya*), on the strength of the testimony of the two girls, the man's admission that he was in charge of the ostrich, and the medical report on the girl's death.[69]

This was a typical case. Because of the strict rules of procedure and evidence, the *qāḍī*, especially in homicide cases, rarely found for the plaintiff.[70] In homicide cases, the councils would not give a decision before the *qāḍī* had issued his sentence. If the sentence was capital punishment by way of retaliation, the council would accept that and submit the dossier for approval to the Supreme Judicial Council. Otherwise, if the *qāḍī* had awarded the bloodprice to the plaintiffs or had dismissed the claim because the victim's heirs had pardoned the killer, the council would sentence the accused to imprisonment on the strength of the criminal code.

Homicide was not the only offence heard by *qāḍī*s. They would typically deal with cases of wounding, sexual offences, scuffles (*ḍarb, muḍāraba*) and public insults (*mushātama, qawl sū'*). There was a clear division of labour between the two types of courts. The *qāḍī* would hear private claims, which could be either punitive (retaliation or *ta'zīr*) or, more commonly, financial such as bloodmoney for killing or wounding or the proper brideprice in case of illicit intercourse with unmarried women. Discretionary punishment awarded by the *qāḍī* consisted in flogging, to be carried out in court immediately after the sentence. Although in 1861 corporal punishment was officially abolished, *qāḍī*s continued for some time to sentence defendants to flogging.

In the following case, tried by a *qāḍī* in 1870, the financial claim for unlawful sexual intercourse ended in a settlement, which was duly recorded by the

69 Peters, 'Islamic and secular criminal law', 79.

70 For one court in Upper Egypt I found that in 5 per cent of all homicide cases the *qāḍī* awarded *diya* and in 2 per cent *qiṣāṣ*. See ibid., p. 90.

qāḍī. But in addition the *qāḍī* sentenced the defendant to a discretionary punishment.

A woman sued a man claiming that he had given her some sweets while they were in her father's house and that they were drugged so that she had fainted after having eaten them.[71] Then the man had taken her on a boat to a villa in the Gharbiyya Province. There he had deflowered her with his member, while she was still unconscious. The defendant admitted that he had deflowered her, but added that he had done so with his finger and not with his member.[72] The plaintiff demanded 12,500 piasters from the defendant, the value of her proper brideprice, as an indemnity for the loss of her virginity. She claimed that her cousin had recently been married for the same amount. The defendant rebutted this claim arguing that this cousin was younger and more beautiful than the plaintiff. Finally the parties agreed on a compensation of 2,500 piasters. The settlement was then ratified by the *qāḍī*, who, in addition, sentenced the man to be flogged for his sinful behaviour. The flogging was carried out during the same session.[73]

The case is interesting because the police and the state councils do not seem to have been involved. Usually such cases would be brought before the *qāḍī* after a police investigation. The *qāḍī* would then adjudicate the compensation, and the punishment would be imposed by the council. But, as is clear from this case, parties could also submit their cases directly to the *qāḍī*. A case of theft, therefore, could be heard before the *qāḍī*, if the parties had not gone to the police, but only wanted to have a decision on ownership or financial compensation. In such cases, the *qāḍī* would routinely give a statement that the conditions of the case did not warrant the infliction of the fixed penalty of amputation. But if he found the defendant otherwise guilty he would sentence him to a discretionary punishment. I have come across only one sentence awarding amputation for theft – which, however, was quashed on appeal. Its proceedings show how the classical repertoire of pleas in *ḥadd* cases were still used to prevent the application of that punishment:

Two men had forced access to the storehouse of a country estate by removing the bricks closing off an opening in the wall and had stolen from it one *ardabb* (198 liters) and eight *kaylāt* (132 liters) of *barsīm* seed. The men were apprehended and confessed to having taken the seed from the storehouse. At the trial the qadi dealt only with the property claim. During the session the defendants returned one *ardabb* of the stolen seed to the owner and promised to hand over the rest after

[71] This is standard: in nearly all cases of illegal defloration tried in Egypt during the nineteenth century, the victim claimed to have been drugged or made drunk before intercourse took place.

[72] This was also a standard phrase in admissions of illegal defloration, used to avert the application of the fixed punishment for fornication.

[73] Peters, 'Islamic and secular criminal law', 85.

they returned to their village. The plaintiff agreed and the qadi gave judgment accordingly. When the sentence was submitted to the provincial mufti (*muftī al-mudīriyya*), he pointed out that the qadi had paid no attention to the criminal aspects of the case and that the *ḥadd* punishment should be applied with regard to that part of the seed that had not been returned during the session. The case was referred back to the qadi, who, on the strength of this *fatwā*, sentenced the two defendants to amputation. Upon appeal, the sentence was reviewed by the Council of Appeal of the Northern Region (*Majlis Isti'nāf Baḥrī*). The *'ulama'* of the Council examined the judgment and found that it could not be upheld for three reasons:

(1) In the plaintiff's claim and the defendants' confessions the word 'taking' (*akhadha*) was used rather than 'stealing' (*saraqa*). This constitutes a well-known uncertainty (*shubha*), which prevents the application of the fixed penalty.

(2) The judgment did not mention whether or not the remainder of the seed, which might have perished or been consumed, still exists. If the seed does no longer exist, the *ḥadd* punishment cannot be enforced since the plaintiff cannot claim the originally stolen goods but only their replacement (*badal*).

(3) The sentence does not mention whether the eight *kaylāt* had been taken from the storehouse at once or in smaller portions. This is also relevant for the application of the *ḥadd* penalty [as the possibility exists that none of the portions amounted to the value of the *niṣāb*, RP].

The Council warned the qadi and the provincial mufti that 'they should be very cautious with regard to this kind of judgment and venture to pronounce it only after having reached complete certainty, for in this type of case a sentence of amputation must not be pronounced as they had done, by [only] dipping the fingertips in the sea of Abū Ḥanīfa's jurisprudence.' In a long exposé, the qadi defended his sentence and then the papers were sent to the '*Diwan*', an undefined higher judicial authority.[74]

Not until 1880 did the Ministry of the Interior decree that thenceforth cases of theft were not to be tried by *qāḍīs*, but by the councils on the basis of statute law and that property claims resulting from theft were to be settled before the *qāḍī* only after the state authorities had investigated the matter.

I have found no evidence that retaliation in cases of wounding or the fixed penalties of amputation or stoning to death were enforced in Egypt after 1830. This does not appear to be founded on legislation or a Khedival injunction but rather on a common understanding. After flogging and caning were abolished in 1861, imprisonment (often in combination with banishment to the Sudan) became the main form of punishment.

The system of double adjudication in certain types of offences continued until 1883 (1889 for Upper Egypt) when French criminal law and procedure

[74] Ibid., pp. 86–7.

was introduced and a new court system was created. Although art. 1 of the Penal Code of 1883 expressly states that this code does not in any way infringe upon the rights to which every person is entitled under the Shariʿa, this provision has never been interpreted, unlike in the Ottoman Empire, as a legal basis for the *qāḍī*'s competence to adjudicate in cases of homicide and wounding. In 1883/1889 Islamic criminal law was totally abolished in Egypt. Only the rule that death sentences must be approved by the State Mufti[75] provides a reminder of the role Islamic criminal law once played in the Egyptian legal system.

[75] Article 381 Code of Criminal Procedure.

CHAPTER 5

Islamic criminal law today

5.1 INTRODUCTION

In 1972 Mu'ammar al-Gaddafi surprised the world by announcing that he had reintroduced the Shari'a provisions on theft and banditry, making these offences punishable by amputation. Observers of the Arab and Muslim world were puzzled, since this return to Islamic criminal law did not fit with the prevailing modernisation theories that were based on the assumption of a continuous and unstoppable spread of secularisation. Most of these observers regarded Islamic criminal law as something of the past, enforced only in traditional countries such as Saudi Arabia, where, they believed, it would in due course disappear under the influence of modernity. No one expected that Gaddafi would inaugurate a trend and that from the 1970s more Muslim countries would adopt Islamic penal codes.

This chapter deals with the role of Islamic criminal law today. In section 5.2 I will deal with the application of Islamic criminal law in Saudi Arabia, as a typical example of a state where Islamic criminal law has continuously been implemented and where conservative religious scholars have effectively barred attempts to codify it. The main focus of this chapter, however, is on the reintroduction of Islamic criminal law. In section 5.3 I will deal with those countries where Islamic criminal law was grafted onto a legal system that was essentially Western. For each country, I will briefly sketch the political circumstances surrounding the introduction of Islamic criminal law and then discuss the contents of these laws, their conformity with classical Islamic criminal law doctrine, and their enforcement. In general I will only mention deviations from the classical doctrine. In the final section I will discuss the points on which these codes violate international human rights standards and develop some thoughts on how greater compliance with human rights standards might be achieved.

In most Muslim countries Westernisation began in the nineteenth century. This process had a great influence in the field of the law. In some other Muslim countries, however, Westernisation did not start until the second half of the twentieth century. Here the legal systems are much less affected by it. Saudi Arabia, Qatar and Yemen are the most prominent examples of such states. In these three countries, Islamic criminal law was never ousted by Western criminal law. If there was modernisation of the law, it did not affect the substantive law, but rather the organisation of the courts, the procedure and the form of the law, i.e. the introduction of codified law. The degree of codification is an indisputable sign of legal modernisation. Of the three countries I mentioned, Yemen is the one in which codification has made the greatest strides: all criminal law has been codified. After the promulgation of the 1994 Yemeni Penal Code (Law 12/1994), and Code of Criminal Procedure (Law 13/1994) and the 1996 Evidence Law (Law 20/1996),[1] Yemeni criminal law very much resembles that prevailing in those countries where Islamic criminal law has been reintroduced. As in Pakistan (see § 5.3.2), the higher courts are resolved to avert the application of severe fixed punishments and commute such sentences pronounced by lower courts into imprisonment.[2] In Qatar,[3] too, the legal system has undergone considerable Western influence. Its legal system is mainly based on statute law and includes a constitution and a penal code. In addition, however, uncodified Shariʿa still plays a role in criminal law, since the Shariʿa courts take cognisance of cases of homicide and wounding as well as of *ḥadd* and related offences, and try such cases under Hanbalite law. Saudi Arabia, finally, is a country where the Shariʿa is the law of the land and state legislation is only allowed to supplement the Shariʿa. This means that Islamic criminal law is applied in full. However, many *taʿzīr* offences are now defined by legislation. The traditional character of the Saudi legal system does not make it entirely static and immutable. On the contrary, interesting developments are taking place with regard to *siyāsa* justice and court organisation, very much resembling what happened in the Ottoman Empire and in nineteenth-century Egypt. In the following section we shall have a closer look at Saudi Arabia as an example of a country where the Shariʿa has traditionally been the law of the land.

Saudi Arabia, Yemen and Qatar are not representative in the Muslim world: in most countries Islamic criminal law was replaced by Western law.

[1] Summary in Eugene Cotran and Chibli Mallat, eds., *Yearbook of Islamic and Middle Eastern Law* (London etc.: Kluwers Law International, 1994–), vol. III (1996), pp. 326–7.

[2] Najeeb Shamiry, 'The rule of law in Yemen: uniting North and South', in *The rule of law in the Middle East and the Islamic world: human rights and the judicial process*, ed. Eugene Cotran and Mai Yamani (London: I. B. Tauris, 2000), pp. 107–27.

[3] Nathan N. Brown, *The rule of law in the Arab world: courts in Egypt and the Gulf* (Cambridge: Cambridge University Press, 1997), p. 180.

However, when Islamist movements gained strength in the Muslim world, the prevailing Westernised legal systems came under attack. The Islamists wanted to establish an Islamic state, and the main characteristic of an Islamic state was, for them, the enforcement of the Shari'a in all domains, including, of course, that of criminal law. The introduction of the Shari'a became the rallying cry of the religiously inspired political movements. The idea of going back to their cultural roots and of imposing Islamic norms on society was appealing to large segments of the population that were opposed to the increasing Western political and cultural influence. In a few countries, as we shall see, Shari'a-based legislation was adopted, whereby criminal legislation usually was the first to be enacted.

The reintroduction of Islamic criminal law is surrounded by a powerful ideological discourse, that was shaped by the propagandists of Islamism but has its roots in deeply felt religious convictions and emotions. The crucial element is that Muslims, in order to be good Muslims, must live in an Islamic state, a state which implements the Shari'a. It is not sufficient that such a state gives Muslims the choice to follow or not to follow the Shari'a; it must actually impose the Shari'a on them, by implementing Islamic criminal law. Preaching and admonition do not suffice, and a big stick is needed to change behaviour in an Islamic direction. Islamic criminal law is a tool to impose an Islamic moral order on society, by enforcing rigorous rules, especially in the fields of sexual morality, blasphemy and the consumption of alcohol and drugs.

The establishment of an Islamic state is presented as a religious duty for all Muslims and as an endeavour that may bring Paradise within their reach. And there is another felicitous prospect connected with it: that of a pious and virtuous community on earth that enjoys God's favour and is actively aided by Him to overcome poverty and humiliation. Such a community will be prosperous and strong. The reintroduction of Islamic criminal law is, from this perspective, a step towards salvation in the Hereafter as well as in this life. It is, therefore, much more than a merely technical reform of penal law. The notions connected with it make the project of enforcing Islamic criminal law attractive to both the ruling elite and large parts of the Muslim population.

For the elite, the re-Islamisation of criminal law may have three advantages: it confers an Islamic legitimacy on their rule; it provides them with a tool of suppression; and it introduces a way of dealing with homicide which, in many regions, is closer to notions of popular justice. Let us first have a look at its role in legitimising regimes. Islamist regimes that come to power as a result of a revolution or coup d'état need to demonstrate immediately that they are making a start on the construction of a real Islamic state by implementing Islamic criminal law. But Islamic criminal law has also been introduced by regimes already in power, as a political expedient to enhance their legitimacy and take the wind out of the sails of the Islamist opposition. Egypt is a case in point, although in the end Islamic criminal law was not implemented. Between 1976 and 1982 enormous efforts were made by various parliamentary committees set up to draft Islamic legislation, including an Islamic criminal code. This was done in order to demonstrate the Islamic character of the state and thus to defend the regime against the ideological attacks of the Islamist opposition. However, the fickle political nature of the process became clear a few years later. When in the early 1980s, after the assassination of President Sadat, the political climate changed and the government decided to take a firm stand against radical Islamist groups, these proposals were officially consigned to the wastepaper basket.[4]

A final ideological motive for a regime to adopt Islamic criminal law is that, in doing so, it makes a clearly anti-Western statement. Islamic criminal law is one of those parts of the Shariʿa that are most at variance with Western law and Western legal notions, much more than for example the private or commercial law of the Shariʿa. In implementing Islamic criminal law, there is a clear emphasis on the fixed punishments, because here the contradictions between Islamic criminal law and Western-type penal law are glaring. The punishments such as amputation of limbs and stoning to death, which go directly back to the sacred texts of Islam, are in conflict with present-day principles of legal punishment, such as the inadmissibility of corporal punishment, nowadays accepted both in the Islamic world and the West. Islamic criminal law, and especially the law of *ḥudūd*, has a highly symbolic value and its introduction is regarded by many Muslims as the litmus test for a real Islamisation of the legal system.

There are two practical aspects that make the implementation of Islamic criminal law an attractive option for political elites in the Muslim world. The first is that it provides an effective instrument of control and repression. The enactment of Islamic criminal legislation has been a pretext for the introduction, on a large scale, of corporal punishment, especially flogging, not only for *ḥadd* crimes, but also for offences that have nothing to do with Islamic criminal law *stricto sensu*. The Nimeiri regime in the Sudan, for instance, introduced flogging as a possible punishment for all

4 See R. Peters, 'Divine law or man-made law? Egypt and the application of the Shari'a', *Arab Law Quarterly* 3 (1988), 231–53.

offences mentioned in the Penal Code. Corporal punishment, especially when administered in public, is an effective instrument of repression. This is not only true with regard to those who are directly subjected to it, but even more so for society as a whole. The spectacle of public executions, amputations and floggings symbolises the supreme power of the regime and the futility of resistance against it.

The second reason why adopting Islamic criminal law might be attractive for a regime is that the way homicide is tried under Islamic criminal law is closer to the sense of justice of large parts of the population in the Islamic world. As we saw, legal proceedings for homicide are based on private rather than state prosecution. The victim's heirs control the process in the sense that they are party to the trial, that prosecution depends on their wills and that they can agree to an extrajudicial settlement. This is different from their position under the Western-inspired codes, where the victim's heirs are not admitted as parties to the criminal trial and are, at best, relegated to the position of witnesses, without a say in the proceedings. The doctrine of Islamic criminal law is attractive in societies where private justice or revenge prevails, because it combines the idea of private prosecution with orderly judicial proceedings.

When Islamic criminal law was reintroduced in the various countries, it did not meet with much opposition. In most countries it was supported by large groups in Muslim society. This is due to the powerful ideological discourse surrounding it, which holds promises for the 'ordinary people'. In the first place, there is the religious aspect, the idea that by implementing Islamic criminal law the community complies with God's wishes and will be rewarded. But on a practical level, Islamic criminal law holds a promise of eliminating crime and corruption as a result of its deterrence and its swift justice. Those who are apprehensive about rising crime rates and corruption will welcome Islamic criminal law as a panacea for the cure of social evils and the restoration of a virtuous society. Its advocates argue that Islamic criminal law offers effective tools to fight crime because it allows the application of severe and painful punishments consisting of whipping, amputation and stoning to death. This is an often-used argument in favour of Islamic criminal law. The amputation of the hand of one thief, it is repeatedly asserted, will deter many others from violating the property of other people. The advocates always contend that the crime rate in countries such as Saudi Arabia, where fixed punishments are carried out, is much lower than elsewhere.

A further advantage mentioned in support of the introduction of Islamic criminal legislation is the fact that trials can be short and justice can be implemented quickly. Advocates of the implementation of Islamic criminal law contrast its expediency with the protracted judicial procedures under Western law, with trials that can drag on for many years. Khomeini expressed the superiority of the Shariʿa in this respect as follows:

> Islamic justice is based on simplicity and ease. It settles all criminal and civil complaints and in the most convenient, elementary, and expeditious way possible. All that is required is for an Islamic judge, with pen and inkwell and two or three enforcers, to go into a town, come to his verdict in any kind of case, and have it immediately carried out.[5]

Such words appeal to a widely felt desire for quick justice and simple and transparent procedures, and a longing for a less complicated and orderly society, where good deeds are immediately rewarded and evil deeds punished right away. Such desires and longings are universal: it has already been noticed that there are great similarities between the portrayal of Islamic justice by Khomeini and other Iranian clerics, and the positive image of the form of justice practised by the heroic sheriff that we know from Wild West pictures, who single-handedly, with only his gun, restores law and order in a little frontier town where crime is rife.[6]

A striking aspect of the way Islamic criminal law is implemented is that it is effected through state legislation. Islamic jurisprudence, the *fiqh*, is, as we saw, essentially a legal doctrine formulated by scholars and not by the state. *Fiqh* is jurists' law. Judges applying the Shariʿa have to consult the scholarly works of jurisprudence, and to select, with regard to the case they must adjudicate, the most authoritative among several opinions with a bearing on the issue. The regimes that reintroduce Islamic criminal law claim that they are returning to the legal system that prevailed before the West began to exert its influence in the Islamic world. This, of course, is illusory. Returning to the pre-colonial past would have meant introducing Islamic criminal law not by legislating it, but by referring the judges to the classical works on *fiqh*. Although this was done in two exceptional cases,[7] introducing Islamic criminal law by statute law has been the rule. This shows that the Western

[5] Khomeini, *Sayings of the Ayatollah Khomeini*, tr. H. Salemson (1979), p. 30, quoted in Graeme Newman, 'Khomeini and criminal justice: notes on crime and culture', *Journal of Criminal Law and Criminology* 73 (1982), 561–81, at p. 561.

[6] Ibid.

[7] In Afghanistan and the United Arab Emirates. When the Taliban came to power in Afghanistan they began to apply Islamic criminal law on the basis of the classical doctrine and did not codify Islamic criminal law. In the UAE, Islamic criminal law was introduced in 1987, when the Federal Penal Code laid down that *ḥadd* offences, homicide and wounding would thenceforth be tried by the Shariʿa courts according to the Shariʿa. See B. S. B. A. al- Muhairi, 'The Islamisation of laws in the UAE: the case of the penal code', *Arab Law Quarterly* 11 (1996), 350–71.

idea that it is the state that lays down the law has been accepted, even by those countries that are re-Islamising their legal systems. The spread of this idea in the Islamic world began in the Ottoman Empire during the second half of the nineteenth century: witness the codifications of parts of the Shariʿa, such as the Mecelle, the Ottoman Civil Code enacted around 1870 and containing Hanafite law, and the various codes of personal status, the first of which was promulgated in 1917.

The advantages of codified law for centralising bureaucratic states, such as the late nineteenth-century Ottoman Empire, are obvious: more legal certainty and predictability of legal decisions as a result of the reduction of judicial discretion and of clear and unambiguous legal provisions. But the most important advantage was the greater control by the state (i.e. the power of the legislature and the executive) of the law. For these reasons Islamic criminal law has been introduced by means of legislation enacted by the state and not by giving authority to the body of classical *fiqh* doctrine. The result of the reintroduction of Islamic criminal law, in most countries, is that something new is created, a form of criminal law consisting of Islamic substantive rules in a Western garb and embedded in a Western-type adjective law, with Western-type courts and Western institutions such as the state prosecutor.

5.2 UNINTERRUPTED APPLICATION OF ISLAMIC CRIMINAL LAW: THE EXAMPLE OF SAUDI ARABIA[8]

The legal system of Saudi Arabia is an exceptional one in the world of Islam. In most countries where the Shariʿa is applied, the state determines which parts of the Shariʿa are enforced. Moreover, in order to assert their power to determine what is law, states as a rule have codified – and thereby modernised – those parts of the Shariʿa that are applied by the courts. In Saudi Arabia, however, the state does not interfere with the substantive laws of the Shariʿa. The Saudi state regards uncodified Shariʿa as the law of the land, and enacted law is subordinate to it. In the following I will discuss some of the special characteristics of Saudi criminal law.

Saudi judges adjudicate cases on the basis of the Hanbalite doctrine and select from the various opinions on the case the one that in their opinion is doctrinally the soundest. That means that they test the opinions found in the classical works of *fiqh* against the sources of the doctrine, i.e. the Koran,

[8] This section is based on Vogel, *Islamic law and legal system.*

the Sunna and the consensus of the early generations of jurisprudents, in order to find the most authentic opinion. Sometimes they practise *ijtihād* and formulate new rules by interpreting the sources. Finding the applicable law is for a Saudi judge a much more complicated process than for judges in other parts of the world where the law is codified. Enacted laws, called *niẓām* (regulation), do exist but cannot be in conflict with the Shariʿa. Article 48 of the Basic Regulation of the Kingdom of Saudi Arabia (1992) formulates this principle as follows: 'The courts shall apply in cases brought before them the rules of the Islamic Shariʿa in agreement with the indications [or proofs] in the Book [the Koran] and the Sunna and the regulations issued by the ruler that do not contradict the Book or the Sunna'.[9] The Saudi Kings, unlike the Ottoman Sultans, have not issued instructions to the *qāḍī*s with regard to the *fiqh* doctrines to be applied and left them totally free in choosing *madhhab*s and opinions for deciding cases. Nevertheless *qāḍī*s as a rule follow the Hanbalite school of jurisprudence. In some cases the Board of Senior ʿUlamaʾ, at the request of the government, issues *fatwā*s imposing certain interpretations of the doctrine on the judiciary. In general, there is a strong sense of independence among the religious scholars staffing the courts, based on their view that the realm of the *fiqh* is their prerogative and that the state should not interfere.

The Shariʿa courts apply the Hanbalite law of *ḥadd* crimes and homicide and wounding. They also try *taʿzīr* offences, for which they may award the death penalty. However, many of those have now been defined in criminal legislation. Thus we find for example penal regulations on bribery, counterfeiting, offences with regard to cheques, drugs abuse and trafficking, and crimes committed by officials. Often these penal statutes stipulate that the offences mentioned in them must be tried before special committees. These regulations, however, have not been collected in a comprehensive penal code.

As under classical Shariʿa, the Saudi courts apply different standards of evidence and rules of procedure, depending on whether they are dealing with *taʿzīr* cases, on the one hand, or retaliation and *ḥadd* offences, on the other. The strict standards of classical *fiqh* are applied in trying the second type of offence. If, during the trial of a *ḥadd* case, the accused retracts his confession, alleging that he was coerced into confessing, the case is dropped. If there is other evidence, he will be given a discretionary sentence. This may save the lives of the accused, as in the following case:

[9] Ibid., p. 4.

Three men had beaten up a young boy, frightened him and then raped him. During the investigation they had confessed to this crime, which, according to a Royal Decree of 1982 [seen below], must be tried as the *ḥadd* crime of banditry and would entail capital punishment or cross-amputation. During the trial session the men withdrew their confessions, claiming that they were illiterate and could not read the confession statement that they had been forced to sign. As a result the charge of banditry was dropped and they were each sentenced to a discretionary punishment of five years' imprisonment and 500 lashes, to be administered in five instalments at two-month intervals.[10]

In this case, the withdrawal of the confession resulted in a lighter punishment. This, however, is not always the outcome. When a band of seven men had abducted women and children, abused them sexually, taken their property, and had, in addition, burgled houses, three of them were, after confessing, given a death sentence for banditry. The other accused retracted their confessions, but to no avail. They were also sentenced to death 'on the ground of the seriousness, the number and the variety of their offences, which are to be classified as "corruption on earth", and also in order to restore security and deter crime'.[11]

Although circumstantial evidence is not admitted to establish guilt in *ḥadd* offences, Saudi judicial practice allows it with regard to drinking alcohol. This offence is fully proven if two qualified witnesses testify that the accused reeked of alcohol. In addition, some judges allow pregnancy as proof of unlawful sexual intercourse. However, in order to avert the fixed punishment it suffices that the woman claims, without further substantiation, to have been raped or to have been impregnated during her sleep.

Ḥadd sentences cannot be rashly pronounced. Judges usually award discretionary punishments: in the year 1403 (1982–3), for example, 4,925 *taʿzīr* sentences for theft were pronounced, as against two sentences of amputation for theft.[12] *Ḥadd* offences are tried in the first instance before a court comprising three judges. They are then heard on appeal by, successively the Board of Review (Hay'at al-Tamyīz) and the Supreme Judicial Council (Majlis al-Qaḍā'al-Aʿlā). Finally, the King reviews the case before ordering execution. Sentences of stoning and amputation are relatively rare: between 1981 and 1992 forty-five judicial amputations were carried out and four death penalties by stoning. In view of the strict requirements of evidence and the multitude of defences based on uncertainty (*shubha*), one cannot but

[10] Muḥammad ibn ʿAbd Allāh ʿUmayrī, *Musqiṭāt ḥadd al-ḥirāba wa-taṭbīqātuhā fī al-Mamlaka al-ʿArabiyya al-Saʿūdiyya* (Riyadh: Akādīmiyat Nāyif al-ʿArabiyya lil-ʿUlūm al-Amniyya, 1999), pp. 194–7.

[11] Ibid., pp. 174–8.

[12] Vogel, *Islamic law and legal system*, p. 247.

conclude that at least some of these *ḥadd* sentences must have been the consequence of voluntary confessions. In some cases this may have been the result of acceptance by the accused of the penalty by way of atonement, induced by the idea that undergoing this divinely instituted punishment in this world will diminish the sufferings of the next. In other cases, however, such sentences may be the result of the ignorance of the accused with regard to the successful defences. It is unlikely that such sentences are based on confessions extracted under torture, for such confessions can be withdrawn during the trial. Moreover, confessions are not always needed since the courts have extensive powers to impose discretionary punishment if full evidence for a *ḥadd* sentence is lacking.

The classical doctrine of *fiqh* gives the ruler extensive powers to exercise *siyāsa* justice for reasons of utility. In Saudi Arabia, the King still uses this power. He pronounces *siyāsa* sentences in cases of urgent public necessity, if the proof of guilt is overwhelming. Prior to issuing *siyāsa* sentences, the King will instruct a Shariʿa court to establish the facts or consult senior *ʿulamāʾ* on the issue. A formal trial will not be required. The King will award a death sentence by *siyāsa* if, for instance, the crime was a particularly heinous one and the law of homicide and *ḥadd* offences would not allow the infliction of a capital sentence. A typical case where the King would use his prerogative is that of a man who kills his children, since a parent may not be sentenced to retaliation for killing his children (see § 2.5.4.4).

During the last two decades it seems that there has been a tendency for the King to withdraw from giving *siyāsa* sentences and to leave the trial of serious crimes to the judiciary. This was heralded by a *fatwā* on the exact meaning of the crime of banditry (*ḥirāba*). In Fatwa No. 85 of the Board of Senior 'Ulama' (*Hayʾat Kibār al-ʿUlamāʾ*), issued on 9 September 1981, the law of *ḥirāba* was authoritatively expounded. The *fatwā* was motivated by reports of an increase in violent crimes in cities, in cases of abduction for sexual purposes and in drug-related offences. The *fatwā* consists of two parts. The first one extends the *ḥadd* offence of banditry by adopting the Malikite definition (see § 2.6.3). The muftis rule that henceforth *qāḍīs* may award the fixed punishments for banditry in cases of armed attacks in cities and that abduction for sexual motives must be put on a par with the taking of property. Further, the *fatwā* stipulates that the punishment imposed for banditry is no longer related to the existence of specific aggravating circumstances in addition to the 'hold-up' and that judges, therefore, are free to choose any of the punishments mentioned in K 5:33–4 (banishment, cross-amputation, death or death with crucifixion). The second part of the *fatwā* deals with the trafficking and smuggling of drugs. It sets forth that these crimes fall under the notion of 'spreading corruption on earth' (K 5:3–4) and provides that the first offence shall entail a severe discretionary punishment (imprisonment, flogging, fine) and that for a second offence the court may impose any penalty, including death. This applies also to drug users who are convicted for the second time. Some months later, a royal decree was enacted confirming the *fatwā*, but laying down that in the cases of abduction, the final choice of punishment is not the *qāḍī*'s but the king's. Giving the courts jurisdiction to try the above-mentioned offences as *ḥadd* crimes was meant to confer greater legitimacy on the death sentences passed in such cases.

On the strength of this *fatwā* and the royal decree confirming it, *ḥadd* sentences for banditry can be awarded by the courts for drug-related offences and in cases of burglary and robbery committed in cities. The following case shows the extent to which the definition of banditry (*ḥirāba*) has now been stretched:

> Three men, two of whom were dressed in women's clothes, including the face veil that is obligatory in Saudi Arabia, had gained access to a home, where, at that moment, only the lady of the house was present. They had phoned her earlier and told her that they had to deliver documents for her husband. Once inside, they had threatened the woman with a knife, taken her jewellery and forced her to undress. Then they had taken pictures of her in the nude with a Polaroid camera. After they had left, they had contacted her by telephone and demanded money in exchange for the picture. Shortly thereafter they were caught and confessed to their crimes. The men were then sentenced to the death penalty for banditry.[13]

Prior to the *fatwā*, such cases committed in cities would be tried by *siyāsa* justice, since they did not fall under the definition of banditry. It is remarkable that cases of this kind are tried and finalised with great speed. Saudi justice is very fast: those who are sentenced to death are executed in a period between four days and three months after committing their crimes.[14]

In order to further modernise criminal justice, the office of public prosecutor was introduced in 1989.[15] In 2001 the Saudi government enacted a code of criminal procedure in 225 articles.[16] An important principle of this law is that no punishment can be inflicted except for crimes prohibited

13 'Umayrī, *Musqiṭāt ḥadd al-ḥirābah*, pp. 201–5.
14 Vogel, *Islamic law and legal system*, p. 261.
15 See Fayṣal b. Ma'īḍ Qaḥṭānī, *Hay'at al-taḥqīq wa-l-iddi'ā' al-'āmm wa-dawruhā fī niẓām al-'adāla al-jinā'iyya fī al-Mamlaka al-'Arabiyya al-Sa'ūdiyya* (Riyadh: Akādīmiyat Nāyif al-'Arabiyya lil-'Ulūm al-Amniyya, 1999).
16 Cotran and Mallat, eds., *Yearbook of Islamic and Middle Eastern Law*, vol. VII (2000–1), p. 276.

by the Shariʿa and Saudi regulations and on the strength of a conviction, based on a final judgment by a court of law issued after due process. It is not clear how this law has affected the royal exercise of *siyāsa* justice. The new code prohibits torture during criminal investigations and gives the accused the right to a lawyer. It is tempting to describe the Saudi legal system as traditional and very similar to the pre-modern Islamic legal system. This, however, is not the case. In spite of its traditional outward appearance, the judicial system has been subjected to an intense process of rationalisation and bureaucratisation, implemented through statute law of which the 2001 Code of Criminal Procedure is the most recent example.

5.3 THE REINTRODUCTION OF ISLAMIC CRIMINAL LAW

Since 1972 seven countries have enacted legislation to reintroduce Islamic criminal law. In this section I will discuss the cases of Libya, Pakistan, Iran, Sudan and Northern Nigeria. I will not discuss Kelantan, one of the federal states of Malaysia, nor the United Arab Emirates. In Kelantan, a Hudud Bill was passed in November 1993, with a codification of the law of *ḥudūd* and retaliation. The law, however, never became effective as it was not approved by the federal government.[17] In the United Arab Emirates, a law was passed in 1978 ordering the Shariʿa courts to hear cases of homicide and wounding according to the Shariʿa rules.[18] I have not been able to find information about its application. I will not discuss the model for a unified Arab penal code drafted in 1986 by the Arab League and incorporating the Islamic provisions on homicide, wounding and the *ḥadd* offences either,[19] since it has not been adopted by any Arab state. Moreover, neither the Sudanese Penal Code of 1991 nor the Yemeni Penal Code of 1994 has been influenced by it.

5.3.1 Libya[20]

As soon as Gaddafi, through a military coup d'état, had seized power in 1969, he made it clear that Islam would be an important source of inspiration for

[17] Mohammad Hashim Kamali, 'Islamic law in Malaysia: issues and developments', in ibid., vol. IV (1997–8), p. 171.

[18] B. S. B. A. al- Muhairi, 'The Federal Penal Code and the aim of unification', *Arab Law Quarterly* 12 (1997), 197–210.

[19] 'Mashr ūʿ qānūn jināʾī ʿArabī muwaḥḥad', in *Wathāʾiq al-dawra al-rābiʿa li-Majlis Wuzarāʾ al-ʿAdl al-ʿArab* (Casablanca: Majlis Wuzarāʾal-ʿAdl al-ʿArab, al-Amāna al-ʿĀmma, 1986).

[20] My principal souces for this section were, apart from the texts of the penal laws, A. E. Mayer, 'Libyan legislation in defense of Arabo-Islamic mores', *American Journal of Comparative Law* 28 (1980), 287 ff.; A. E. Mayer, 'Reinstating Islamic criminal law in Libya', in *Law and Islam in the Middle East*, ed. D. H. Dwyer (New York: Bergin & Garvey, 1990), pp. 99–114.

him. He almost immediately banned alcoholic beverages and, from 1971, he introduced legislation laying down that stipulations of interest were null and void. In the same year a committee was set up to prepare the Islamisation of the Libyan legal system. The committee's activities resulted in four laws with regard to the *ḥadd* crimes and related offences, enacted between 1972 and 1974. They dealt with theft and robbery (Law 148 of 11 October 1972); illegal sexual intercourse (Law 70 of 20 October 1973); unfounded accusations of fornication (Law 52 of 16 September 1974); and, finally, the drinking of alcoholic beverages (Law 89 of 20 November 1974). In 1994 a very brief law (Law 6/1994, containing only eight sections) ordered the courts to follow the classical rules of retaliation and bloodmoney in homicide cases.[21] The existing Penal Code was amended to adapt to these new laws, but remained further in force.

The *ḥudūd* laws essentially follow Malikite doctrine, the *madhhab* prevailing in Libya. The laws also contain provisions based on *taʿzīr* for offences resembling *ḥadd* crimes, such as those punishing minors for committing *ḥadd* crimes and those penalising the production and sale of alcoholic beverages. On four points the laws deviate from classical doctrine. First, criminal responsibility begins at the age of eighteen and not at puberty as in the classical doctrine. Second, a bandit who has not taken property or another person's life is sentenced to imprisonment instead of banishment and a bandit who has both killed and plundered is punished with the death penalty only and his body is not publicly exposed (crucified) (art. 5, Law 148/1972). Third, if a person who has already been punished with amputation commits a second theft or banditry, he will not be sentenced to further amputations but to imprisonment until he repents, with a minimum of three years (art. 13, Law 148/1972). Fourth, unlawful sexual intercourse is only punished with flogging, and not with stoning to death. Here the legislator followed the text of K 24:2, which only mentions flogging, and not the classical doctrine (see § 2.6.4). In addition the court may impose imprisonment (art. 2, Law 70/1973). Article 407 was added to the Penal Code, laying down that illegal sexual intercourse is also punishable with a maximum of five years' imprisonment. Until 1998 the offence did not have to be proven according to the strict rules of evidence of the Shariʿa but could be established according to the rules of evidence of the Code of Criminal Procedure (art. 10, Law 70/1973). In 1998, the law was amended on this issue and required that thenceforth unlawful sexual intercourse be

[21] English translation in Cotran and Mallat, eds., *Yearbook of Islamic and Middle Eastern Law*, vol. I (1994), pp. 543–4.

proven on the basis of the classical rules, or by any other scientific method of proof.[22] Regarding the other *ḥadd* crimes, the laws stipulate that the Islamic rules of evidence are to be followed.

The new legislation was to be applied by the existing courts, and no special tribunals were created. The death penalty and amputation may only be carried out after the case has been reviewed on appeal (art. 19, Law 148/1972). Judicial amputation must be carried out under anaesthesia by a surgeon (art. 21, Law 148/1972). Until recently, no sentences of amputation were passed and carried out. This was possibly due to the fact that this legislation was to be applied by the normal judiciary, trained in Western jurisprudence. It would seem that those judges were not very enthusiastic about imposing mutilating punishments. However, according to disquieting reports of human rights organisations, the first judicial amputation occurred on 3 July 2003, when the sentences of four robbers to cross-amputation were carried out.[23]

5.3.2 Pakistan[24]

In 1977, General Zia ul-Haq, supported by the Islamist organisation Jamāʿat-i Islāmī, seized power. Soon afterwards, in February 1979, he announced a programme of legal Islamisation. The Constitution was amended by adding article 203-D, establishing a Federal Shariat Court that, at the request of a citizen or the government, must examine 'whether or not any law or provision of a law is repugnant to the injunctions of Islam, as laid down in the Holy Quran and the Sunna' and can rescind laws found to be in conflict with Islam. Further parts of the Islamisation programme were the introduction of a ban on interest, the collection of *zakāt* tax and, finally, the enactment of Islamic criminal legislation. This last plan

[22] Ibid., vol. V (1998–9), p. 289.

[23] Amnesty International, *Annual Report 2003*, Libya. See http://web.amnesty.org/report 2003/Lby-summary-eng.

[24] Apart from the texts of the relevant legislation I have made use of Mohammad Amin, *Islamization of laws in Pakistan* (Lahore: Sang-e-Meel Publishers, 1989); C. Bouma, 'Pakistan's Islamization 1977–1988: the Zia era in retrospect', *al-Mushir* 31 (1989), 9–27; D. P. Collins, 'Islamization of Pakistan law: a historical perspective', *Stanford Journal of International Law* 24 (1987), 511–85; Asma Jahangir and Hina Jilani, *The Hudood Ordinances, a divine sanction?: a research study of the Hudood Ordinances and their effect on the disadvantaged sections of Pakistan society* (Lahore: Rhotas Books, 1990); C. H. Kennedy, 'Islamic legal reform and the status of women in Pakistan', *Journal of Islamic Studies* 2 (1991), 45–55; C. H. Kennedy, 'Islamization in Pakistan: the implementation of Hudud Ordinances', *Asian Surveys* 33 (1988), 309–10; R. Mehdi, *The Islamization of the law in Pakistan* (Richmond: Curzon, 1994); R. Patel, *Islamisation of laws in Pakistan?* (Karachi: Faiza Publishers, 1986), Anita M. Weiss, ed., *Islamic reassertion in Pakistan: the application of Islamic laws in a modern state* (Syracuse, NY: Syracuse University Press, 1986).

was realised immediately, for, on 9 February 1979, five presidential decrees were enacted with provisions regarding *ḥadd* crimes[25] and the execution of the penalty of flogging.[26] In addition, three amendments were added in 1980, 1982 and 1986 to the Pakistan Penal Code (1860) criminalising the defiling, by words or acts, of the Prophet Mohammed and his wives and relatives and the desecration of the Koran. The amendment of 1986 made such defiling of the Prophet a capital offence. Finally, in 1990, the Qisas and Diyat Ordinance was passed, amending the Pakistan Penal Code so as to bring it in conformity with the Shariʿa law of homicide and wounding.[27] A further amendment of the Pakistan Penal Code, enacted in 1991, provided that, as in the classical doctrine of *fiqh,* criminal responsibility begins with puberty, but at the latest with eighteen years for males and sixteen years for females (s. 229 Penal Code).

The new criminal laws follow the classical, mainly Hanafite, doctrine. Fixed punishments can only be carried out after the case has been tried on appeal by the Federal Shariat Court. In addition to the *ḥadd* crimes, the ordinances contain provisions regarding discretionary punishment, imposing penalties for related acts. It is striking that the punishment for such acts is nearly always flogging, often in combination with imprisonment. In cases of banditry, the punishment for merely frightening persons, without killing or taking property, is not exile, as the classical doctrine has it, but a maximum of thirty lashes and imprisonment of at least three years 'until the court is satisfied of his being sincerely penitent' (art. 17.1 Offences Against Property (Enforcement of Hudood) Ordinance). Exposure of the dead body (crucifixion) is not mentioned as an additional punishment in cases of banditry with homicide and plunder.

The rules concerning unlawful sexual intercourse are identical with the classical doctrine. If the offence is established in court but without a confession or the four male eyewitnesses required by the Shariʿa, the accused can be punished with a *taʿzīr* penalty of ten years' imprisonment and thirty lashes (art. 10, Offences of Zina (Enforcement of Hudood) Ordinance). Rape (*zinā bil-jabr*), defined as intercourse with a man or woman without

[25] These are the following decrees: Offences Against Property (Enforcement of Hudood) Ordinance, 1979; Offences of Zina (Enforcement of Hudood) Ordinance, 1979; Offences of Qazf (Enforcement of *ḥadd*) Ordinance, 1979; Prohibition (Enforcement of *ḥadd*) Ordinance, 1979. Texts in: Government of Pakistan, *New Islamic Laws: Enforcement of Hudood Ordinance 1979* (Lahore: Lahore Law Times Publications, n.d.), 87 pp.

[26] Execution of the Punishment of Whipping Ordinance, 1979. This was repealed in 1996 by the Abolition of Whipping Act, which abolished whipping for all offences except those mentioned in the 1979 Hudood Ordinances. See Cotran and Mallat, eds., *Yearbook of Islamic and Middle Eastern Law*, vol. V (1998–9), p. 447, n. 21.

[27] Text in Mehdi, *Islamization*, pp. 298–323.

or against his/her consent or with his/her consent if this has been obtained under duress or by fraud, is mentioned as a separate offence, with the same punishment as the one for unlawful sex, if proven according to the Shariʿa. This means that rape is very difficult to establish. If the offender is not a *muḥṣan*, the court can sentence him, in addition to the hundred lashes, to 'such other punishment, including the sentence of death, as the Court may see fit having regard to the circumstances of the case' (art. 6, Offences of Zina (Enforcement of Hudood) Ordinance). Homosexual acts as such are not made punishable in this Ordinance; they were already offences under section 377 of the Pakistan Penal Code. The articles regarding the offence of unfounded accusation of fornication contain a novel rule, not found in the classical law books: the punishment lapses if the accusation was made for the public good or to a person who has lawful authority over the defendant (art. 3, Offences of Qazf (Enforcement of *ḥadd*) Ordinance). This means that women's sexual acts may be reported with impunity to their fathers or husbands, however unfounded and slanderous they may be. The number of lashes for drinking alcoholic drinks is forty (art. 8, Prohibition (Enforcement of *ḥadd*) Ordinance). Pakistani non-Muslims can be punished by a *taʿzīr* punishment of five years' imprisonment and/or thirty lashes if they drink alcoholic beverages, unless they do so as a part of a religious ceremony. Non-Muslim foreigners can be sentenced to the same punishment but only if they drink alcohol in public.

The enactment of the Criminal Law (2nd Amendment) Ordinance of 1990 concerning retaliation and bloodmoney was a direct result of a decision by the Shariat Bench of the Supreme Court ruling that the law of homicide of the Pakistani Penal Code was not in accordance with the Islamic law of manslaughter and therefore null and void.[28] A bill to remedy this, containing the Hanafite doctrine of homicide and wounding, had been published in 1981 and had generated a great deal of public discussion. The provisions that women were not allowed to testify in retaliation cases and that the bloodprice of a woman was half that of a man were, in particular, criticised by many. Nevertheless the Bill was passed in 1990. In some sections, e.g. the one on the value of bloodmoney for homicide, the law does not give details but refers to the 'Injunction of Islam as laid down in the Holy Qur'an and Sunnah' (art. 323). There are some minor deviations from the classical doctrine. For instance, the liability of the solidarity group of the accidental killer for the victim's bloodprice is not mentioned, nor is

[28] *Gul Hassan Khan* v. *The Government of Pakistan*, PLD 180 Peshawar 154. Mentioned in Mehdi, *Islamization*, p. 237 n. 77.

the *qasāma* procedure. Moreover, the law is silent on the requirement of equivalence in bloodprice between victim and killer for the enforcement of retaliation.

In 1984, the government enacted the Qanun-e Shahadat (Law of Evidence) Order. This is essentially a rearrangement of the existing Law of Evidence Act of 1872, except that articles 3 and 17 introduced Islamic rules by stipulating that the court shall determine whether a person is a competent witness in accordance with the qualifications prescribed by the Koran and the Sunna and, where no such competent witness is forthcoming, the court may take the evidence of any witness available. This means that essentially the Shariʿa rules regarding evidence by witnesses is now part of the Pakistan legal system. In addition, the Hudood Ordinances give specific rules concerning the proof of *ḥadd* offences.

A specific Pakistani element in the re-Islamisation of criminal law is the enactment of laws against the Ahmadiyya sect. The adherents of this sect consider themselves Muslims but are nor recognised as such by the Muslim majority. The first overtly anti-Ahmadiyya law (Ordinance XX, adding articles 298-B and 298-C to the Penal Code) was passed in 1984. It prohibited Ahmadis, among other acts, to refer to their places of worship as mosques, to recite the Islamic call for prayer and to present themselves as Muslims. These acts were punishable with up to three years' imprisonment. Two years later a further amendment was added (art. 295-C). It made 'defiling the sacred name of the Holy Prophet Muḥammad' an offence punishable with death or life imprisonment. Since a large number of the Ahmadis recognise a prophet after Mohammed (who for Muslims is the last of all prophets), almost all tenets of faith of such Ahmadis or even the admission of being such an Ahmadi could be regarded as falling under this provision. With regard to this last law, the Federal Shariat Court in 1990 directed the government to pass legislation to remove life imprisonment as a punishment for this offence, since in the classical doctrine defiling the Prophet is a capital offence only. However, the legislature has not passed the necessary law. So far no death sentences have been awarded under this provision, but by the end of 2003 more than a hundred Ahmadis have been charged with this offence and are awaiting trial.[29]

The Federal Shariat Court and the Shariat Bench of the Supreme Court have given several fundamental rulings in the field of criminal law. The issue of the first case decided by the Federal Shariat Court was the validity

[29] Mohamed S. M. Eltayeb, *A human rights approach to combating religious persecution: cases from Pakistan, Saudi Arabia and Sudan* (Antwerp: Intersentia, 2001), pp. 81–92.

of the Pakistani Penal Code (which is based on the Indian Penal Code of 1860). This was challenged on the grounds that it was not in conformity with the rules of the classical doctrine of Islamic law. The court rejected this approach, and stated that

> the language of the Constitution does not warrant any attempts at harmonising the laws with any particular jurisprudence (fiqh) or jurisprudence of any particular school of thought or sect . . . It appears that reference to any particular doctrinal approach (fiqh) has been eliminated deliberately so as to enable the Courts to test the validity of a law only on the criteria of commendments [*sic*] laid down in the Holy Quran and the Sunnah of the Prophet.[30]

A year later the Federal Shariat Court was requested to give a ruling on the question of whether or not the punishment of lapidation was repugnant to the injunctions of Islam, since it is not mentioned in the Koran. The court answered this question in the affirmative and argued that K 24:2, which deals with the punishment of fornicators, only mentions flogging and not lapidation, thus putting aside the relevant *ḥadīth*s and the classical doctrine (see §§ 2.4.11.2 and 2.6.4). This decision was not to the liking of General Zia ul-Haq, who immediately replaced the judges sitting on the court and amended the Constitution to allow the court to re-hear the case. The court, in its new composition, set its previous decision aside and ruled according to the classical doctrine.[31] In spite of this decision, no sentence of death by stoning has been carried out in Pakistan.

Another important decision with far-reaching effects was pronounced in 1998. Lower courts would often sentence wives to a *taʿzīr* punishment for unlawful sexual intercourse on the mere accusation of their husbands. In order to put an end to this practice, the Supreme Court ruled that in such cases the *liʿān* procedure (mentioned in art. 14 of the Offences of Qazf (Enforcement of *ḥadd*) Ordinance, 1979) must be initiated. This means that if a husband accuses his wife of adultery, he must swear four oaths to corroborate his accusation. If the wife then rejects the accusation and swears five oaths to this effect, the marriage is dissolved and no criminal charges can be instigated against her.[32]

The change of membership of the Federal Shariat Court has not prevented it from exercising a moderating influence on the application of the *ḥadd* laws. The court is loath to apply the severe fixed penalties. In a 1986

[30] *Muḥammad Riaz* v. *Federal Government*, PLD 1980, FSC 1, quoted in Collins, 'Islamization', p. 571.

[31] *Hazoor Bakhsh* v. *Federal Government of Pakistan*, PLD 1981, FSC 145; PLD 1983, FSC 255 (1982). Quoted in Collins, 'Islamization', pp. 572–4.

[32] *Riaz* v. *Station House Officer, Police Station Jhang City*, PLD 1998, Lah 35. Quoted in Cotran and Mallat, eds., *Yearbook of Islamic and Middle Eastern Law*, vol. V (1998–9), p. 448.

decision, the court stated 'that not only the maximum benefit of every reasonable doubt will be extended to the accused, but an effort, too, will be made not to inflict a *ḥadd* as long as it may be avoided by all legitimate and established means'.[33] That this is indeed the prevailing judicial practice is corroborated by a study of the decisions of the Federal Shariat Court. Stoning has not been awarded by any court. The few amputation sentences passed by lower courts have all been quashed by the Federal Shariat Court and, usually, commuted to *ta'zīr* sentences.[34]

So far, the Pakistani way of enforcing Islamic criminal law has been careful and controlled, except with regard to the blasphemy laws directed against the Ahmadiyya sect. Mutilating punishments and death by stoning have not been inflicted; only flogging was frequently practised. However, the Abolition of Whipping Act of 1996 has greatly reduced the instances of corporal punishment. We must conclude that in Pakistan, as in Libya, the introduction of the *ḥudūd* had a highly symbolic character and did not result in a drastic change of the penal system. The introduction, however, of the Islamic law of homicide and wounding did bring significant legal change, in the direction of greater conformity with custom.

5.3.3 Iran[35]

Soon after the victory of the Islamic revolution in Iran at the beginning of 1979, revolutionary Islamic courts were set up. The law regulating the establishment of these courts, enacted in June 1979, provided that they had jurisdiction to try political crimes such as homicide committed to support the Pahlavi regime or to oppress the people; unlawful detention and torture; certain grave economic offences; conspiracy; armed rebellion; terror; destruction of installations; espionage for foreign powers; armed theft and similar violent acts; and, finally, drug-related crimes. The law did not define these crimes or specify their penalties, but directed the

33 *Ghulam Ali* v. *The State*, PLD 1986, SC 741. Quoted in Mehdi, *Islamization*, p. 113.

34 Jahangir and Jilani, *The Hudood Ordinances*; Kennedy, 'Islamization'.

35 In addition to the text of the Iranian Penal Code, I used Newman, 'Khomeini and criminal justice'; B. L. Ottley, 'The revolutionary courts of Iran: Islamic law of revolutionary justice?', *Newsletter of International Law* 4 (1980), 1–8; P. Saney, 'Die Strafrechtsordnung Irans nach der islamischen Revolution', *Zeitschrift für die Gesamte Strafrechtswissenschaft* 97 (1985), 436–53; S. Tellenbach, 'Zur Re-Islamisierung des Strafrechts in Iran', *Zeitschrift für die Gesamte Strafrechtswissenschaft* 101 (1989), 188–205; S. Tellenbach (tr. and introd.), *Strafgesetze der islamischen Republik Iran* (Berlin etc.: Walter de Gruyter, 1996); and S. Tellenbach, 'Zur Strafrechtspflege in der islamischen Republik Iran', in *Beiträge zum islamischen Recht IV*, ed. S. Tellenbach and T. Hanstein (Frankfurt am Main: Peter Lang, 2004).

courts to apply Islamic law. The decisions of these courts were final and not subject to appeal. The revolutionary courts tended to expand their jurisdiction. As early as 1981, they began to try sexual offences and other *ḥadd* crimes, and the first sentences of amputation and lapidation were carried out. Very often the charge on which convictions were based was phrased in words taken from K 5:33, such as 'fighting God and His Messenger' (*muḥārabat Allāh wa-rasūlihi*) and 'spreading corruption on earth' (*al-saʿy fī l-arḍ fasād*^{an}). On such charges the courts could impose punishments such as cross-amputation and the death penalty. However, when the Islamisation of the ordinary court system progressed, the revolutionary courts restricted themselves to political cases.

In 1982 and 1983 four laws were enacted to codify Islamic criminal law. These laws were (1) the Law Concerning *Ḥudūd* and *Qiṣāṣ* and Other Relevant Provisions (25-8 1982); (2) the Law Concerning *Diyat* (15-12 1982); (3) the Law Concerning Islamic Punishments, containing general provisions (13-10 1982); and (4) the Law Concerning Provisions on the Strength of *taʿzīr* (9-8 1983). The last-mentioned law was roughly identical with the Penal Code in force before the revolution, except that for some fifty offences, e.g. for driving a car without a driver's licence (art. 156), the punishment of flogging was introduced. With the exception of the *taʿzīr* law of 1983, these laws were incorporated into one criminal code, enacted in 1991.[36] In 1996 the law of *taʿzīr* was replaced by a new law, which was then inserted into the Iranian Penal Code as chapter 5.[37]

The 1991 Penal Code contains a section with general provisions (arts. 1–62); the law of *ḥudūd* crimes (arts. 63–203); the law of homicide and wounding (retaliation for homicide and wounding, arts. 204–93) and bloodmoney (arts. 294–494). All this is based on Shiite doctrine. Remarkably, apostasy is not mentioned as a *ḥadd* crime. This, however, does not mean that an apostate is left without punishment, because article 289 of the Code of Criminal Procedure lays down that sentences in criminal matters must mention the article on which the conviction is founded but that the courts must apply the Shariʿa in cases in which the code does not give a ruling. Death sentences for apostasy have been pronounced on the strength of this rule. Criminal liability begins at puberty (art. 49), which, according to the Iranian Civil Code (art. 1210) is set at nine years for girls and fifteen years for boys. There have been reports of offenders executed for crimes committed when younger than eighteen years.

36 German translation in Tellenbach, *Strafgesetze*.

37 Cotran and Mallat, eds., *Yearbook of Islamic and Middle Eastern Law*, vol. III (1996), pp. 342–51.

The chapter on *ḥadd* crimes mentions not only these crimes themselves, but also related offences punishable by *ta'zīr*. The section on sexual offences (*zinā* and related offences such as homosexuality) is very detailed and contains seventy-six articles (63–138). They include provisions regarding homosexual acts and pandering. The definition of the offence of 'armed disturbance of the peace (*muharaba*)' (which, in Sunnite law, is restricted to armed banditry), has been extended to include some offences of a highly political character, such as membership of groups espousing armed rebellion, planning and financially supporting the overthrow of the Islamic government and willingness to occupy important posts in a government after the overthrow of the Islamic regime (arts. 186–8). These acts can, therefore, be punished with death, crucifixion and cross-amputation. The penalty for drinking alcoholic beverages is eighty lashes. Non-Muslims can be sentenced to the same punishment if they drink in public (art. 174, Explanation).

With regard to the law of homicide, a judge who pronounces a sentence of retaliation may allow one of the prosecutors to carry out the execution (art. 265). The Iranian Penal Code is the only one that specifies that a woman's bloodprice is only half that of a man (art. 300). Under Shiite law (see § 2.5.4.2), which applies here, this means that if the heirs of a murdered woman demand the death penalty of her male killer, they have to pay 75 million riyal (*c.* €7,750), which is half the bloodprice of a male Muslim. When, in 2003, such a case arose the state offered to pay part of this sum. A few months before, at the instigation of some female members of parliament, a draft law was passed to abolish this difference in bloodprice because it violates a basic human rights principle. However, the Council of Guardians, which must approve laws before they can be put into force, has refused to do so. The campaign for equal rights is supported by some mollas, who are also in favour of putting an end to the difference in the bloodprice between Muslims and non-Muslims.[38]

Reports by human rights organisations indicate that all punishments mentioned in the law are actually applied, with the possible exception of crucifixion, although the Penal Code mentions this punishment, which consists of tying the convict to a cross, leaving him there for three days and taking him down after that period, even if he has not died in the mean time (art. 207). Human rights organisations have reported numerous instances of lapidation, judicial amputations and floggings, sometimes carried out

[38] See 'Iran girl's murder spurs debate over bloodmoney', *Women's e-news*, 12 January 2003; BBC News, World Edition, 4 November 2002, http://news.bbc.co.uk/2/hi/middle_east/2395867.stm.

before the execution of a death sentence. In order to facilitate the amputation of the four fingers of the right hand, the fixed punishment for theft under Shiite law, the Judicial Police have designed a special device, which, in May 1986, was demonstrated to journalists, officials and prisoners, in the prison of Mashhad.[39] Amputation for theft was still practised in early 2003. An interesting event took place at the end of 2002. According to press reports, the head of the judiciary told the judges on 29 December of that year to cease pronouncing stoning sentences.[40] This announcement was to be followed by legal measures, but by early 2005 no Bill had been introduced in this matter.

The chapter on *ta'zīr*, enacted in 1996 and replacing the 1983 law, substituted corporal punishment for many offences with imprisonment and fines. On the other hand, it now includes more typically religious offences. It makes blasphemy against the prophets, the Shiite Imams and the granddaughters of the Prophet punishable offences, as well as the practising of *ribā*, i.e. contracts in the basis of interest. Moreover it forbids women to go about in public without modest dress (including the headscarf). Finally it expressly allows a husband to kill his wife and her lover, if he catches them *in flagrante*. If he knows, however, that his wife acted under coercion, he may only kill her rapist (art. 630).

In general, the code sticks to the strict rules of evidence of classical *fiqh*. However, with regard to certain fixed punishments and death sentences by way of retaliation, a judge may sentence on the basis of his own knowledge as stipulated in classical Shiite doctrine. If he does so, he must mention the source of his knowledge in the sentence (arts. 120, 199.3, 231). It is not clear how this affects legal practice. Moreover, in cases of homicide, sentences, including death sentences, may be passed on the strength of the *qasāma* procedure (art. 239–256).

Compared to Saudi Arabia, many sentences of amputation and stoning have been given, especially during the first decade after the revolution. In view of the many restraints put by the Shari'a on the application of fixed punishments, it is doubtful whether all these convictions were obtained in conformity with the Shari'a, which stipulates that testimonies and confessions made under duress are not valid. Since the testimonies of eyewitnesses are generally difficult to find, it seems evident that most sentences were pronounced on the strength of confessions and that one may have justified doubts as to whether these were obtained without undue pressure, as

39 R. Peters, 'The Islamization of criminal law: a comparative analysis', *Welt des Islams* 34 (1994), 246–74, at p. 262.

40 *The Guardian*, 30 December 2002.

heavy reliance on confession as a means of proving crime can be an incentive for the police to apply torture to the suspect during the preliminary investigation.

Generally speaking, penal practice in Iran became highly politicised after the revolution and was used by the revolutionary courts to suppress any form of opposition. This was done on the basis of the classical Shiite doctrine. This came to an end in 1982–3 with the enactment of criminal laws, to be implemented by regular (as opposed to revolutionary) courts, whose staff had been replaced by supporters of the new regime. The judiciary is, therefore, controlled by conservative 'ulamā' and the liberalisation of the recent years has not affected the legal institutions. The courts are generally willing to assist the conservative factions in their morality campaigns and prosecution of critical intellectuals for blasphemy or apostasy.

5.3.4 Sudan[41]

During the 1970s the regime of al-Nimeiri, who had seized power in 1969, began to steer a more Islamic course aimed at strengthening the power base of the regime. It wanted to get rid of its nationalist and leftist image, so as to secure financial help from Saudi Arabia and the USA. Domestically, the regime solicited the support of the Muslim Brothers. In order to implement article 9 of the Constitution of 1973, laying down that the Shari'a was the principal source of legislation, a Committee for Law Revision was set up in 1977 to prepare the Islamisation of Sudanese law. However, the proposals drafted by the committee, dealing, among other topics, with bans on alcoholic drinks, interest and the introduction of *zakāt* tax, were shelved. The presidential decree of 8 September 1983, introducing Islamic legislation, came, therefore, as a complete surprise.

The decree brought into force the Penal Code, the Criminal Procedure Act, the Judgments (Basic Rules) Act and the Evidence Act. In 1984 the

[41] Apart from the texts of the relevant codes, I consulted for this section C. Fluehr-Lobban, 'Islamization in Sudan: a critical assessment', *Middle East Journal* 44 (1990), 611–24; al-Mukāshifī Ṭāhā Kabbāshī, *Taṭbīq al-Sharī'a al-Islāmiyya fī al-Sūdān bayn al-ḥaqīqa wa-l-ithāra* (Cairo: Al-Zahrā'li-l-I'lām al-'Arabī, 1986); Olaf Köndgen, *Das islamisierte Strafrecht des Sudan von seiner Einführung 1983 bis Juli 1992* (Hamburg: Deutsches Orient-Institut, 1992); Aharon Layish and Gabriel W. Warburg, *The re-instatement of Islamic law in Sudan under Numayri: an evaluation of a legal experiment in the light of its historical context, methodology, and repercussions* (Leiden: E. J. Brill, 2002), Safiya Safwat, 'Islamic laws in the Sudan', in *Islamic law: social and historical contexts*, ed. A. Al-Azmeh (London: Routledge, 1988), pp. 231–50; Abdel Salam Sidahmed, 'Problems in contemporary applications of Islamic criminal sanctions: the penalty for adultery in relation to women', *BRISMES* 28, 2 (2001), 187–204; and A. M. Tier, 'Islamization of the Sudan laws and Constitution: its allure and its impracticability', *Verfassung und Recht in Übersee* 25 (1992), 199–219.

Civil Transactions Act and the Civil Procedure Act were enacted. The new Penal Code included, apart from the offences included in the previous Penal Code, the law of *ḥadd* crimes and the Islamic provisions on homicide and wounding. Moreover, it did away with the system of specified and well-defined punishments for *taʿzīr* offences. Most offences defined in the code were to be punished with public flogging, and/or imprisonment, and/or a fine, without further quantification of the punishment. As a consequence, the often subtle differences in the definitions of the offences, copied from the 1974 Penal Code, became meaningless since the differences in punishments to which they were related had disappeared in the 1983 Penal Code. In view of the widespread criticism of the 1983 Sudanese Penal Code on the grounds of its technical flaws and its deviation from classical *fiqh*, a new Penal Code (Law 8/1991) was enacted in January 1991.

In general the 1983 Sudanese Penal Code applied to Muslims and non-Muslims alike. However, in several provisions of the code, non-Muslims were treated differently from Muslims. For instance, the former were allowed to drink alcohol in private (arts. 443–4). Some other offences entailed different penalties for non-Muslims. Thus, a non-Muslim having unlawful sexual intercourse with another non-Muslim would be punished according to his own religious laws. And if these do not provide punishment, they would be sentenced to a maximum of eighty lashes and a fine and one year's imprisonment, whereas Muslims could be punished with death or a hundred lashes, depending on whether or not they are *muḥṣan*.

The 1983 Sudanese Penal Code did not exhaustively list all punishable offences. Article 458.3 laid down that if a defendant cannot be sentenced to a fixed punishment because of uncertainty (*shubha*), the court may impose any punishment that it sees fit, even if the act as such is not mentioned in the code. Moreover, article 3 of the 1983 Judgments (Basic Rules) Act stipulated that, in the absence of an applicable legislative provision, the judge must apply Islamic law. On the strength of this article the leader of an Islamic movement, advocating an alternative way of interpreting the Koran, was sentenced to death for apostasy in 1985, although apostasy was not mentioned as a crime in the Sudanese Penal Code. There have also been convictions for arranging loans on interest, in spite of the fact that the 1983 Sudanese Penal Code did not make it a punishable offence.

Those who drafted the 1983 Penal Code evidently wanted to extend the scope of fixed punishments. This was done by broadening the definitions, by applying fixed punishments to offences other than the traditional *ḥadd* crimes, and by relaxing the rules of evidence. The definition of theft (art. 320 Sudanese Penal Code (1983)) was much wider than the classical one. For the application of the punishment of amputation the code did not require that the theft be surreptitious or that the thief take the stolen object from a safe place. This implies that the scope of behaviour punishable with amputation was greatly widened. On the strength of section 320 Sudanese Penal Code (1983) the bookkeeper of a state school, who had embezzled money by putting fictitious persons on the list of employees and pocketing their salaries, was sentenced to amputation, a punishment that was carried out immediately after conviction in the first instance.[42] Such a sentence is in conflict with the classical doctrine on two scores: the bookkeeper did not take the money surreptitiously from a safe place; and the money he took was state money, a circumstance typically regarded as a *shubha* preventing the application of a *ḥadd* since the thief might have believed that he was entitled to take his share from the common property of all Muslims (see § 2.6.2). Article 318A (Sudanese Penal Code (1983)), dealing with the offence of procuring, is another instance of the introduction of *ḥadd*-type punishments for offences that are not *ḥadd* offences in classical *fiqh*. It stipulates that second offenders shall be punished by death with crucifixion or cross-amputation, precisely the punishment for robbery in the *fiqh*. Another example is section 457, punishing with the fixed penalties for robbery (death, death with crucifixion, cross-amputation or life imprisonment) participation in a criminal organisation that has been established to violate the Penal Code or any other law, and whose acts pose a danger to persons, properties, or public order, or which corrupt public life. The infliction of fixed penalties was facilitated by the Evidence Act of 1983, which relaxed the rules for establishing *ḥadd* crimes. If the two (or, in cases of unlawful sex, four) Muslim male witnesses of good reputation, required by the classical doctrine, are not available, the offence may be proved by the testimony of other witnesses at the discretion of the court (arts. 77, 78 Evidence Act). Moreover, circumstantial evidence is now admitted in many cases. Thus, pregnancy of an unmarried woman counts as evidence of the offence of unlawful intercourse (art. 77 Evidence Act) and possession of stolen goods as evidence of theft. In addition to the widening of the definitions of *ḥadd* offences and the lowering of the standards for proving them, the code made punishable with *ta'zīr* many acts resembling *ḥadd* offences or related thereto. Even attempted unlawful intercourse became a punishable offence. It was sufficient for a conviction that a man and a woman were seen together in public and could not prove that they were

[42] Text of the sentence of the Court of Appeal in Kabbāshī, *Taṭbīq al-Sharī'a*, pp. 78–84.

legally married or were related in such a manner that marriage between them was unlawful (*maḥārim*).

In one instance the judiciary restricted the working of the law. In explaining articles 318 (1) and 430 of the 1983 Penal Code regarding unlawful sexual intercourse, the Supreme Court, in a 1985 decision, abandoned the Sunnite definition of *muḥṣan* (i.e. a person who has had intercourse within a valid marriage) in favour of the Shiite opinion that *muḥṣan* is a person who is actually married. The Supreme Court ruled that a divorcée is neither a *muḥṣan* (to be punished with stoning) nor a person who was never legally married (to be punished with one hundred lashes), and must therefore be sentenced to a discretionary rather than a *ḥadd* penalty.[43] This ruling takes the sting out of article 77 of the Evidence Act, which provides that extramarital pregnancy is proof of unlawful sexual intercourse with regard to unmarried women. Since unmarried women, according to the Supreme Court, are not *muḥṣan*, extramarital pregnancy, if used as evidence for unlawful intercourse, cannot result in a stoning sentence.

With regard to the law of homicide and wounding, it is noteworthy that difference in status no longer plays a role. For the application of retaliation the Hanafite position has been adopted, with the result that a Muslim may be executed for killing a non-Muslim. The code specifies the amount of the bloodprice without reference to a Muslim male (arts. 251 ff.), which might imply that the bloodprice of men and women, Muslims and non-Muslims, is the same. There is no support for this position in the classical doctrine. The liability for bloodmoney always rests on the culprit himself; the solidarity group (*ʿāqila*) is not mentioned.

From September 1983, the execution of corporal punishments was embarked upon with great energy. On 9 December of that year the first judicial amputation was carried out. In 1984 at least sixty-five judicial amputations took place, among which there were twenty cross-amputations (i.e. amputation of the right hand and the left foot). The total number of amputations carried out in the period from September 1983 to April 1985, when the Nimeiri regime was overthrown, varies according to different reports between 96 and 120. Corporal punishments were usually carried out in public, under the supervision of a physician. I have not found reports of execution of the death penalty by stoning. It seems that the courts would sometimes pronounce death sentences by hanging for unlawful sexual intercourse. Flogging was widely applied, often in combination with prison sentences. On 15 June 1984 a person was sentenced to death with

[43] Sidahmed, 'Contemporary applications'.

crucifixion, i.e. exposure of his body after execution. However, the last part of the punishment could not be carried out because, according to the prison director, 'the machinery was not available'.[44]

In April 1985, Nimeiri's regime was overthrown in a coup d'état. Although the new government suspended the execution of judicial amputations, the courts continued to pronounce such sentences under the 1983 Sudanese Penal Code. In August 1986, a resolution moved by the National Islamic Front demanding the immediate execution of all amputation sentences was defeated in Parliament. However, in June 1989 another coup d'état strengthened the position of the National Islamic Front. Apparently, one of the motives behind the coup was to prevent the abolition of the 1983 Penal Code. Fixed punishments were again carried out and hangmen were sent to Saudi Arabia for training in amputation. In January 1990, two men who had been convicted for robbery six years before were crucified.

Because of the serious criticism of the 1983 Penal Code, a new Sudanese Penal Code was enacted in 1991, together with a new Criminal Procedure Act. The code stipulates that for the time being the provisions regarding drinking and trading in alcohol, selling meat that has not been ritually slaughtered, apostasy, *ḥadd* offence of theft, *qadhf* and the punishments for unlawful sexual intercourse and retaliation will not be applied in the south (art. 5.3). Criminal liability begins with puberty, but not before the age of fifteen and no later than the age of eighteen (arts. 3 and 9).

The interpretation given by the Supreme Court of the notion of *iḥṣān* as being actually married is now included in the code (art. 146). The 1991 Sudanese Penal Code is, to the best of my knowledge, together with the Yemeni Penal Code (art. 259) the only modern Shariʿa penal codes to include a provision on apostasy. It is punishable with death, unless the apostate repents and returns to Islam (art. 126). Further differences from the previous code are the reintroduction of the liability of the solidarity group (*ʿāqila*), whose definition is extended to include not only the male agnatic relations, but also the third-party insurance of the perpetrator and his employer in case someone is killed or wounded by a person who is carrying out occupational duties (art. 45.2).

In general the new Sudanese Penal Code is more in agreement with the classical doctrine than the old one, especially with regard to the definitions of the *ḥadd* offences. However, the 1983 Judgment (Basic Rules) Act is still effective, which means that the courts can convict persons for acts

44 Amnesty International, *Annual Report 1985*, Sudan, p. 98.

that do not fall under the wording of the Penal Code, but are punishable under the Shariʿa. Since the 1983 Evidence Act with its relaxed standards of proof for *ḥadd* offences remains in force, such *ḥadd* offences can be easily established in court. Indeed, such punishments are still being enforced: on 25–27 January 2001, five men suffered cross-amputation after being sentenced for banditry.[45] There are no indications that the government or the judiciary want to put an end to the enforcement of the severe fixed penalties.

5.3.5 Northern Nigeria[46]

The most recent instance of return to Islamic criminal law took place in Northern Nigeria. As in the United States, the states of the Federal Republic of Nigeria have the power to enact legislation in the domain of criminal law. The introduction of Shariʿa penal codes is, therefore, a matter for the separate states of the federation. On 27 January 2000, Zamfara, a state in the predominantly Muslim north, enacted the first Shariʿa Penal Code in Northern Nigeria, having first established Shariʿa courts to implement it. The example of Zamfara was followed in May by Niger state, where the government, like that in Zamfara, fully supported the re-Islamisation of the legal system. Other Northern states, prompted by popular pressure, followed suit. In Katsina and Sokoto, Shariʿa criminal sentences were pronounced and executed (in one case a sentence of amputation of the right hand was carried out) even before a Shariʿa penal code came into force, on the strength of the Shariʿa courts laws, which stipulate that the Shariʿa courts must apply the provisions of the Koran and *ḥadīth* and those found in the traditional authoritative Malikite works of law. By April 2002, twelve Northern states had introduced Shariʿa criminal law by setting up Shariʿa courts with jurisdiction in criminal matters and promulgating Shariʿa penal codes.[47] These codes include the Malikite law of *ḥudūd*, homicide and wounding, and, under the heading of *taʿzīr*, most offences mentioned in the 1959 Penal Code. Although these codes differ in their details, they concur in closely following Malikite doctrine.

45 Amnesty International, Annual Report 2002, Sudan. See http://web.amnesty.org/report2002/afr/sudan.

46 For this section I relied on Ruud Peters, *Islamic criminal law in Nigeria* (Ibadan: Spectrum Books, 2003).

47 Bauchi, Borno, Gombe, Jigawa, Kaduna, Kano, Katsina, Kebbi, Niger, Sokoto and Yobe. The Shariʿa penal codes of most of these states follow the example of the Zamfara code with minor changes. Whereas Kano has enacted an independent Shariʿa Penal Code, Niger has implemented Shariʿa criminal law by adding amendments to the 1959 Penal Code for Northern Nigeria.

The reintroduction of Islamic criminal law in Northern Nigeria is constitutionally more complicated than its implementation elsewhere. Nigeria is a multi-religious state, and the federal Constitution explicitly forbids the federation of states to accept an official state religion. Among Nigerian constitutional lawyers there is disagreement about whether or not the implementation of Shariʿa criminal law can be seen as the adoption of a state religion. In the other countries where Shariʿa criminal law has been implemented there is no such constitutional problem, since their constitutions lay down that Islam is the religion of the state. In addition there are other points on which the newly promulgated Shariʿa penal codes are in conflict with the constitution. I will return to this point below.

Except in Zamfara and Niger state, the state governments were not enthusiastic about Islamisation of the legal system, but were forced to enact it under popular pressure. Large sections among the Muslims of the North supported the introduction of Islamic criminal law. Although religious zeal played a role, there were more important social and political factors. The most prominent one was that many believed that Islamic criminal law would be the answer to widespread criminality and government corruption. Further, support for Islamic criminal law was a protest against federal politics. Since the end of military dictatorship in 1997, the centre of gravity of Nigerian politics had moved to the mainly non-Muslim South. The Islamisation movement was a reaction against this: a challenge to federal politics and an attempt to reassert Muslim political power. In addition, there was a widespread belief that imposing Islamic norms on public life, by banning the drinking of alcohol and closing bars and by putting an end to prostitution, would secure God's help in making the Nigerian Muslims stronger. Finally, as in most other countries where Islamic criminal law has been introduced, it was regarded as a conscious reassertion of cultural roots against Western political and cultural dominance.

The Shariʿa penal codes apply to Muslims as well as to non-Muslims who desire to be tried under these codes and present a written document of consent to the court (art. 5 Zamfara Sharia Courts Establishment Law (1999)).[48] Others, i.e. in practice all non-Muslims, are tried by magistrates' courts under the 1959 Penal Code. Criminal liability for *ḥudūd* begins with puberty (art. 71 Zamfara Shari'ah Penal Code), which means that children below the age of eighteen can be sentenced to death and amputation.

48 In the following I will refer only to the Zamfara legislation, which, with minor modifications, has been adopted by most states, rather than listing the articles of all Shariʿa penal codes.

An important effect of the Islamisation of criminal law is that the codes are not regarded as exhaustive. Acts not mentioned in the codes may also be punishable offences, if they are so under classical Islamic criminal law. Most of the new codes contain the following provision:

> Any act or omission which is not specifically mentioned in this Shari'ah Penal Code but is otherwise declared to be an offence under the Qur'an, Sunnah and *Ijtihad* of the Maliki school of Islamic thought shall be an offence under this code and such act or omission shall be punishable:
> (a) With imprisonment for a term which may extend to 5 years, or
> (b) With caning which may extend to 50 lashes, or
> (c) With fine which may extend to N[aira] 5,000.00 or with any two of the above punishments.[49]

A few codes contain provisions about the applicability of the Islamic rules of evidence. That most codes are silent on this point, although it is an essential part of the laws of fixed penalties and retaliation, must be attributed to a conscious omission by the various legislators. They must have been aware of the fact that according to the federal Constitution of Nigeria legislation in the field of evidence is a federal matter. By now it has become clear that the Shariʿa courts follow the Malikite doctrine with regard to evidence. This means that unlawful intercourse may also be proven by extramarital pregnancy. In 2002 two divorced women (Safiyyatu Hussaini in Sokoto state and Amina Lawal in Katsina state) were sentenced by lower Shariʿa courts to be stoned to death for unlawful sexual intercourse, on the strength of pregnancy without being married. Both sentences, however, were quashed on appeal. This was partly for technical reasons: they were charged with having had unlawful sexual relations at a time that the Shariʿa Penal Code in their states had not yet been promulgated. But more importantly, both Shariʿa courts of appeal ruled that pregnancy of a divorced woman is, in and by itself, not sufficient evidence of unlawful sexual intercourse, in view of the Malikite doctrine that the maximum period of gestation is five years.[50]

In some codes certain offences are equated with theft and can also be punished by amputation. Most penal codes make the kidnapping of a child under seven (or before puberty in some codes) punishable by amputation. The Zamfara Shari'ah Penal Code (art. 259) has a clause imposing amputation as the penalty for forgery of documents if the value they represent

[49] Zamfara Shari'ah Penal Code, section 92. Other penal codes contain a similar section.

[50] For a detailed discussion of the Safiyyatu Hussaini case, see Rudolph Peters, 'The re-Islamization of criminal law in Northern Nigeria and the judiciary: the Safiyyatu Hussaini case', in *Dispensing justice in Islamic courts*, ed. M. K. Masud, R. Peters and D. Powers (Leiden: Brill, forthcoming).

is more than the *nisāb*. The Kano Penal Code has made embezzlement of public funds or of funds of a bank or company by officials and employees an offence punishable by amputation (art. 134B). For these provisions there is some support from less authoritative Malikite opinions, which regard amputation as a lawful punishment for these offences, not as a fixed but as a discretionary penalty. This may result in more frequent enforcement of amputation, since, for these offences, the strict conditions for the application of the fixed penalty for theft, a critical constituent of this part of the law, do not seem to apply here.

The law of homicide and wounding follows the classical doctrine closely. Some codes specify that the killer can be sentenced to be executed in the same way as he killed his victim. As in Malikite law, 'heinous murder' (*qatl ghīla*, defined as 'the act of luring a person to a secluded place and killing him' (art. 50 Zamfara Shari'ah Penal Code)) is a capital offence for which the position of the prosecutors is irrelevant. A striking omission in the Northern Nigerian Shariʿa penal codes is that they are silent on the requirement of equivalence in value between victim and killer or attacker (see § 2.5.4.2). It is to be expected that on this point the courts will apply Malikite doctrine.

Several cases of judicial amputation have been reported. It seems that in many cases the culprit did not lodge an appeal against the sentence in the first instance, either as a result of social pressure from friends and acquaintances who argued that he would not be a good Muslim if he opposed the sentence, or because of his belief that undergoing the punishment in this life would ease his sufferings in the Hereafter. In passing a sentence of retaliation for manslaughter, the *qāḍī* may order that the perpetrator is to be executed in the same way as he has killed his victim. At least one such sentence has been pronounced.[51] A few sentences of retaliation for wounding have been pronounced. On 26 May 2001 Ahmed Tijani was sentenced in Malunfashi, Katsina, to have his right eye removed after blinding a man in an assault. The victim was given the choice between demanding 'an eye for an eye' and fifty camels. In a bizarre case, a forty-five-year-old man was sentenced in January 2003 by the Upper Sharia Court in Bauchi to have his right leg removed from the knee (without anaesthesia or painkillers, as the court directed) for having done the same to his wife, whom he had accused of overexposing herself to a doctor when she received an injection.

[51] Zamfara Shari'ah Penal Code, section 240. In November 2001, a Katsina Shariʿa court sentenced Sani Yakubu Rodi to be stabbed to death in the same way as he had killed his victims. At the time of writing I do not know whether the sentence has been carried out.

I have no information on whether these sentences have actually been carried out.

The enforcement of the new Shari'a penal codes is sometimes problematic due to the structure of the Nigerian federation. The police force is a federal institution, and police personnel often work outside their home states. This means that in Muslim states there are also many non-Muslim policemen, who are not overzealous in tracing specific Shari'a offences. Indeed, there have been reports of police stations in the North that began to function as beer parlours after the prohibition of drinking alcohol was enforced. This lax attitude on the part of the police resulted in vigilantism: Muslims, discontented with the level of enforcement of Islamic criminal law, set up what they called *ḥisba* groups and started patrolling urban neighbourhoods, attacking places where they suspected that alcohol was served or prostitutes were plying their trade. To counter this phenomenon, some states established official *ḥisba* organisations that would function in close cooperation with the police.

The reintroduction of Islamic criminal law in the North is surrounded by political and legal complications. It will remain a bone of contention between the Muslim North and the rest of Nigeria. One of the major legal problems is that the Shari'a penal codes are on several scores at variance with the Nigerian federal Constitution. The first controversy is whether the introduction of these laws can be reconciled with the secular character of the Nigerian state. Article 10 of the Constitution reads: 'The Government of the Federation or of a State shall not adopt any religion as State religion.' The issue, however, is not as clear as it *prima facie* would seem to be, since the Shari'a has for a long time been accepted as a part of the legal systems of the Northern states in the domain of family, civil and commercial law. There is no doubt, however, about the unconstitutionality of the implicit introduction of the Malikite law of evidence: the Constitution stipulates that legislation on evidence is a prerogative of the federal legislature. Finally, the Shari'a penal codes are in conflict with several human rights guaranteed in the federal Constitution. We will return to this issue in the following section, dealing with Islamic criminal law and human rights. So far the Federal Supreme Court has not had the opportunity to rule on the constitutionality of the Shari'a penal codes. Since it is expected that the court will find many of the provisions of these codes unconstitutional, there are widespread fears that such a decision might fuel the antagonism between the North and the South, even to the point of endangering the existence of the federation.

5.4 ISLAMIC CRIMINAL LAW AND HUMAN RIGHTS STANDARDS

The implementation of Islamic criminal law in recent decades has raised the question of its compatibility with universal human rights standards. Judging classical Islamic law–or other pre-modern legal systems, for that matter–by the standards of the modern doctrine of human rights is, obviously, anachronistic and futile. It is perfectly legitimate, however, to scrutinise the recently enacted Islamic penal codes for their compatibility with universal human rights standards. In this section I will do so to identify the areas of conflict. Moreover, I will develop some thoughts on the perspectives of a greater compliance with universal human rights norms by the states that have introduced Islamic criminal law. My point of reference will be the international human rights conventions that have been drafted and are implemented under the aegis of the United Nations. Unlike the Universal Declaration of Human Rights of 1948, these conventions are binding upon their signatories, in spite of the fact that the sanctions on violations are minimal. Nevertheless, their signatories show their commitment to human rights. The instruments relevant to this study are: the 1966 International Covenant on Civil and Political Rights (ICCPR); the 1979 Convention for the Elimination of All Forms of Discrimination against Women (CEDAW); the 1984 Convention against Torture and Other Cruel, Inhuman and Degrading Treatment or Punishment (CAT); and the 1989 Convention on the Rights of the Child (CRC).

The legitimacy of modern human rights discourse is often challenged by Muslims with the argument that human rights are a Western invention and based on a Western discourse that does not take into account the cultural specificity of the Muslim world or non-Western cultures in general. Yet most Muslim states have by now become signatories to human rights conventions, showing their acceptance of international human rights discourse, even if they have not yet ratified the treaties. Table 5.1 shows which conventions have been signed by the countries that implement Islamic criminal law. Interestingly, most of them acceded to the ICCPR and the CAT without reservations regarding articles that are at variance with the Shariʿa.

5.4.1 Violations of international human rights standards

Although Islamic criminal law protects a number of important fundamental rights, such as the right to life and the integrity of the body, the Shariʿa

Table 5.1: *States enforcing Shari'a criminal law as signatories to international human rights conventions*

	ICCPR 1966	CEDAW 1979	CAT 1984	CRC 1989
Iran	1976	–	–	1994/sh
Libya	1996/a	1989/a/sh*	1989/a	1993/a
Nigeria	1993/a	1995	2001	1991
Pakistan	–	1996/a/sh	–	1996/sh
Saudi Arabia	–	2000/sh	1997/a	1996/a/sh
Sudan	1986/a	–	1986/a	1990

/a indicates signature or accession without ratification.
/sh indicates a reservation with regard to the articles that are at variance with the Shari'a.
/sh* indicates a 'Shari'a reservation' only with regard to family law and succession.

criminal law as applied today is in conflict with human rights standards in the following areas:

(a) the ban on cruel, degrading or inhuman punishment;
(b) the principle of *nulla poena sine lege*, i.e. that punishment may be awarded on the strength of a law defining the offence and its punishment;
(c) the principle that all persons are equal before the law;
(d) freedom of religion and freedom of expression;
(e) the basic right of children not to be subjected to the death penalty, life imprisonment and cruel, degrading or inhuman punishment.

Cruel, degrading or inhuman punishment is outlawed by the ICCPR (art. 7) and the CAT. Articles 1 (1) and 16(1) of the CAT stipulate that no person shall be subjected to torture or to cruel, inhuman or degrading punishments and that states shall take measures to prevent public servants from committing acts of torture or administering such punishment. Here we have, it would seem, one of the most conspicuous areas of conflict between the Shari'a penal codes and human rights principles. It is surprising, therefore, that Libya, Saudi Arabia and Sudan have acceded to the CAT, without any reservations, in spite of the fact that their legal systems allow severe punishments such as amputation and execution by stoning. A plausible explanation is that since the CAT does not define the notion of cruel, inhuman or degrading punishment, these states can argue that the Shari'a penalties, as they are based on God's law, cannot be regarded as cruel, inhuman or degrading. However, the prevailing interpretation of cruel, inhuman or degrading punishment is that it includes all forms of corporal punishment. The Special Rapporteur on Torture and Cruel, Degrading and Inhuman Treatment or Punishment to the UN Commission on Human Rights formulated this principle as follows:

> Corporal punishment is inconsistent with the prohibition of torture and other cruel, inhuman, and degrading treatment or punishment enshrined, inter alia, in the Universal Declaration of Human Rights, the International Covenant on Civil and Political Rights, the Declaration on the Protection of All Persons from Being Subjected to Torture and Other Cruel, Inhuman or Degrading Treatment or Punishment and the Convention against Torture and Other Cruel, Inhuman or Degrading Treatment or Punishment.[52]

International human rights organisations such as Amnesty International and Human Rights Watch hold that flogging, the amputation of limbs and retaliation for grievous hurt such as blinding or the pulling out of teeth are indeed a form of cruel, inhuman or degrading punishment. The same is true with regard to certain modes of carrying out the death penalty, such as stoning and crucifixion (at least if the latter punishment is taken to mean that the convict is subjected to it while alive, as is the case in Iran), execution in the same way as the culprit killed his victim (mentioned in the Sudanese Penal Code and some Northern Nigerian Shariʿa penal codes) or execution by one of the victim's heirs (which, according to the Iranian Penal Code, the court may allow).

The main principle of modern criminal law is that a person shall not be convicted of a criminal offence and punished for it unless that offence is defined and the penalty therefore is prescribed in national or international law. This was regarded as so important that it was raised to the status of a human rights principle. It is included in article 15 of the ICCPR. This norm is violated by many states that have implemented Islamic criminal law. In classical *fiqh* the principle is not known, except with regard to the law of homicide, wounding and *ḥadd* punishments: on the strength of *taʿzīr* and *siyāsa* any act could be punished if the court or the executive qualified it as sinful or contrary to the interests of state or society. This situation still prevails in Saudi Arabia, where only a small part of criminal law is codified. The countries where Islamic criminal law has recently been implemented by legislation seem to comply with the principle of legality. However, in the penal codes of Iran, Sudan and several Northern Nigerian states, we

[52] Report of the Special Rapporteur, Commission on Human Rights, 53rd Session, Item 8(a), UN Doc. E/CN.4/1997/7 (1997). In a 2003 resolution the commission formulated the principle slightly less categorically when it reminded governments 'that corporal punishment, including of children, can amount to cruel, inhuman or degrading punishment or even to torture' (Commission on Human Rights resolution 2003/32).

find provisions to the effect that the courts can inflict penalties for acts that are punishable under the Shariʿa, even if they are not punishable under statute law. As a result, persons have been sentenced to death for apostasy in Iran and in Sudan (under the 1983 Sudanese Penal Code), although the penal codes of these countries do not contain provisions making this a punishable offence. With regard to these cases, it is a moot point whether or not they constitute violations of the *nulla poena* principle, as it could be argued that apostasy, although not included in the penal code, is an offence under the Shariʿa. However, in view of the discretionary powers to inflict punishment conferred by the Shariʿa on judges and officials, the provisions could be used to punish persons for acts not previously defined as offences.

One of the most prominent human rights principles is that all persons are equal before the law and entitled to the same legal protection. The ICCPR stipulates that 'all persons shall be equal before the courts and tribunals' (art. 14) and that 'all persons are equal before the law and are entitled without any discrimination to the equal protection of the law' (art. 26). Under classical Islamic law, as under other pre-modern legal systems, the principle of legal equality of persons is not recognised. The new Islamic penal codes follow the classical doctrine and violate the principle of legal equality by provisions that discriminate on the basis of gender and religion.

In classical Shariʿa criminal law men and women are treated differently with regard to evidence and bloodmoney. The testimony of a man has twice the strength of that of a woman. Instead of the testimonies of two male witnesses required for conclusive evidence, the testimonies of one man and two women or the testimonies of four women may be used in court. However, with regard to *ḥadd* offences and retaliation, the testimonies of female witnesses are not admitted at all. These rules are now included in most recent Shariʿa codes. A further rule that puts women in an inferior legal position is the Malikite rule, adopted in the Sudan and Northern Nigeria, that pregnancy of an unmarried woman is regarded as conclusive proof of unlawful sexual intercourse. A final point of gender discrimination with regard to evidence is the way law enforcers deal with women who report rape. In some countries, such a report is regarded as confession to unlawful sexual intercourse. In order not to be punished, the woman must show that she did not give her consent. Moreover, if she names her attacker and cannot establish, according to the strict rules of the Shariʿa, that he has had intercourse with her, she is liable to the fixed punishment for defamation (*qadhf*).

The second domain in which women are legally discriminated against is the law of homicide and wounding. Under classical Islamic law, the bloodprice of a woman is half that of a man. Most Shariʿa penal codes are silent on the issue and specify only the bloodprice of a Muslim man, implying by the use of the words 'Muslim man' that the bloodprice for women and non-Muslims is different. The Sudanese Penal Code (both the 1983 and 1991 codes) defines the upper limit of the bloodprice without reference to a Muslim male, which probably implies that no distinction is made between men and women. Only the Iranian code explicitly lays down that a woman's bloodprice is only half that of a man. Moreover, in Iran the Shiite doctrine is applied that if the killer's bloodprice is of a higher value than the victim's, retaliation is conditional on the payment of the difference by the victim's heirs to the killer's heirs. Thus, if a woman is killed by a man, her heirs can only demand retaliation if they are willing to pay half the value of the full bloodprice to the heirs of the killer (art. 258 Iranian Penal Code). A final form of gender discrimination is found in article 630 of the same code. This section expressly allows a husband to kill his wife and her lover, if he catches them *in flagrante*. There is no provision in the Iranian Penal Code granting the wife the same right with regard to her husband.

Under classical Islamic criminal law, Muslims and non-Muslims do not always have the same rights. Different treatment exists in the fields of evidence, the law of retaliation and bloodmoney, and with regard to the application of certain fixed penalties. Under classical Islamic law the testimonies of non-Muslim witnesses are not admitted in court. Although the newly enacted codes are silent on this point, it is plausible that in court practice this rule will be followed. The classical schools of jurisprudence differ on the amount of the bloodprice for non-Muslims, but are in agreement that it is lower than that of a Muslim. None of the Shariʿa penal codes is explicit on this point. But here the same reasoning applies as that I mentioned above when discussing the bloodprice of women: the codes only mention the bloodprice of Muslim males, from which it can be inferred that the bloodprice of a non-Muslim has a different value. It is plausible that the rules of classical doctrine would be applied, which would theoretically mean that in non-Hanafite countries (such as Libya or Northern Nigeria) a Muslim cannot be sentenced to death if he kills a non-Muslim. I have, however, no information on whether or not this rule is actually being applied. In Iran, a Muslim who has killed a non-Muslim can be sentenced to death only if the victim's heirs pay the difference in bloodprices. Another problem exists in Iran with regard to adherents of the Bahai religion, who are not regarded as protected subjects, *dhimmīs*, since the Bahai religion is not recognised under Iranian law. If a Muslim kills a Bahai, retaliation is not possible, neither can the victim's heirs claim bloodmoney. A final issue where non-Muslims are put in an inferior position to Muslims is the law of *qadhf* (unfounded allegation of unlawful sexual intercourse). Some Shariʿa penal codes protect only Muslims against this form of defamation and not non-Muslims (e.g. art. 5 Pakistan, Offence of Qazf (Enforcement of *ḥadd*) Ordinance, 1979). Others are silent on this point. In some cases the discrimination between Muslims and non-Muslims works in favour of the latter: the Northern Nigerian Shariʿa penal codes apply only to Muslims and not to non-Muslims. The latter fall under the 1959 Northern Nigerian Penal Code. The result is that the same offence, e.g. theft or unlawful sexual intercourse, incurs a much more severe punishment for Muslims than for non-Muslims. In Iran non-Muslims will only be punished for drinking alcohol if they do so publicly, whereas for Muslims drinking alcohol is always a punishable offence (Iranian Penal Code, art. 174).

Freedom of religion implies not only that one can freely practise one's religion, but also that one is free to change one's religion. Both the 1994 Yemeni Penal Code (art. 259) and the 1991 Sudanese Penal Code (art. 126) make apostasy from Islam a punishable offence. In accordance with classical doctrine, it incurs the death penalty. That the other Shariʿa penal codes do not list apostasy as a punishable offence does not mean that in those countries apostates will not be prosecuted. In Iran, persons have been sentenced to death for apostasy, not on the strength of the Iranian Penal Code, but of uncodified Shariʿa. That similar sentences were pronounced by Saudi courts is no surprise, as uncodified Shariʿa is the law of the land. Most Northern Nigerian penal codes contain an article allowing the courts to inflict punishment for acts that are not mentioned in the penal codes, but are nevertheless punishable under the Shariʿa. Theoretically these sections could be used to punish apostasy. However, if a person were charged with apostasy, he could plead that the Shariʿa court has no jurisdiction over him, as he has abandoned Islam. Moreover, he could argue that prosecution for apostasy is unconstitutional since the Nigerian federal Constitution recognises the right to change one's religion.

One of the problems connected with apostasy is that its definition is not clear-cut. Of course, if one publicly renounces Islam and embraces another religion, the situation is clear. However, apostasy may also be the result of acts or utterances implying it,[53] in which case the act of apostasy

[53] Peters and de Vries, 'Apostasy in Islam'.

can only be established by inference and interpretation. This can become a weapon in the hands of conservative *'ulamā'* for silencing adherents of more liberal interpretations of Islam. This happened, for example, in the case of the Egyptian Koran scholar Naṣr Ḥāmid Abū Zayd, who in 1995 was declared an apostate by an Egyptian court of appeal on the basis of his novel interpretations of the Koran. Although in Egypt apostasy is not a punishable offence, a court sentence establishing it entails serious consequences in one's personal life, since for one thing the apostate's marriage is dissolved.[54] In Iran, an academic who had criticised the Iranian *'ulamā'* for aspiring to total political and religious control, for their arbitrary rule and for putting the believers in the position of 'monkeys' who can only blindly imitate was sentenced to death for apostasy on 9 November 2002 by a court on which only conservative mollas sat. Fortunately, the sentence was repealed on review in early 2003.[55]

Blasphemy by insulting a prophet (*sabb al-nabī*) is a serious offence in the classical doctrine, incurring the death penalty for the perpetrator. Some Shari'a penal codes include express provisions making this or similar acts punishable offences. Such provisions are not necessarily in conflict with the principle of freedom of religion. However, if they are consistently applied against certain religious groups, their enforcement can be regarded as a violation of this principle. This is the case in Pakistan, where blasphemy laws are used to persecute adherents of the Ahmadiyya movement. The Iranian Penal Code deals with blasphemy in articles 513–15. These sections (not found in the 1983 *ta'zīr* law) stipulate that blasphemy against prophets, Shiite imams and the religious leadership incurs a punishment of one to three years' imprisonment, unless the act can be classified as insulting the Prophet, in which case it is a capital offence. It is clear that these articles can be used to curtail freedom of expression.

A final violation of human rights standards is the minimum age for criminal liability. In classical doctrine, this age is set at puberty, or at fifteen years (eighteen years according to the Malikites; nine years for girls according to the Shiites), whichever comes first (see § 2.3.2.1). Some Shari'a penal codes follow the same system, but with varying minimum ages. Pakistan has set the age at eighteen for men and sixteen for women (art. 29 Pakistani Penal Code), Iran at fifteen for men and nine for women (art. 49 Iranian Penal Code and 1210 Iranian Civil Code), Sudan between fifteen and eighteen.

[54] See Kilian Bälz, 'Submitting faith to judicial scrutiny through the family trial: the Abû Zaid case', *Die Welt des Islams* 37 (1997), 135–56.

[55] Human Rights Watch press release, 9 November 2002. See http://hrw.org/press/2002/11/iranacademic.htm.

Most Northern Nigerian Shari'a penal codes stipulate that criminal liability for *ḥudūd* crimes begins with puberty. This means that in all these countries children under eighteen years old can be sentenced to capital punishment and to cruel, inhuman and degrading penalties, which violates article 37 of the CRC.

5.4.2 Strategies for human rights enforcement

It is clear that the recently enacted Shari'a penal codes are in conflict with international human rights conventions in several areas. Some will argue that this is unavoidable, since Islam and the Shari'a are incompatible with what they regard as essentially Western values such as democracy and human rights. I reject this position: Islam and the Shari'a are not monolithic but diverse, and it is therefore impossible to apply such generalising statements to them. Moreover, they are open to development and not per se identical with the views and interpretations of classical religious scholars. Finally, human rights principles are not Western principles but universal and should be implemented everywhere, although there should be some room for culturally and locally defined interpretations. As a consequence, it is obligatory to raise the question of whether the violations of the human rights norms found in the Shari'a penal codes can be remedied and what the possibilities are that the states that enacted these codes will replace or amend these laws in order to comply with international human rights standards.

Let us first look at the constraints in order to identify the possible obstacles, traps and pitfalls. Departing from these constraints, we can search for strategies to achieve a greater or full human rights compliance. The first constraint is the fact that, as I argued at the beginning of this chapter, the implementation of Islamic criminal law is more than a merely technical law reform or a change in the law introduced for reasons of practical expediency. The main motivations behind the implementation of Islamic criminal law are political and cultural. The politicians and legislators who introduced it have proclaimed their commitment to a special interpretation of Islam and to the establishment of an Islamic state based on that interpretation. At the same time, it constitutes a conscious rejection of legal notions and human rights standards that are allegedly Western and not universal. The lawmakers wish to convey the message that the Shari'a, being God's law, is superior to man-made law. Thus, objecting to the Shari'a penal codes and their practical enforcement will be countered with the argument that human rights conventions are made by man, whereas the Shariʿa is based on divine revelation. I shall revert to this issue later.

A further complication is mistrust with regard to human rights policies. The human rights policies of most Western countries can be criticised on two grounds: first, they are motivated by considerations of power politics rather than by a serious concern for human rights; and, second, many Western countries themselves do not comply with human rights norms. Countries such as the United States have subordinated their human rights policy to their foreign policy and regard it as an instrument to ensure their political and economic interests. The United States (and other Western countries, for that matter) apply double standards: they tend to target only countries with which they do not have good relations with sanctions aimed at enforcing human rights compliance, while turning a blind eye to the violations of human rights norms committed by friendly nations. This is not conducive to the acceptance of human rights standards by those states against which such sanctions are directed. Many Muslims, if confronted with Western criticism that the Shariʿa penal codes violate international human rights norms, will be quick to point this out and stress the violations of human rights principles by Western states, especially where Muslims are concerned. The United States, they assert, has lost its credibility on this score by keeping hundreds of persons imprisoned in Guantánamo Bay while denying them their basic rights and through the torture of Iraqi prisoners. And the same is true for France, which infringes on freedom of religion by banning headscarves in state schools. These objections, however justified they may be, obscure the real issues: that human rights are not a Western ploy to subject the rest of the world but represent universal values and that it is desirable to comply with the international human rights conventions.

These anti-Western feelings in most Muslim countries and this prevailing mistrust of human rights campaigns and policies are obstacles on the path towards greater compliance with human rights norms in those countries that have enacted Shariʿa penal codes. Is it possible to overcome these obstacles? Some would argue that this can be achieved if one or more Western powers put political and economic pressure on the countries where Islamic criminal law is implemented, with the aim of forcing them to repeal or change the Shariʿa penal codes. Such a course of action, however, is doomed to failure, if for no other reason than that a government which yields to this pressure and abolishes the Shariʿa will lose its legitimacy and commit political suicide. Once the Shariʿa has been put into force in a certain domain of the law, the way back is nearly impossible, because repealing parts of the Shariʿa would be regarded as tantamount to apostasy. Moreover, because of the positive connotations that accompanied its introduction (see § 5.1) its abolition would be opposed by important sections of the population and could easily be exploited by Islamist groups to topple the government. The responsible ministers might well become easy targets for assassination by radical Muslims on the grounds of their alleged apostasy. For the same reasons a campaign launched by Western human rights organisations and directed against the Shariʿa would not be successful.

In order to avoid all semblance of Western interference and to enhance the chances of success it is advisable that campaigns for greater compliance with universal human rights standards be organised by local human rights groups with diversified international support. They should be the main actors and remain independent from foreign sponsors. If they appear to be controlled by specific foreign powers or organisations, they will lose their domestic credibility. Their strategy should be aimed at creating support and acceptance for human rights issues. However, this is not easy to achieve, for ideological and religious reasons. If human rights activists argue that certain fixed penalties are cruel, degrading and inhuman, advocates of the Shariʿa penal codes would retort that such punishments are prescribed in God's revelation and are therefore divine institutions that are above criticism. Moreover, they often claim that human rights are a Western ploy aimed at undermining Islam by attacking its strongest base: the Shariʿa. In order to take the edge off this criticism, and make it acceptable to large parts of the Muslim population, a human rights discourse must be constructed, based on the international human rights conventions but with an Islamic legitimacy.

Several Islamic human rights proclamations already exist. They have adopted the terminology of modern human rights discourse, but stipulate that these rights are recognised only if they are not in conflict with the Shariʿa. A typical provision in such a declaration is article 12 (a) of the Universal Islamic Declaration of Human Rights, which says in its English version: 'Every person has the right to express his thoughts and beliefs so long as he remains within the limits of the Law.' This restriction seems to be identical with those found in human rights conventions allowing that, on certain grounds, human rights may be restricted by enacted laws. However, in the Arabic text of this declaration the word Shariʿa is used (and not *qānūn*). This is problematic because it could mean that the right to freedom of religion is restricted by the classical rules concerning the *dhimmīs* (the protected non-Muslim residents), which for instance put serious restrictions on the building of churches and synagogues or on the rights of religions other than Christianity and Judaism. Moreover, in view of the existence of various schools of jurisprudence and their diverse interpretations, the phrase the 'limits of the Shari'a' is not sufficiently precise to warrant restrictions in the applicability of human rights. Although some of these declarations expressly forbid the use of torture, none of them stipulates that cruel, inhuman or degrading punishments are unlawful.[56] Since these Islamic human rights declarations are effective only within the confines set by the Shari'a, it is doubtful whether they can offer remedies in cases where legislation based on the Shari'a is at variance with universal human rights standards.

I would argue that, in order to remedy the human rights violations related to the implementation of Islamic criminal law, there is no other choice but to stimulate debates among Muslims on the interpretation of the religious sources with the aim of providing greater legitimacy for human rights norms. Such an endeavour should be aimed in the first place at modifying the Shari'a penal codes in order to bring them into agreement with human rights standards. But at the same time they should provide Islamic legitimisation for such changes. As we saw in the first chapter, Islamic legal doctrine is not an unequivocal law code. The drafters of the Shari'a penal codes have made choices between opinions and interpretations on separate issues. This process of selection must become more transparent, so that the drafters and supporters of the present codes cannot counter any opposition to them with the argument that the codes embody God's law and that such opposition is tantamount to heresy. Within the heritage of classical legal doctrine, and by using methods of interpretation, it is possible to redefine the codes in such a way that they do not violate basic human rights.

Another, perhaps more daring, approach is a campaign for suspending the law of *ḥadd* until there is an Islamic society based on social justice that has eliminated poverty and want, and is ruled by a just Islamic government. This argument was first put forward by the Egyptian Muslim Brothers in the 1940s.[57] They argued that it is unfair to punish a thief with amputation if he has been driven to his crime by poverty and hunger or to apply the fixed penalty for unlawful intercourse if people lack the financial means to enter into marriage. Since the countries that have enacted Shari'a penal

56 Sami A. Aldeeb Abu-Sahlieh, *Les musulmans face aux droits de l'homme* (Bochum: Verl. Dr. Dieter Winkler, 1994), pp. 71–2.

57 R. P. Mitchell, *The Society of the Muslim Brothers* (London: Oxford University Press, 1969), pp. 240–1, quoting Hasan al-Banna', Sayyid Qutb and 'Abd al-Qadir 'Awda.

codes are still far away from these ideals, there are good reasons for not enforcing the law of *ḥadd*.

In order to develop these interpretations and opinions, local human rights organisations should cooperate with practical lawyers and specialists in *fiqh* and explore the possibilities offered by the classical doctrine of Islamic law to prevent the application of the severe corporal and mutilating penalties, in the same way as the Pakistani higher courts do. The latter activity is not aimed at structural legal change. On the other hand, it can be of great value in the day-to-day legal process and may help many persons who otherwise would be exposed to cruel punishment or death sentences.

CHAPTER 6

Conclusion

In the foregoing chapters I have expounded the doctrine, the practice and the modern history of Islamic criminal law. By way of conclusion I will highlight the central themes of each chapter and try to connect the separate topics. The doctrine of Islamic criminal law is technically quite complicated, especially because its three domains are governed by different rules of procedure and evidence. However, the rules of these domains serve similar aims. Criminal law is meant to protect the central interests and values of society. By analysing the provisions of Islamic criminal law, we gain insight into these values, or at least into those values held dear by those who formulated and elaborated the doctrine. Because of its precise definitions of crimes, Islamic criminal law in its narrow sense (i.e. the law of retaliation and of *ḥadd* crimes) is the most suitable object of such an analysis.

Protection of life and the integrity of the body is central among the values safeguarded by Islamic criminal law. The law of homicide and wounding imposes serious sanctions on those who violate these fundamental rights: capital punishment or retaliatory mutilation if the infraction was deliberate, and otherwise financial compensation. However, at the same time, it is clear that the Shariʿa regards these rights as private, to the extent that prosecution depends entirely on the will of the victim or his heirs. The state only interferes as a referee, to supervise the correct applications of the law during the trial and the execution of the sentence. A similar system of trying homicide existed in western Europe in the Middle Ages. Such systems originated in societies where the state was absent or weak and the accepted reaction to manslaughter was revenge on the killer's tribe, taken by the victim's next of kin. With the emergence of strong states in western Europe the state took over the prosecution of homicide and private prosecution disappeared. In the Muslim world this did not happen, although strong states did arise. One of the factors that may explain the preservation of the classical law of homicide until the nineteenth century was the distrust of the state felt by the Islamic scholars. By requiring the consent of the victim's heirs for the imposition of a death sentence on the killer, they tried to restrict the state's power over life and death.

The law of *ḥadd* is also essential for understanding the basic values protected by the Islamic criminal law, in spite of the fact that its harsh punishments were seldom inflicted. Its importance lies in the fact that the *ḥadd* offences and their punishments proclaim that certain interests and values are crucial to society. If infractions of these interests and values could not be punished with a fixed punishment, law enforcers could inflict punishment at their discretion. The significance of the law of *ḥadd* crimes lies not so much in the rules of *ḥadd* themselves, but in the implicit instructions to the law enforcers to punish all acts violating values protected by the rules of *ḥadd* offences.

The law of *ḥadd* protects four central interests and values of society: public order, private property, sexual order and personal honour. Those who violate these interests – such as bandits, thieves, those who offend against sexual mores and slanderers – are threatened with severe punishments. The prohibition of alcoholic beverages can be understood in various ways. One is the protection of social order since drunkenness often results in criminal behaviour. Furthermore the ban underscores the value of reason, since drunkenness makes a person lose his reason. Another, more sociological, explanation is that the ban on alcohol protects Muslim identity and the coherence of Muslims in societies where Muslims and non-Muslims live together, as, just like other dietary rules, it hinders social contacts with followers of other religions.

A careful reading of the classical texts on the legal doctrine and *fatwā* collections may tell us a great deal about the legal practice and the historical context. However, documentary sources will give us more detailed information on and a deeper insight into the operation of the legal system. These, unfortunately, are rare for the period before the sixteenth century. They exist, however, in great quantity in the Ottoman archives, where we find a wealth of judicial records going back to the sixteenth century. For that reason I selected the Ottoman Empire as the context for the investigation of the practice of Islamic criminal law. In doing so, I could build on the excellent studies on Ottoman law based on court records kept in the Turkish archives.

I have shown that the *qāḍīs*' courts faithfully applied Hanafite criminal law, but that, in addition, a sizeable part of criminal law enforcement was carried out by executive officials, who were not fully bound to the prescriptions of Islamic criminal law, although they operated within the parameters of Islamic legality. They would impose and carry out punishments at their discretion on the basis of *siyāsa,* as recognised by the doctrine of the *fiqh*. Higher officials, such as provincial governors, could even impose capital punishment and had to approve death sentences of lower officials and courts. However, the actions of these officials were not entirely arbitrary. In the first place, they were obligated to follow the enacted laws (*qānūn*) in carrying out their task. For instance, the fines they were allowed to collect from offenders were prescribed in detail in these laws, which also laid down rules for the delimitation of the jurisdictions of the *qāḍī* and these executive officials. The *qāḍī* would first investigate a case, and if he decided that he could not pronounce a sentence on the strength of the legal doctrine, he would draw up a report of the testimonies and other available information and send it to the executive officials to further investigate the case and impose punishment on the strength of *siyāsa*. The *qāḍī* would also monitor the subsequent proceedings: for instance, the executive officials were not to torture or imprison a suspect without his permission.

The values and interests protected by Ottoman criminal law were the same as those underlying the classical doctrine of the Shariʿa. However, there were two additional interests safeguarded by the law, interests that appear to have been very important in the Ottoman system. One was the protection of the state. The Sultan and his high-ranking representatives could sentence to death persons who formed a threat to the political order. The second one is the protection of social cohesion and morality. As we have seen, the inhabitants of a neighbourhood or village could initiate a procedure before the *qāḍī* in order to force people to depart if their behaviour was in the community's eyes unacceptable.

Summarising the role of the Shariʿa in this criminal law system, one can conclude that the classical Hanafite doctrine was applied in full, and that, apart from that, the executive officials charged with maintaining law and order were required to ask the *qāḍī*'s approval in many situations. Since the latter would apply Islamic rules of evidence and procedure and, in general, Islamic norms, the impact of Islamic criminal law went beyond the cases adjudicated in the *qāḍīs*' courts. The *qāḍīs* thus conferred Islamic legality on the whole system of criminal law enforcement.

The subject of chapter 4 was the eclipse of Islamic criminal law as a result of Westernisation and modernisation. In most countries under colonial rule this happened by merely abolishing it and replacing it with Western-type penal codes. In a few other countries, where Western influence was absent or small, Islamic criminal law continued to be applied. The focus of this chapter, however, was on those countries where attempts were made to 'modernise' Islamic criminal law, either by altering Islamic criminal law itself, or by regulating *siyāsa* justice by setting up a parallel judiciary next to the Shariʿa court system, to apply newly enacted penal codes.

The attempts by British colonial administrators to modernise or 'domesticate' Islamic criminal law ended in the creation of a system that was Islamic in all but name. Islamic criminal law was changed to fit British notions of justice. The severe *ḥadd* penalties were not enforced and sentences awarding them were commuted to imprisonment. The law of homicide and wounding was stripped of characteristic elements such as private prosecution and the defences that could be put forward to avert capital punishment or retaliation for wounding. In the end, this newly created law was replaced by modern penal codes.

In the Ottoman Empire and Egypt (which was an autonomous part of the Ottoman Empire with its own legal system), Islamic criminal law was left intact during the period of reform. Modernisation took place mainly in the field of *siyāsa* justice. Here modern notions of penal law were gradually introduced: the idea of legality (i.e. that punishment may only be imposed on the strength of a legal enactment defining the offence and specifying its punishment); the notion of impartiality of the law and equality of legal subjects; that of public prosecution of crime; and that of due process. But although Islamic criminal law was left intact, it was still affected by the new developments. The Shariʿa judiciary became bureaucratised and procedures were introduced to supervise the *qāḍīs*' courts so as to secure a correct application of the Hanafite doctrine. The severe *ḥadd* penalties ceased to be enforced, although, unlike flogging, they were never officially abolished. However, in those countries too Islamic criminal law was in the end abolished and replaced with Western-inspired penal codes.

The re-emergence of Islamic criminal law, the main focus of chapter 5, is one of the most striking phenomena in the recent history of the Shariʿa. Islamic criminal law was regarded by many as a phenomenon of the past. Many Western observers believed that in those few countries where it was still in force Islamic criminal law would eventually be abolished. However, from the 1970s the number of countries applying Islamic criminal law slowly increased. The attitude of the regimes that have recently come to promulgate Shariʿa penal codes and legislation differed from that adopted by Islamic governments of the past. For the latter, the Islamic legal order was a matter of fact; for the former it was an expression of cultural and political assertion against Western hegemony. It became a symbol for the Islamicity of a regime and its steadfastness against Western pressures. Because of the powerful ideology connected with the implementation of Shariʿa penal law, large segments of the population are in favour of it. A complicating factor is that campaigns for human rights are perceived in these countries as Western assaults on Islamic identity.

It is precisely this ideological element that creates an obstacle to legal change. Abolishing Islamic criminal law after its introduction is regarded by many as religiously forbidden, and doing so would seriously undermine a regime's legitimacy. This poses problems in the domain of compliance with internationally accepted human rights standards. Most countries that have enacted Shariʿa penal codes are signatories to the main human rights conventions. Yet these new Shariʿa penal codes violate human rights principles on a number of issues. Since abolition of Shariʿa criminal law in the countries where it has recently been introduced is no option, the solution must be sought within an Islamic framework, for instance by reinterpreting the textual sources or by going back to the abundance of opinions found in the classical works on jurisprudence with the aim of selecting those that are most in conformity with the demands of modern society.

Glossary of technical terms

actus reus	act containing all elements of a punishable offence and imputable to the person who has committed it
ʿadl	good reputation or rectitude of a witness required for the validity of his testimony
akçe	Ottoman silver coin
alkali	Northern Nigerian term for *qāḍī*
amāra	indication, circumstantial evidence
ʿamd	(criminal) intent
ʿāqila	solidarity group liable for bloodmoney if one of its members commits homicide
arsh	financial compensation (*diya*) for injuries
bayt al-māl	public treasury
dhimmī	protected non-Muslim subject of an Islamic state
dinar	gold coin
dirham	silver coin
Dīvān-i Hümayūn	Ottoman Empire: imperial Divan presided over by the Grand Vizier
diya	bloodmoney or bloodprice, the financial compensation for homicide and injuries
diya mughallaẓa	enhanced financial compensation for certain types of homicide
ehl-i fesād	literally, 'people of corruption'; Ottoman expression for repeated offenders and known criminals
ehl-i ʿörf	Ottoman expression for the executive officials
fatwā	legal opinion without binding force given by a mufti in answer to a question stating a concrete case (which does not necessarily have to be based on actual facts)

Federal Shariat Court	Federal court in Pakistan, established in 1979 to examine whether or not enacted laws were repugnant to Islam and to hear on appeal cases involving *ḥadd* penalties
fermān	Ottoman Empire: sultanic order
fiqh	Islamic jurisprudence, legal doctrine
ghurra	financial compensation for the loss of a foetus
ḥabs	imprisonment, detention
ḥadd (plural: *ḥudūd*)	fixed punishment for certain crimes (*ḥadd* crimes), mentioned in the Koran and *ḥadīth*
ḥadīth	formally transmitted words or behaviour of the Prophet Mohammed, one of the sources of Islamic jurisprudence
ḥaqq Allāh (plural: *ḥuqūq al-Allāh*)	claim of God, representing the public interest
ḥaqq al-ʿibād (plural: *ḥuqūq al-ʿibād*)	claim of a human being (as opposed to a claim of God)
ḥarbī	non-Muslim residing outside the territory of Islam (i.e. in the *dār al-ḥarb,* the Abode of War)
ḥirāba	the *ḥadd* crime of robbery, banditry, one of the *ḥadd* offences, synonymous with *muḥāraba* and *qaṭʿ al-ṭarīq*
ḥirz	custody, specifically a safe place where movable property is kept
ḥisba	office of the *muḥtasib* (q.v.)
ḥüccet (*ḥujja*)	document issued by a *qāḍī* containing depositions about a certain case or issue (Ottoman legal practice)
ḥudūd	see *ḥadd*
ḥukm	final sentence of a *qāḍī*
ḥukūmat ʿadl	financial compensation for injuries based on an assessment of the disability caused by the injury and not on the tariff list for standard injuries
ḥuqūq al-Allāh	see *ḥaqq Allāh*
ḥuqūq al-ʿibād	see *ḥaqq al-ʿibād*
ʿidda	period after the dissolution of a marriage during which a woman may not remarry

iʿdhār	opportunity given by the *qāḍī* to the party against whom evidence is introduced during a trial to challenge that evidence
ifsād	spreading corruption (on earth), synonymous with *saʿy bi-l-fasād* (q.v.)
iḥṣān	the quality of being *muḥṣan* (q.v.)
ijmāʿ	consensus of Islamic scholars
ikrāh	coercion, duress
iʿlām	document containing the final sentence of a *qāḍī*
iqrār	admission, confession
irtidād	apostasy, synonymous with *ridda* (q.v.)
ʿiṣma	inviolability of a person's life, property and freedom resulting from the protection offered by the state
jāʾifa	a wound in the body that reaches one of the inner cavities
jald	flogging
kaffāra	expiation for accidental homicide, as well as for breaking the fast of Ramadan or breaking an oath
kefīl (*binnefs*)	guarantor, a person who guarantees to the authorities that another person (*mekfūl)* will appear before the authorities when summoned
khaṭaʾ	mistake, accident
lawth	circumstantial or incomplete evidence against a person making him a suspect of manslaughter
liʿān	procedure in which a husband, under oath, accuses his wife of adultery and denies the paternity of any children to which she will give birth, answered by an oath of innocence sworn by his wife; the effect of the procedure is that their marriage is dissolved and that he is legally not the father of any children borne by her afterwards
mahr al-mithl	proper brideprice, i.e. the average brideprice a woman of a particular social status, age etc. would receive upon marriage
majlis (plural: *majālis*)	Egyptian judicial councils applying enacted laws, established in the early 1850s
Majlis al-Aḥkām	Egyptian Supreme Judicial Council, established in 1849
maʾmūma	a head wound reaching the cerebral membrane

mawlā	patron, the former owner of a slave
Mecelle	Ottoman Civil Code based on the Shariʿa and enacted between 1867 and 1872
Meclis-i Vālā-yi Aḥkām-i ʿAdliye	Ottoman Supreme Judicial Council, established in 1838
mens rea	blameworthiness of the defendant consisting in the state of mind required for a conviction
mūḍiḥa	wound laying bare the bone
muḥāraba	see *ḥirāba*
muḥṣan	personal qualities, variously defined by the schools of jurisprudence, that cause the fixed penalty for unlawful sexual intercourse to be increased to death by stoning instead of 100 lashes
muḥtasib (Ottoman, *müḥtesib*)	market inspector, official with the power to impose immediate punishment, supervising trade, public space, public morals and the observance of religious duties
munaqqila	injury whereby a bone is displaced
murtadd	apostate
mustaʾmin	*ḥarbī* (q.v.) temporarily admitted to Muslim territory and enjoying full protection of life, property and freedom
müttehem (Arabic, *muttaham*)	suspected person
nafy	banishment, exile
nāʾib	deputy *qāḍī*
niṣāb	minimum value of stolen goods required for the infliction of the fixed penalty for theft
niẓām	enacted decree (Saudi Arabia)
Niẓāmat ʿAdālat	High Court in British India, operative before 1858 and applying Islamic law
Niẓāmiye courts	Ottoman state courts applying enacted laws, established in 1864
ʿörf	administrative law; torture (Ottoman legal practice)
qadhf	calumny, defamation: the *ḥadd* offence of an unfounded accusation of unlawful sexual intercourse
qāḍī	single judge applying the Shariʿa

qānūn	enacted law
qānūnnāme	enacted law code
qasāma	procedure based on the swearing of fifty oaths aimed at establishing liability for a homicide with an unknown perpetrator
qaṭʿ	amputation of the right hand from the wrist (or the four fingers of the right hand)
qaṭʿ min khilāf	cross-amputation, i.e. amputation of the right hand and the left foot
qaṭʿ al-ṭarīq	see *ḥirāba*
qatl bi-sabab	indirect killing, i.e. the killing of a person without acting directly against the victim's body
qatl ghīla	heinous murder
qatl khaṭaʾ	accidental or unintended homicide
qawad	retaliation for homicide or wounding, synonymous with *qiṣāṣ* (q.v.)
qiṣāṣ	retaliation for homicide or wounding, synonymous with *qawad* (q.v.)
rajm	stoning to death, the fixed penalty for unlawful sexual intercourse committed by a *muḥṣan*
ridda	apostasy, synonymous with *irtidād* (q.v.)
sabb al-nabī	insulting the Prophet, a capital offence
Ṣadr Niẓāmat ʿAdālat	see Niẓāmat ʿAdālat
sāʿī bi-l-fasād	spreader of corruption, cf. K 5:33
ṣāḥib al-madīna	head of the police in Muslim Spain
ṣāḥib al-shurṭa	head of the police
ṣāḥib al-sūq	the *muḥtasib* in Muslim Spain
ṣalb	crucifixion
sariqa	theft
saʿy bi-l-fasād	spreading corruption, synonymous with *ifsād* (q.v.)
Şeyh ül-Islâm	the supreme mufti of the Ottoman Empire, also acting, during the nineteenth century, as Minister of Justice
shahāda	testimony
shahāda ʿalā al-shahāda	indirect testimony, i.e. testimony regarding another person's statement

shibh ʿamd	pseudo-intent or semi-intent, which exists if a person causes the death of another person by a deliberate act, although the instrument used is not indicative of the intent to kill
shubha	uncertainty regarding the unlawfulness of an act
shurb khamr	drinking wine and, by extension, any alcoholic beverage
shurṭa	police
siyāsa (Ottoman, *siyāset*)	discretionary justice exercised by the head of state and executive officials, not restricted by the rules of the Shariʿa
subaşı	head of the police (Ottoman Empire)
ṣulḥ	amicable settlement out of court between parties
taʾdīb	corrective punishment
taghrīb	banishment, exile
tashhīr	punishment consisting in exposing a person to public scorn
tawba	repentance
taʿzīr	discretionary, corrective punishment
wakīl (Ottoman, *vekīl*)	legal agent
walī al-dam (plural: *awliyāʾ al-dam*)	private prosecutor, i.e. the relatives of a victim of homicide
zinā	unlawful sexual intercourse, illicit sex, fornication
zindīq	apostate posing as a Muslim

Bibliography

Ābī, Ṣāliḥ ʿAbd al-Samīʿ al-, *Jawāhir al-iklīl sharḥ Mukhtaṣar Khalīl*, 2 vols. (Cairo: ʿĪsā al-Bābī al-Ḥalabī, n.d.).

Abū Zahra, Muḥammad, *al-Jarīma wa-al-ʿuqūba fī al-fiqh al-Islāmī*, 2 vols. (Cairo: Dār al-Fikr al-ʿArabī, n.d.).

Akgündüz, Ahmed, *Mukayeseli Islam ve Osmanlı hukuku külliyatı* (Diyarbakır: Dicle Üniversitesi Hukuk Fakültesi Yayınları, 1986), xxxvi, 1,000 pp.

Osmanlı kanunnāmeleri ve hukukī tahlilleri. Birinci kitap: Osmanlı hukuna giriş ve Fātih devri kanunnāmeleri (Istanbul: Faysal Eğitim ve Yardimlaşma Vakfi, 1990), 710 pp.

Akgündüz, Ahmet et al., *Şerʿiye sicilleri. C. 1: Mahiyeti, toplu kataloğu ve seçme hükümler. C. 2: Seçme hükümler* (Istanbul: Türk Dünyası Araştirmaları Vakfı, 1988–9).

Akhoundi, Mahmoud, *De l'influence de la tradition religieuse sur le droit pénal de l'Iran* (Teheran: Imprimerie de l'Université Téhéran, 1961), 146 pp.

Aldeeb Abu-Sahlieh, Sami A., *Les musulmans face aux droits de l'homme,* (Bochum: Verl. Dr. Dieter Winkler, 1994), 610 pp.

ʿAlī Efendi, *Fatāwā ʿAlī Efendi*, 2 vols. (Istanbul: n.p., n.d.).

Amin, Mohammad, *Islamization of laws in Pakistan* (Lahore: Sang-e-Meel Publishers, 1989), xi, 257 pp.

Anderson, J. N. D., *Islamic law in Africa* (London: HMSO, 1954), viii, 409 pp.

An-Na'im, A. A., 'The Islamic law of apostasy and its modern applicability: a case from the Sudan', *Religion: Journal of Religion and Religions* 16 (1986), 197–224.

Arcas Campoy, M., 'La penalizacíon de las injurias en el derecho maliki', *Boletín de la Asociación Espanola de Orientalistas* 30 (1994), 209–17.

Arévalo, R., *Derecho penal islámico* (Tanger: F. Erola, 1939), 188 pp.

ʿAsqalānī, Ibn Ḥajr al-, *Bulūgh al-marām min adillat al-aḥkām* (Cairo: Dār al-Kitāb al-ʿArabī, n.d.), 286 pp.

Atallah, Borham, 'Le droit pénal musulman ressuscité', *Annuaire de l'Afrique du Nord* 13 (1974), 227–52.

ʿAwda, ʿAbd al-Qādir, *al-Tashrīʿ al-jināʾī al-Islāmī muqāranan bi-l-qānūn al-waḍʿī*, 2 vols. (Cairo: Dār al-Turāth, n.d.).

Bābartī, Muḥammad al-, *al-ʿInāya sharḥ al-hidāya*, 10 vols. (Cairo: Dār al-Fikr, n.d.).

Baer, G., 'Tanzimat in Egypt – the penal code', *Bulletin of the School of Oriental and African Studies* 26 (1963), 29–49.

'The transition from traditional to Western criminal law in Turkey and Egypt', *Studia Islamica* 45 (1977), 139–58.

Bälz, Kilian, 'Submitting faith to judicial scrutiny through the family trial: the Abû Zaid case', *Die Welt des Islams* 37 (1997), 135–56.

Bambale, Yahaya Yunusa, *Crimes and punishment under Islamic law* (Kaduna (Nigeria): Infoprint Publishers, 1998), 150 pp.

Banerjee, Tapas Kumar, *Background to Indian criminal law*, repr. edn. (Calcutta: R. Cambray, 1990; first publ. 1963), xviii, 402 pp.

Bassiouni, M. Cherif, ed. *The Islamic criminal justice system* (London etc.: Oceana Publications, 1982), xiv, 255pp.

Bayındır, Abülaziz, *Islam muhakeme hukuku: Osmanlı devri uygulaması* (Istanbul: Islami Ilimler Araştırma Vakfı, 1986), xvi, 288 pp. (Islami İlimler Araştırma Vakfı Yayınları, 7).

Beck, S. (tr.), 'Das afghanische Strafgesetzbuch vom Jahre 1924. Aus dem persischen übersetzt und mit einer allgemeinen Einleitung in die afghanische Strafgesetzgebung versehen', *Die Welt des Islams* 11 (1928), 67–157.

Bouma, C., 'Pakistan's Islamization 1977–1988: the Zia era in retrospect', *al-Mushir* 31 (1989), 9–27.

Brown, Nathan N., *The rule of law in the Arab world: courts in Egypt and the Gulf* (Cambridge: Cambridge University Press, 1997), xvii, 258 pp. (Cambridge Middle East Studies, 6).

Bucknill, John A. Stratchey, and Haig Apisoghom S. Utidjian, *The imperial Ottoman penal code: a translation from the Turkish text, with latest additions and amendments together with annotations and explanatory commentaries upon the text and containing an appendix dealing with the special amendments in force in Cyprus and the judicial decisions of the Cyprus courts* (London: Oxford University Press, 1913), xix, 243 pp.

Calero, M. I., 'La justicia. Cadíes y otros magistrados', in *El Reino nazarí de Granada (1232–1492), política, instituciones, espacio y economía,* edited by M. J. Viguera (Madrid: Espasa-Calpe, 2000), 365–427 (Historia de España Menéndez Pidal, VIII, 4).

Çavuşzāde, Meḥmed ʿAzīz, *Dürr al-ṣukūk*, 2 vols. (Istanbul: Maṭbaʿa-yi ʿĀmira, 1871–2 (1288 H)).

Chalmeta, P., 'Acerca de los delitos de sangre en al-Andalus durante el califato', in *El saber en al-Andalus: textos y estudios, II*, edited by J. M. Carabaza and A. T. M. Essay (Seville: Universidad de Sevilla, Secretariado de Publicaciones, 1999), 45–64.

Cin, Halil, and Ahmet Akgündüz, *Türk-İslām hukuk tarihi*, 2 vols. (Istanbul: Timaş Yayınları, 1990).

Colebrooke, James Edward, *Digest of the regulations and laws, enacted by the Governor-General in Council for the civil government of the territories under the Presidency of Bengal arranged in alphabetical order*, 2 vols. (Calcutta: n.p., 1807).

Collins, D. P., 'Islamization of Pakistan law: a historical perspective', *Stanford Journal of International Law* 24 (1987), 511–85.

Cotran, Eugene, and Chibli Mallat, eds., *Yearbook of Islamic and Middle Eastern Law* (London etc.: Kluwers Law International, 1994–).

Court of Nizamut Adawlut, *Reports of criminal cases, 1805[–11]* (n.p.: n.p., n.d.).

d'Ohsson, Ignace Mouradgea, *Tableau général de l'empire othoman*, 3 vols. (Paris: Imprimerie F. Didot, 1788–1820).

Düstur, 2nd edn., ([Istanbul]: Maṭbaʿa-yi ʿĀmira, 1866 (1282 H.)), vol. I, 904 pp.

Ebussuud Efendi and Mehmet Ertuğrul Düzdağ, *Şeyhülislam Ebussuud Efendi Fetvaları ışığında 16. asır Türk hayatı*, 2nd edn. (Istanbul: Enderun Kitabevi, 1983), 245 pp.

Eichmann, F., *Die Reformen des osmanischen Reiches mit besonderer Berücksichigung des Verhältnisses der Christen des Orients zur türkischen Herrschaft* (Berlin: Verlag der Nicolaischen Buchhandlung, 1858), 461 pp.

El-Baradie, A., *Gottes-Recht und Menschen-Recht: Grundlagenprobleme der islamischen Strafrechtslehre* (Baden-Baden: Nomos, 1983), 245 pp. (Rechtsvergleichende Untersuchungen zur gesamten Strafrechtswissenschaft, 3/14).

El Hour, R., 'The Andalusian qāḍī in the Almoravid period: political and judicial authority', *Studia Islamica* 90 (2000), 67–83.

El-Nahal, Galal H., *The judicial administration of Ottoman Egypt in the seventeenth century* (Minneapolis etc.: Bibliotheca Islamica, 1979), ix, 109 pp. (Studies in Middle Eastern History, 4).

Eltayeb, Mohamed S. M., *A human rights approach to combating religious persecution: cases from Pakistan, Saudi Arabia and Sudan* (Antwerp: Intersentia, 2001), xii, 245 pp.

Ergene, Boğaç, *Local court, provincial society and justice in the Ottoman Empire: legal practice and dispute resolution in Çankırı and Kastamonu (1652–1744)* (Leiden: Brill, 2003), x, 236 pp. (Islamic Law and Society, 17).

Fahmy, Khaled, 'The anatomy of justice: forensic medicine and criminal law in nineteenth-century Egypt', *Islamic Law and Society* 6 (1999), 224–71.

'The police and the people in nineteenth century Egypt', *Die Welt des Islams* 39 (1999), 340–77.

Fierro, M., 'El proceso contra Ibn Hatim al-Tulaytuli (años 457/1064–464/1072)', in *Estudios onomastico-bibliográficos de al-Andalus*, edited by M. Marín (Madrid: Consejo Superior de Investigaciones Cientificas, 1994), 187–214.

Fisch, J., *Cheap lives and dear limbs: the British transformation of the Bengal criminal law 1769–1817* (Wiesbaden: Steiner, 1983), vii, 154 pp. (Beiträge zur Südasienforschung, 79).

Fluehr-Lobban, C., 'Islamization in Sudan: a critical assessment', *Middle East Journal* 44 (1990), 611–24.

García Gómez, Emilio, 'Sobre la diferencia en el castigo de plebeyos y nobles', *al-Andalus* 36 (1971), 71–9.

Gerber, Haim, *State, society and law in Islam: Ottoman law in comparative perspective* (Albany: State University of New York Press, 1994), 233 pp.

Ginio, Eyal, 'The administration of criminal justice in Ottoman Selanik (Salonica) during the eighteenth century', *Turcica* 30 (1998), 185–210.

Gledhill, Alan, *The penal codes of Northern Nigeria and the Sudan* (London: Sweet & Maxwell, 1963), lii, 820 pp. (Law in Africa, 8).

Gökçen, Ahmet, *Tanzimat dönemi Osmanlı ceza kanunları ve bu kanunlardaki ceza müeyyidleri* (Istanbul: Ahmet Gökçen, 1989), xv, 174 pp.

Grant, Charles, *Observations on the state of society among the Asiatic subjects of Great Britain with respect to morals and on the means of approving it. Written chiefly in 1792* ([London]: House of Commons, 1813), 116 pp.

Hakim, J. el-, *Le dommage de source delictuelle en droit musulman: survivance en droit syrien et libanais* (Paris: Librairie générale de droit et de jurisprudence, 1971), 220 pp. (Université Saint Joseph, Beyrouth. Annales de la Faculté de Droit et des Sciences Economiques de Beyrouth, 40).

Hallaq, W., *Authority, continuity and change in Islamic law* (Cambridge: Cambridge University Press, 2001), xiv, 269 pp.

'Murder in Cordoba: ijtihad and ifta' and the evolution of substantive law in medieval Islam', *Acta Orientalia* 55 (1994), 55–83.

Hamo, Ahmed Ali, *Lectures on the criminal law of the Sudan, 1991* (Khartoum: International Printing House, 1992), 172 pp.

Hardy, M. J. L., *Blood feuds and the payment of bloodmoney in the Middle East* (Beirut: Catholic Press, 1963), 106 pp.

Harington, John Herbert, *An analysis of the laws and regulations enacted by the Governor General in Council, at Fort William, in Bengal, for the civil government of the British territories under that Presidency* (London: A. J. Valpy, 1821), xx, 645 pp.

Hassan, N., and I. Itscherenska, 'Zur Revitalisierung des islamischen Strafrechts in Iran', *Asien, Afrika, Lateinamerika* 13 (1985), 58–68.

Heidborn, A., *Droit public et administratif de l'Empire Ottoman*, 2 vols. (Leipzig: C. W. Stern, 1908–9).

Heyd, Uriel, *Studies in old Ottoman criminal law*, edited by V. L. Ménage (Oxford: Oxford University Press, 1973), xxxii, 340 pp.

Ḥillī, Jaʿfar b. al-Ḥasan al-, *Sharāʾiʿ al-Islām fī masāʾil al-ḥalāl wa-l-ḥarām*, 4 vols. (n.p.: n.p., 1969).

Ḥilmī, ʿÖmer, *Miʿyār-i ʿadālet* (Istanbul: Bosnawī Ḥajjī Muḥarrem Efendi, 1881–2 (1301 H)), 86 pp.

Horster, Paul, *Zur Anwendung des islamischen Rechts im 16. Jahrhundert: die juridischen Darlegungen* (maʿruzat) *des Schejch ül-Islam Ebu Su'ud* (Stuttgart: Kohlhammer, 1935), 112 pp.

Ibn Farḥūn, *Tabṣirat al-ḥukkām fī uṣūl al-aqḍiya wa-manāhij al-aḥkām*, 2 vols (Cairo: Maktabat al-Kulliyyāt al-Azhariyya, 1986).

Ibn Ḥanbal, Aḥmad, *Musnad*, 6 vols. (Cairo: al-Maṭbaʿal-Maymūniyya, 1985).

Ibn Māja, *Sunan* (Cairo: Dār al-Ḥadīth, 1998), 554 pp.

Ibn Qudāma, ʿAbd Allāh, *al-Mughnī*, edited by Muḥammad Sālim Muḥaysin and Shaʿbān Muḥammad Ismāʿīl, 11 vols. (Beirut: Dār Iḥyāʾal-Turāth al-ʿArabī, n.d.).

Ibn Rushd, Muḥammad b. Aḥmad, *Bidāyat al-mujtahid wa-nihāyat al-muqtaṣid*, 2 vols. (Cairo: Muṣṭafā al-Bābī al-Ḥalabī, 1960).
Idrīs, ʿAwaḍ Aḥmad, *al-Diya bayn al-ʿuqūba wa-l-taʿwīḍ fī al-fiqh al-Islāmī al-muqāran* (Beirut: Dār wa-Maktabat al-Hilāl, 1986), 637 pp.
ʿIllaysh, Muḥammad, *Fatḥ al-ʿalī al-mālik fī al-fatwā ʿalā madhhab al-Imām Mālik*, 2 vols. (Cairo: Maṭbaʿa al-Taqaddum al-ʿIlmiyya, 1902–3).
Imber, Colin, *Ebu's-Suʿud: the Islamic legal tradition* (Edinburgh: Edinburgh University Press, 1997), xii, 288 pp. (Jurists: Profiles in Legal Theory).
Studies in Ottoman history and law (Istanbul: Isis, 1996), iv, 337 pp.
'Zina in Ottoman law', in *Contributions à l'histoire économique et sociale de l'Empire Ottoman* (Leuven: Peeters, 1981), 59–92.
Ipşirli, Mehmet, 'XVI. Asrının ikinci yarısında kürek cezasi ili ilgili hükümler', *Tarih Enstitüsü Dergisi* 12 (1982), 204–48.
Jabartī, ʿAbd al-Raḥmān al-, *ʿAjāʾib al-āthār fī al-tarājim wa-l-akhbār*, 4 vols. (Bulaq: n.p., 1879–80).
Jacob, G., 'Türkische Sittenpolizei im 16. Jahrhundert', *Der Islam* 11 (1921), 254–9.
Jahangir, Asma, and Hina Jilani, *The Hudood Ordinances, a divine sanction?: a research study of the Hudood Ordinances and their effect on the disadvantaged sections of Pakistan society* (Lahore: Rhotas Books, 1990), 420 pp.
Jallād, Fīlīb, *Qāmūs al-idāra wa-l-qaḍāʾ*, 4 vols. (Alexandria: al-Maṭbaʿa al-Bukhāriyya, 1890–2).
Jallaf, Muhammad ʿAbd al-Wahhâb, 'La justicia: cadíes y otros magistrados', in *Los Reinos de Taifas: al-Andalus en el siglo XI*, edited by María Jesus Viguera Molins (Madrid: Espasa-Calpe, 1994), 163–90 (Historia de España Menéndez Pidal, VIII, 1).
Jazīrī, ʿAbd al-Raḥmān al-, *Kitāb al-fiqh ʿalā al-madhāhib al-arbaʿa. Al-juzʾ al-khāmis: al-ʿuqūbāt al-sharʿiyya* (Cairo: Dār al-Irshād, n.d.), 404 pp.
Jennings, Ronald C., 'Kadi, court, and legal procedure in 17th c. Ottoman Kayseri' *Studia Islamica* 48 (1978), 133–72.
'Limitations of the judicial powers of the kadi in 17th c. Ottoman Kayseri' *Studia Islamica* 50 (1979), 151–184.
Johansen, B., *Contingency in a sacred law: legal and ethical norms in the Muslim fiqh* (Leiden: Brill, 1999), xiii, 521 pp. (Studies in Islamic Law and Society, 7).
'Eigentum, Familie und Obrigkeit im hanafitischen Strafrecht. Das Verhältnis der privaten Rechte zu den Forderungen der Allgemeinheit in hanafitischen Rechtskommentaren', *Die Welt des Islams* 19 (1979), 1–73.
'Zu den Gleichheitsbegriffen im hanafitischen Strafrecht', in *XX. Deutscher Orientalistentag . . . 1977 in Erlangen: Vorträge*, edited by W. Voigt (Wiesbaden: Steiner, 1980), 226–7 (Zeitschrift der deutschen morgenländischen Gesellschaft. Supplemente, 4).
'Der ʿisma Begriff im hanafitischen Recht', in *Actes du VIIIe congrès international des arabisants et islamisants* (Aix-en-Provence: Edisud, 1978), 89–108.
'Zum Prozessrecht der ʿuqubat', in *XIX Deutscher Orientalistentag 1975, Freiburg i.B.* (Stuttgart: Steiner Verlag, 1977), 477–86 (Zeitschrift der deutschen morgenländische Gesellschaft. Supplement III, 1).

'Secular and religious elements in Hanafte law: functions and limits of the absolute character of government authority', in *Islam et politique au maghreb*, edited by E. Gellner and J.-C. Vatin (Paris: Editions du Centre de la Recherche Scientifique, 1981), pp. 282–303.

'Signs as evidence: the doctrine of Ibn Taymiyya (1263–1328) and Ibn Qayyim al-Jawziyya (d. 1351) on proof', *Islamic Law and Society* 9, 2 (2002), 168–93.

'The valorization of the human body in Muslim Sunni law', in B. Johansen, A. Singer and D. J. Stewart, *Law and society in Islam* (Princeton: Markus Wiener, 1996), 71–112.

Jones-Pauly, C., 'Use of the Qurān in key Pakistani court decisions on zinā and qadhf', *Arabica* 47 (2000), 539–53.

Kabbāshī, al-Mukāshifī Ṭāhā, *Taṭbīq al-Sharīʿa al-Islāmiyya fī al-Sūdān bayn al-ḥaqīqa wa-l-ithāra* (Cairo: Al-Zahrā' li-l-Iʿlām al-ʿArabī, 1986), 133 pp.

Kamali, Mohammad Hashim, 'Islamic law in Malaysia: issues and developments', In *Yearbook of Islamic and Middle Eastern Law*, edited by Cotran and Mallat, vol. IV (1997–1998), 153–79.

Karibi-Whyte, A. G., *History and sources of Nigerian criminal law* (Ibadan: Spectrum Law Publishers, 1993), xxii, 281 pp. (Spectrum law series).

Keay, E. A., and S. S. Richardson, *The native and customary courts of Nigeria* (London etc.: Sweet & Maxwell, 1966), xxxii, 381 pp.

Kennedy C. H., 'Islamic legal reform and the status of women in Pakistan', *Journal of Islamic Studies* 2 (1991), 45–55.

'Islamization in Pakistan: the implementation of Hudud Ordinances', *Asian Surveys* 33 (1988), 309–10.

Köndgen, Olaf, *Das islamisierte Strafrecht des Sudan von seiner Einführung 1983 bis Juli 1992* (Hamburg: Deutsches Orient-Institut, 1992), 145 pp. (Mitteilungen des Deutschen Orient-Instituts, 43).

Krcsmarik, J., 'Beiträge zur Beleuchtung des islamischen Strafrechts, mit Rücksicht auf Theorie und Praxis in der Türkei', *Zeitschrift der deutschen morgenländischen Gesellschaft* 108 (1904), 69–113, 316–62, 539–81.

Kudūsī, Meḥmed b. Aḥmad al-, *Natījat al-fatāwā*, 2nd edn. (Istanbul: n.p., 1848–9), 635 pp.

Kusha, Hamid Reza, *The sacred law of Islam: a case study of women's treatment in the criminal courts of Iran* (Aldershot: Ashgate, 2002),xi, 314 pp.

Lagardère, V., 'La haute judicature à l'époque almoravide en al-Andalus', *al-Qantara* 7 (1986), 135–228.

Lāyiḥat zirāʿat al-fallāḥ wa-tadbīr aḥkām al-falāḥ, 2nd edn. (Bulaq: Dār al-Ṭibāʿa al-ʿĀmira al-Mīriyya, 1840–1).

Layish, Aharon, and Gabriel W. Warburg, *The re-instatement of Islamic law in Sudan under Numayri: an evaluation of a legal experiment in the light of its historical context, methodology, and repercussions* (Leiden: E. J. Brill, 2002), xxi, 348 pp. (Studies in Islamic Law and Society, 16).

Mahdī, Muḥammad al-ʿAbbāsī al-, *al-Fatāwā al-Mahdiyya fī al-waqāʾiʿ al-Miṣriyya*, 7 vols. (Cairo: Maṭbaʿat al-Azhar, 1884 (1301 H)).

Mahmud, Abdulmalik Bappa, *A brief history of Shari'ah in the defunct Northern Nigeria* (n.p.: n.p., 1988), 61 pp.

Majumdar, Niharkana, *Justice and police in Bengal, 1765–1793: a study of the Nizamat in decline* (Calcutta: Mukhopadhyay, 1960), xiii, 351 pp.

Maqṣūdī, Muḥammad Aḥmad ʿAlī, *al-Niẓām al-jināʾī wa-l-ijrāʾāt al-jināʾiyya: dirāsa taṭbīqiyya wa-taḥlīliyya ʿalā al-waḍʿ fī al-Mamlaka al-ʿArabiyya al-Saʿūdiyya* ([Riyadh]: Kinda lil-Nashr wa-al-Tawzīʿ, 2001), 285 pp. (Silsilat al-Kutub al-Qānūniyya).

'Mashrūʿ qānūn jināʾī ʿArabī muwaḥḥad', in *Wathāʾiq al-dawra al-rābiʿa li-Majlis Wuzarāʿ al-ʿAdl al-ʿArab.* (Casablanca: Majlis Wuzarāʾ al-ʿAdl al-ʿArab, al-Amāna al-ʿĀmma, 1986).

Māwardī, ʿAlī b. Muḥammad al-, *al-Aḥkām al-sulṭaniyya* (Cairo: Muṣṭafā al-Bābī al-Ḥalabī, 1966), 264 pp.

Mayer, A. E., 'Le droit musulman en Libye à l'âge du "Livre Vert"', *Magreb-Machrek* 13 (1981), 5–22.

'Libyan legislation in defense of Arabo-Islamic mores', *American Journal of Comparative Law* 28 (1980), 287–313.

'Reinstating Islamic criminal law in Libya', in *Law and Islam in the Middle East*, edited by D. H. Dwyer (New York: Bergin & Garvey, 1990), 99–114.

Mehdi, R., *The Islamization of the law in Pakistan* (Richmond: Curzon, 1994), 329 pp. (monograph series: Nordic Institute of Asian Studies, 60).

Mitchell, R. P., *The Society of the Muslim Brothers* (London: Oxford University Press, 1969), xix, 349 pp.

Molina Lopez, Emilio, 'L'attitude des juristes de al-Andalus en matière de droit pénal: à propos d'une publication récente sur le thème', in *Actes du VIIe Colloque Universitaire Tuniso-Espagnol sur le patrimoine andalous dans la culture arabe et espagnole (Tunis 3–10 février 1989)* (Tunis: CERES, 1991), 155–91.

Muhairi, B. S. B. A. al-, 'The Federal Penal Code and the aim of unification', *Arab Law Quarterly* 12 (1997), 197–210.

'The Islamisation of laws in the UAE: the case of the penal code', *Arab Law Quarterly* 11 (1996), 350–71.

Müller, Christian, *Gerichtspraxis im Stadtstaat Córdoba: Zum Recht der Gesellschaft in einer malikitisch-islamischen Rechtstradition des 5./11. Jahrhunderts* (Leiden: E. J. Brill, 1999), xx, 468 pp. (Studies in Islamic Law and Society, 10).

'Judging with God's law on earth: judicial powers of the qadi al-jamāʿa of Cordoba in the fifth/eleventh century', *Islamic Law and Society* 7 (2000), 122–59.

Mumcu, Ahmet, *Osman devletinde siyaseten katl* (Ankara: Ankara Universitesi, Hukuk Fakültesi, 1963), xxiii, 260 pp. (Ankara Üniversitesi, Hukuk Fakültesi yayınlarından, 180).

Newman, Graeme, 'Khomeini and criminal justice: notes on crime and culture', *Journal of Criminal Law and Criminology* 73 (1982), 561–81.

Nord, E., *Das Türkische Strafgesetzbuch vom 28. Zilhidje 1274 (9. August 1858)* (Berlin: Guttentag, 1912), 107 pp. (Sammlung ausserdeutscher Strafgesetzbücher in deutscher Übersetzung, 34).

Nūr, 'Awad al-Hasan al-, *al-Qānūn al-jinā'ī al-Sūdānī 1991: sharḥ al-qism al-'āmm wa-l-ḥudūd* (Khartoum: n.p., 1992), 246 pp.

Ottley, B. L., 'The revolutionary courts of Iran: Islamic law of revolutionary justice?' *Newsletter of International Law* 4 (1980), 1–8.

Patel, R., *Islamisation of laws in Pakistan?* (Karachi: Faiza Publishers, 1986), 238 pp.

Peirce, Leslie, *Morality tales: law and gender in the Ottoman court of Aintab* (Berkeley etc.: University of California Press, 2003), xv, 460 pp.

Peters, Rudolph, 'Administrators and magistrates: the development of a secular judiciary in Egypt, 1842–1871', *Die Welt des Islams* 39 (1999), 378–97.

'The codification of criminal law in 19th century Egypt: tradition or modernization?', in *Law, society, and national identity in Africa*, edited by J. M. Abun-Nasr et al. (Hamburg: Buske, 1991), 211–25 (Beiträge zur Afrikaforschung, 1).

'Divine law or man-made law? Egypt and the application of the Shari'a', *Arab Law Quarterly* 3 (1988), 231–53.

'Egypt and the age of the triumphant prison: judicial punishment in nineteenth century Egypt', *Annales Islamologiques* 36 (2002), 253–85.

'"For his correction and as a deterrent example for others": Meḥmed 'Alī's first criminal legislation (1829–1830)', *Islamic law and Society* 6 (1999), 164–93.

Islamic criminal law in Nigeria (Ibadan: Spectrum Books, 2003), viii, 87 pp.

'Islamic and secular criminal law in nineteenth century Egypt: the role and function of the qadi', *Islamic Law and Society* 4, 1 (1997), 80–90.

'The Islamization of criminal law: a comparative analysis', *Die Welt des Islams* 34 (1994), 246–74.

'Murder on the Nile: homicide trials in 19th century Egyptian Shari'a courts', *Die Welt des Islams* 30 (1990), 95–115.

'The re-Islamization of criminal law in Northern Nigeria and the judiciary: the Safiyyatu Hussaini case', in *Dispensing justice in Islamic courts*, edited by M. K. Masud, R. Peters and D. Powers (Leiden: Brill, 2005) (Studies in Islamic Law and Society).

'What does it mean to be an official madhhab: Hanafism and the Ottoman Empire', in *The Islamic school of law: evolution, devolution, and progress*, edited by P. Bearman, R. Peters and F. Vogel (Cambridge, MA: Harvard University Press, 2005).

Peters, Rudolph, and Gert J. J. de Vries, 'Apostasy in Islam', *Die Welt des Islams* 17 (1976–7), 1–25.

Pickthall, Mohammed Marmaduke, *The meaning of the glorious Koran: an explanatory translation* (New York: Mentor Books, n.d.).

Qaḥṭānī, Fayṣal b. Ma'īḍ, *Hay'at al-taḥqīq wa-l-iddi'ā' al-'āmm wa-dawruhā fī niẓām al-'adāla al-jinā'iyya fī al-Mamlaka al-'Arabiyya al-Sa'ūdiyya* (Riyadh: Akādīmiyat Nāyif al-'Arabiyya lil-'Ulūm al-Amniyya, 1999), 445 pp.

Qānūn al-'Uqūbāt (8 Rajab 1265 [30 May 1849]) (Bulaq: Dār al-Ṭibā'a al-'Āmira al-Mīriyya, 1849), 41, 43 pp.

Qarāfī, Aḥmad b. Idrīs, *Anwār al-burūq fī anwā' al-furūq*, 4 vols. (Beirut: 'Ālam al-Kutub, n.d.).

Qırımīzāde Efendi, Ahmed Reşīd, *Mesā'ili cināyete müta'alliq Qırımīzāde mecmu'ası* (Istanbul: n.p., 1288 [1871]), 301 pp.

Repp, Richard, 'Qanun and Shari'a in the Ottoman context', in *Islamic law: social and historical contexts*, edited by A. Al-Azmeh (London: Routledge, 1988), 124–46.

Rodríguez, F., 'Instituciones judiciales: cadíes y otras magistraturas', in *El retroceso territorial de al-Andalus. Almorávides y almohades. siglos XI al XIII*, edited by M. J. Viguera (Madrid: Espasa-Calpe, 1997), 435–546 (Historia de España Menéndez Pidal, VIII, 2).

Safwat, Safiya, 'Islamic laws in the Sudan', in *Islamic law: social and historical contexts*, edited by A. Al-Azmeh (London: Routledge, 1988), 231–50.

Sāmī, Amīn, *Taqwīm al-Nīl*, 3 vols. (Cairo: Maṭba'at al-Kutub al-Miṣriyya, 1928–36).

Saney, P., 'Die Strafrechtsordnung Irans nach der islamischen Revolution', *Zeitschrift für die Gesamte Strafrechtswissenschaft* 97 (1985), 436–53.

Selle, F., *Prozessrecht des 16. Jahrhunderts im osmanischen Reich: auf Grund von Fetwas der Scheichülislame Ebüssuud und anderer unter er Regierung des Sultans Süleiman des Prächtigen* (Wiesbaden: Harrassowitz, 1962), ii, 112 pp.

Serrano, Delfina, 'Legal practice in an Andalusan-Maghribi source from the twelfth century CE: the *Madhāhib al-Ḥukkām fī Nawāzil al-Aḥkām*', *Islamic Law and Society* 7 (2000), 187–235.

'Twelve court cases on the application of penal law under the Almoravids', in *Dispensing justice in Islamic courts*, edited by M. K. Masud, R. Peters and D. Powers (Leiden: Brill, 2005).

'La violación en derecho malikí: doctrina y práctica a partir de tres fetuas de los siglos X a XII d.C.', in *Matrimonio y sexualidad. Normas, prácticas y transgresiones en la Edad Media y principios de la Epoca Moderna*, edited by Martine Charageat (Madrid: Casa de Velázquez, 2003), 125–48 (Dossier de Mélanges de la Casa de Velázquez. Nouvelle Série, 33 (1)).

Shādhilī, Fattūh 'Abd Allāh, *Jarā'im al-ta'zīr al-munaẓẓama fī al-Mamlaka al-'Arabiyya al-Sa'ūdiyya* (Riyadh: Jāmi'at al-Malik Sa'ūd, 'Imādat Shu'ūn al-Maktabāt, 1989), 12, 422 pp.

Shamiry, Najeeb, 'The rule of law in Yemen: uniting North and South', in *The rule of law in the Middle East and the Islamic world: human rights and the judicial process*, edited by Eugene Cotran and Mai Yamani (London: I. B. Tauris, 2000), 107–27.

Shaykhzāde (d. 1667), *Majma' al-anhur fī sharḥ multaqā al-abḥur* (*li-Ibrāhīm al-Ḥalabī, d. 1549*), 2 vols. (Istanbul: Maṭba'a-yi 'Āmira, 1883–4 (1301 H)).

Sidahmed, Abdel Salam, 'Problems in contemporary applications of Islamic criminal sanctions: the penalty for adultery in relation to women', *BRISMES* 28, 2 (2001), 187–204.

Singha, Radhika, *A despotism of law: crime and justice in early colonial India* (Delhi etc.: Oxford University Press, 1998), xxix, 342 pp.

Skipwith, Fulwar, *The magistrate's guide; being an abridgment of the criminal regulations and acts of the circular orders and constructions; and of the cases decided and reported by the Court of Nizamut Adawlut, under the Presidency of Fort William, in Bengal* (Calcutta: G. H. Huttman, Bengal Military Orphan Press, 1843), 240 pp.

Tabi'u, Muhammad, 'Constraints in the application of Islamic law in Nigeria', in *Islamic law in Nigeria: application and teaching*, edited by S. Khalid Rashid (Lagos etc.: Islamic Publications Bureau, 1986), 75–85.

'The impact of the repugnancy test on the application of Islamic law in Nigeria', *Journal of Islamic and Comparative Law* (Zaria) 18 (1991), 53–76.

Tellenbach, Silvia, 'Zur Re-Islamisierung des Strafrechts in Iran', *Zeitschrift für die Gesamte Strafrechtswissenschaft* 101 (1989), 188–205.

'Zur Strafrechtspflege in der islamischen Republik Iran', in *Beiträge zum islamischen Recht IV*, edited by Silvia Tellenbach and Thoralf Hanstein (Frankfurt a.M.: Peter Lang, 2004), 45–58.

Tellenbach, Silvia, (tr. and introd.), *Strafgesetze der islamischen Republik Iran* (Berlin etc.: Walter de Gruyter, 1996), xiv, 189 pp. (Sammlung ausserdeutschen Strafgesetzbücher in deutscher Übersetzung, 106).

Tier, A. M., 'Islamization of the Sudan laws and Constitution: its allure and its impracticability', *Verfassung und Recht in Übersee* 25, 2 (1992), 199–219.

Turkumānī, Adnān Khālid, *al-Ijrā'at al-jinā'iyya al-Islāmiyya wa-taṭbīqātuhā fī al-Mamlaka al-'Arabiyya al-Sa'udiyya* (Riyadh: Akādīmiyat Nāyif al-'Arabiyya lil-'Ulūm al-Amniyya, 1999), 487 pp. (Akādīmiyat Nāyif al-'Arabiyya lil-'Ulūm al-Amniyya, Markaz al-Dirāsāt wa-al-Buḥūth, 225).

Tyan, Emile, *Histoire de l'organisation judiciaire en pays de l'islam*, 2nd rev. edn. (Leiden: E. J. Brill, 1960), 673 pp.

'Umayrī, Muḥammad ibn 'Abd Allāh, *Musqiṭāt ḥadd al-ḥirābah wa-taṭbīqatuha fī al-Mamlaka al-'Arabiyya al-Sa'ūdiyya* (Riyadh: Akādīmiyat Nāyif al-Arabiyya lil-'Ulūm al-Amniyya, 1999), 244 pp. (Akādīmiyat Nāyif al-'Arabiyya lil-'Ulūm al-Amniyya, Markaz al-Dirāsāt wa-al-Buḥūth, 216).

Uzunçarşılı, İsmail Hakkı, *Osmanlı devletinin ilmiye teşkilâtı* (Ankara: Türk Tarih Kurumu Basımevi, 1988), viii, 349 pp.

Vogel, Frank E., *Islamic law and legal system: studies of Saudi Arabia* (Leiden: Brill, 2000), xx, 404 pp. (Studies in Islamic Law and Society, 8).

Wansharīsī, Aḥmad b. Yahyā al-, *al-Mi'yār al-mu'rab wa-l-jāmi' al-mughrib 'an fatāwā 'ulamā' Ifrīqiyya wa-l-Maghrib*, 13 vols. (Beirut: Dār al-Gharb al-Islāmī, 1981).

Weiss, Anita M., ed., *Islamic reassertion in Pakistan: the application of Islamic laws in a modern state* (Syracuse, NY: Syracuse University Press, 1986), xix, 146 pp.

Young, G., *Corps de droit ottoman: recueil des codes, lois, règlements, ordonnances et actes les plus importants du droit intérieur et d'études sur le droit coutumier de l'Empire Ottoman*, 7 vols. (Oxford: Clarendon Press, 1905–6).

Yūsuf, Yāsīn ʿUmar, *al-Naẓariyya al-ʿāmma li-l-qānūn al-jināʾī al-Sūdānī li-sanat 1991* (Beirut: Dār wa-Maktabat al-Hilāl, 1993), 256 pp.
Zafar, Emmanuel, *Law and Practice of Islamic hudood*, 2nd edn. (Lahore: Khyber Law Publishers, 2002), vi, 1103, 23 pp.
Zaghlūl, Aḥmad Fatḥī, *al-Muḥāmāh* (Cairo: Maṭbaʿat al-Maʿārif, 1900), 434 + 211 (app.) + 8 pp.

Suggestions for further reading

GENERAL

In Western languages there are very few works presenting a survey of the doctrine of Islamic criminal law, apart from general works on Islamic law and the relevant entries of the *Encyclopaedia of Islam*. A succinct and reliable survey is Bambale, *Crimes and punishment under Islamic law* (1998). Bassiouni, *The Islamic criminal justice system* (1982) contains contributions on many important aspects of Islamic criminal law. They are, however, of varying quality. In German there is Krcsmarik, 'Beiträge zur Beleuchtung des islamischen Strafrechts, mit Rücksicht auf Theorie und Praxis in der Türkei' (1904, but still valuable) and El-Baradie, *Gottes-Recht und Menschen-Recht: Grundlagenprobleme der islamischen Strafrechtslehre* (1983). In Spanish, finally we have Arévalo, *Derecho penal islámico* (1939). For those who read Arabic, many detailed surveys of the classical rules are available, the most important of which are: Abū Zahra, *al-Jarīma wa-al-ʿuqūba fī al-fiqh al-Islāmī*; ʿAwda, *al-Tashrīʿ al-jināʾī al-Islāmī muqāranan bi-l-qānūn al-waḍʿī*; and Jazīrī, *Kitāb al-fiqh ʿalā al-madhāhib al-arbaʿa. Al-juzʾ al-khāmis: al-ʿuqūbāt al-sharʿiyya.* For a deeper understanding of the doctrine and especially its historical context, the studies of Baber Johansen are indispensable: 'Zum Prozessrecht der ʿuqubat' (1977); 'Der ʿiṣma Begriff im hanafitischen Recht' (1978); 'Eigentum, Familie und Obrigkeit im hanafitischen Strafrecht' (1979); 'Zu den Gleichheitsbegriffen im hanafitischen Strafrecht' (1980); 'Secular and religious elements in Hanafite law' (1981); 'The valorization of the human body in Muslim Sunni law' (1996); and 'Signs as evidence: the doctrine of Ibn Taymiyya (1263–1328) and Ibn Qayyim al-Jawziyya (d. 1351) on proof' (2002). Most of these have been collected in Johansen, *Contingency in a sacred law: legal and ethical norms in the Muslim fiqh* (1999).

THE IMPLEMENTATION OF ISLAMIC CRIMINAL LAW IN THE PRE-MODERN PERIOD

For the Ottoman Empire, the essential work is Heyd, *Studies in old Ottoman criminal law* (1973). On Ottoman legislation there is Repp, '*Qānūn* and shariʿa in the Ottoman context' (1988). For court practice and procedure we have Selle, *Prozessrecht des 16. Jahrhunderts im osmanischen Reich* (1962), the studies of Jennings, 'Kadi, court, and legal procedure in 17th c. Ottoman Kayseri' (1978) and 'Limitations of the judicial powers of the kadi in 17th c. Ottoman Kayseri' (1979), and Bayındır, *Islam muhakeme hukuku: Osmanlı devri uygulaması* (1986). Studies on judicial practice based on court records and fatwās are: Horster, *Zur Anwendung des islamischen Rechts im 16. Jahrhundert* (1935); El-Nahal, *The judicial administration of Ottoman Egypt in the seventeenth century* (1979); Gerber, *State, society and law in Islam: Ottoman law in comparative perspective* (1994); Ginio, 'The administration of criminal justice in Ottoman Selanik (Salonica) during the eighteenth century' (1998); Imber, *Studies in Ottoman history and law* (1996); Imber, *Ebu's-Su'ud: the Islamic legal tradition* (1997); Ergene, *Local court, provincial society and justice in the Ottoman Empire: legal practice and dispute resolution in Çankırı and Kastamonu (1652–1744)* (2003); and Peirce, *Morality tales: law and gender in the Ottoman court of Aintab* (2003).

In this book I have chosen to focus on the Ottoman system of criminal law. The only other area in the Islamic world about which there currently exists a considerable amount of scholarship on criminal judicial practice is Islamic Spain. Those interested in this region I can refer to García Gómez, 'Sobre la diferencia en el castigo de plebeyos y nobles' (1971); Lagardère, 'La haute judicature à l'époque almoravide en al-Andalus' (1986); Molina Lopez, 'L'attitude des juristes de al-Andalus en matière de droit pénal: à propos d'une publication récente sur le thème' (1991); Arcas Campoy, 'La penalizacíon de las injurias en el derecho maliki' (1994); Fierro, 'El proceso contra Ibn Hatim al-Tulaytuli (años 457/1064–464/1072)' (1994); Hallaq, 'Murder in Cordoba: ijtihad and ifta'and the evolution of substantive law in medieval Islam' (1994); Jallaf, 'La justicia: cadíes y otros magistrados' (1994); Rodríguez, 'Instituciones judiciales: cadíes y otras magistraturas' (1997); Chalmeta, 'Acerca de los delitos de sangre en al-Andalus durante el califato'(1999); Calero, 'La justicia. Cadíes y otros magistrados' (2000); El Hour, 'The andalusian qādī in the Almoravid period: political and judicial authority' (2000); Müller, *Gerichtspraxis im Stadtstaat Córdoba: Zum Recht der Gesellschaft in einer malikitisch-islamischen Rechtstradition des 5./11. Jahrhunderts* (1999); Müller, 'Judging with God's law on earth: judicial powers of the *qāḍī* al-jamāʿa of Cordoba in the fifth/eleventh century' (2000); and Serrano's publications, 'Legal practice in an Andalusan-Maghribi source from the twelfth century CE: The *Madhāhib al-Hukkām fī Nawāzil al-Ahkām*' (2000); 'La violación en derecho malikí: doctrina y práctica a partir de tres fetuas de los siglos X a XII d.C.' (2003); and 'Twelve court cases on the application of penal law under the Almoravids' (2005).

THE ECLIPSE OF ISLAMIC CRIMINAL LAW

On early colonial India there are the historical studies of Majumdar, *Justice and police in Bengal, 1765–1793: a study of the Nizamat in decline* (1960); Fisch, *Cheap lives and dear limbs: the British transformation of the Bengal criminal law 1769–1817* (1983); and Singha, *A despotism of law: crime and justice in early colonial India* (1998). The texts of the regulations enacted by the British are published in Colebrooke, *Digest of the regulations and laws, enacted by the Governor-General in Council* (1807); Harington, *An analysis of the laws and regulations enacted by the Governor General in*

Council (1821); and Skipwith, *The magistrate's guide* (1843). Decisions of the Niẓāmat 'Adālat can be consulted in Court of Nizamut Adawlut, *Reports of criminal cases, 1805[–11]* (n.d.).

On the application of Islamic criminal law in Northern Nigeria before the introduction of the 1959 Penal Code there is Anderson, *Islamic law in Africa* (1954); Tabi'u, 'Constraints in the application of Islamic law in Nigeria' (1986); Mahmud, *A brief history of Shari'ah in the defunct Northern Nigeria* (1988); Karibi-Whyte, *History and sources of Nigerian criminal law* (1993); and Keay and Richardson, *The native and customary courts of Nigeria* (1996).

The legal history of the nineteenth-century Ottoman Empire is a neglected field. Some information can be found in Cin and Akgündüz, *Türk-İslām hukuk tarihi* (1990). Still useful is Heidborn, *Droit public et administratif de l'Empire Ottoman* (1909). The texts of the subsequent penal codes are published in Akgündüz, *Mukayeseli Islam ve Osmanlı Hukuku külliyatı* (1986). Translations of the 1858 Penal Code are found in Bucknill and Utidjian, *The imperial Ottoman penal code* (1913) and Young, *Corps de droit ottoman* (1905–6).

For nineteenth-century Egypt we have the following studies: Baer, 'Tanzimat in Egypt – the penal code' (1963) and 'The transition from traditional to Western criminal law in Turkey and Egypt' (1977); Fahmy, 'The police and the people in nineteenth century Egypt' (1999) and 'The anatomy of justice: forensic medicine and criminal law in nineteenth-century Egypt' (1999); and Peters, 'Murder on the Nile: homicide trials in 19th century Egyptian Shari'a courts' (1990); 'The codification of criminal law in 19th century Egypt: tradition or modernization?' (1991); 'Islamic and secular criminal law in nineteenth century Egypt: the role and function of the *qāḍī*' (1997); 'Administrators and magistrates: the development of a secular judiciary in Egypt, 1842–1871' (1999); '"For his correction and as a deterrent example for others": Meḥmed 'Alī's first criminal legislation (1829–1830)' (1999); and 'Egypt and the age of the triumphant prison: judicial punishment in nineteenth century Egypt' (2002). The texts of the nineteenth-century penal codes have been published in Zaghlūl, *al-Muḥāmāh* (1900) and Jallād, *Qāmūs al-idāra wa-l-qaḍā'* (1890–2).

ISLAMIC CRIMINAL LAW TODAY

For recent developments, the contributions and annual updates of the *Yearbook of Islamic and Middle Eastern Law* are indispensable.

On Saudi Arabia, there is the fundamental study by Vogel, *Islamic law and legal system: studies of Saudi Arabia* (2000). In Arabic we have Shādhilī, *Jarā'im al-ta'zīr al-munaẓẓama fī al-Mamlaka al-'Arabiyya al-Sa'ūdiyya* (1989); Turkumānī, *al-Ijrā 'āt al-jinā'iyya al-Islāmiyya wa-taṭbīqātuhā fī al-Mamlaka al-'Arabiyya al-Sa'ūdiyya* (1999); and Maqṣūdī, *al-Niẓām al-jinā'ī wa-l-ijrā'āt al-jinā'iyya: dirāsa taṭbīqiyya wa-taḥlīliyya 'alā al-waḍ' fī al-Mamlaka al-'Arabiyya al-Sa'ūdiyya* (2001).

The re-Islamisation of Libya has been analysed by Mayer, 'Libyan legislation in defense of Arabo-Islamic mores' (1980); 'Le droit musulman en Libye à l'âge du "Livre Vert"' (1981); and 'Reinstating Islamic criminal law in Libya' (1990).

A French translation of the relevant laws was published by Atallah, 'Le droit pénal musulman ressuscité'(1974).

There is much more literature on the re-Islamisation of criminal law in Pakistan: Patel, *Islamisation of laws in Pakistan?* (1986); Zafar, *Law and practice of Islamic hudood* (2002); Collins, 'Islamization of Pakistan law: a historical perspective' (1987); Kennedy, 'Islamization in Pakistan: the implementation of Ḥudūd Ordinances' (1988); Kennedy, 'Islamic legal reform and the status of women in Pakistan'(1991); Amin, *Islamization of Laws in Pakistan* (1989); Bouma, 'Pakistan's Islamization 1977–1988: the Ziā era in retrospect' (1989); Jahangir and Jilani, *The Hudood Ordinances, a divine sanction?* (1990); Mehdi, *The Islamization of the law in Pakistan* (1994); Zafar, *Law and practice of qiṣāṣ and diyat* (1992); and Jones-Pauly, 'Use of the Qurān in key Pakistani court decisions on zinā and qadhf' (2000).

On Iran there are the following studies: Newman, 'Khomeini and criminal justice: notes on crime and culture' (1982); Saney, 'Die Strafrechtsordnung Irans nach der islamischen Revolution' (1985); Hassan and Itscherenska, 'Zur Revitalisierung des islamischen Strafrechts in Iran' (1985); Tellenbach, 'Zur Re-Islamisierung des Strafrechts in Iran' (1989); Kusha, *The sacred law of Islam: a case study of women's treatment in the criminal courts of Iran* (2002); and Tellenbach, 'Zur Strafrechtspflege in der islamischen Republik Iran' (2004). A German translation of the Iranian Penal Code was published by Tellenbach, *Strafgesetze der islamischen Republik Iran* (1996).

As to Sudan, the fundamental work on the Shariʿa Penal Code of 1983 is Layish and Warburg, *The re-instatement of Islamic law in Sudan under Numayri* (2002). Other studies are An-Na'im, 'The Islamic law of apostasy and its modern applicability: a case from the Sudan'(1986); Safwat, 'Islamic laws in the Sudan' (1988); Fluehr-Lobban, 'Islamization in Sudan: a critical assessment' (1990); Köndgen, *Das islamisierte Strafrecht des Sudan von seiner Einführung 1983 bis Juli 1992* (1992); and Tier, 'Islamization of the Sudan laws and Constitution: its allure and its impracticability'(1992). On the new Penal Code of 1991 we have Nūr, *al-Qānūn al-jināʾī al-Sūdānī 1991: Sharḥ al-qism al-ʿāmm wa-l-ḥudūd* (1992); Hamo, *Lectures on the criminal law of the Sudan, 1991* (1992); Yūsuf, *al-Naẓariyya al-ʿāmma li-l-qānūn al-jināʾī al-Sūdānī li-sanat 1991* (1993); and Sidahmed, 'Problems in contemporary applications of Islamic criminal sanctions: the penalty for adultery in relation to women' (2001).

For Northern Nigeria one can consult Peters, *Islamic criminal law in Nigeria* (2003) and 'The re-Islamization of criminal law in Northern Nigeria and the judiciary: the Safiyyatu Hussaini case' (2005).

Index

Printed in Great Britain
by Amazon

56723273R00130